Microsoft® SQL Server® 2008 R2

Master Data Services: Implementation & Administration

Tyler Graham
Suzanne Selhorn

New York Chicago San Francisco Lisbon
London Madrid Mexico City Milan
New Delhi San Juan Seoul Singapore
Sydney Toronto

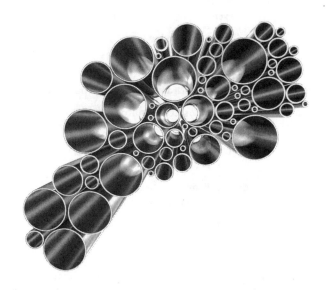

The McGraw·Hill Companies

Cataloging-in-Publication Data is on file with the Library of Congress

McGraw-Hill books are available at special quantity discounts to use as premiums and sales promotions, or for use in corporate training programs. To contact a representative, please e-mail us at bulksales@mcgraw-hill.com.

Microsoft® SQL Server® 2008 R2 Master Data Services: Implementation & Administration

1234567890   DOC DOC   10987654321

ISBN   978-0-07-175623-5
MHID   0-07-175623-X

Contents

Foreword

In the last few weeks I have received duplicate mailings from my bank. My doctor confused my records with another patient, also "D. Farmer." A carrier delivered a ceiling fan, ordered online, with a remote control that does not match it; and the next day delivered a pair of shoes of the right brand, the right color, the right size, but the wrong model.

I doubt that I am especially unlucky: we have all had similar experiences. The retailers, manufacturers, and service providers on the other side of these mishaps all have something in common—problems with *master data*.

That these problems are so familiar is a sign that they are pervasive. And over the years we, in the world of data management, have tried to solve them in many ways. We created reference data sets, but often ended up with multiple reference sets covering the same field confusingly. We built data warehouses to drive reporting and analytics, and thought to use them as our "single version of the truth." However, the data warehouse was populated and maintained on a different cycle, and for different purposes, than our line-of-business applications, and the data was not a suitable source for operational use.

In recent years, however, a body of practice has emerged that is aptly named "master data management," or MDM. Practitioners don't stop at just compiling a reference data set, but implement architectures, data-driven processes, practices, and policies that oversee the entire lifecycle of data.

Tyler Graham has been at the forefront of this new practice. Tyler has seen the start of the master data management movement as a consultant solving complex issues for enterprise customers. He has also worked on software solutions, with the vendor Stratature, building an agile and effective MDM solution. More recently, Tyler has been at Microsoft building their Master Data Services platform, which brings master data capabilities to every user of the SQL Server database. Working with him at Microsoft, Suzanne Selhorn has been documenting the technologies and the practices that Tyler's team has been building.

So, I don't think you could find a more able pair of authors to introduce you to Microsoft SQL Server's Master Data Services. This book covers everything you need to know: identifying systems that source or require master data; handling the data itself; establishing roles and practices for the "data stewards" and others who manage the processes; and naturally there is a wealth of practical advice on the Master Data Services platform itself.

You'll find this book to be an invaluable guide to a challenging subject area, and a fascinating technology.

–Donald Farmer
Product Advocate for QlikView, QlikTech

Acknowledgments

I would like to thank the entire MDS team for making this book and product possible. I would like to thank the light of my life, Tera, who put up with late nights and grumpy days throughout this process. And finally my children, who lost more than a few sessions of catch for this work.

–Tyler Graham

I would like to thank Tyler and everyone at McGraw-Hill for this amazing opportunity and great learning experience. I'd also like to thank Pam Matthews for being an invaluable MDS resource and for always being willing to share her knowledge. Thanks to Mike and Lucy Selhorn for being my loving and silly family. Thanks to Jill Thomasino for being a remarkable writing mentor and friend. And finally, thanks to Clair Turner, Reagan Templin, dark chocolate, and red wine—I couldn't have done it without you!

–Suzanne Selhorn

Introduction

The release of SQL Server 2008 R2 Master Data Services is the beginning of a new, more accessible era for master data management. Because of price and complexity, most solutions on the market today are geared toward large corporations and require dedicated consulting teams to implement. MDS, a feature of SQL Server Enterprise Edition, was built to democratize this process, providing MDM capabilities to a larger audience for a fraction of the price. MDS is meant to be rapidly deployed to any size organization and can solve a variety of master data challenges.

This book is intended for anyone interested in the features of MDS. It is meant to be used as an introduction, a learning tool, a training guide, and a reference manual. Even if you have no experience with MDS, each chapter builds on the previous chapter, so by the end of the book, you should be able to complete a majority of the tasks needed for a working MDS implementation. If you are a consultant with prior experience in the master data management market, you should find value in the product overview and web service examples, which allow you to adapt your existing MDM practice to support MDS.

Master Data Services is composed of some simple-to-understand components that can be used in a variety of ways. In order to provide the clearest understanding for new users, most of the book shows examples of standard, straightforward implementations. Complex examples and edge cases have been omitted from the book for fear of confusing the message. These complex topics are addressed in various resources you can find on the Internet, including the MDS team blog, www.mdsmodeler.com, and www.mdsuser.com.

What You'll Learn in this Book

The intent of this book is to get you up and running with MDS. By reading it, you should become familiar with MDS-specific terminology (models, entities, attributes) and learn how to use MDS to solve your business problems. Each chapter introduces you to basic concepts, shows you how to use the Master Data Manager web application to perform related tasks, and gives you examples to complete the related tasks programmatically by using the web service.

While the book provides advice on how to create a solution specific to your organization, implementing any master data management (MDM) solution requires buy-in from many people across the organization. Doing the work to create models that will work for you and getting agreement that the MDS system is truly the system of record is more than half the battle. The book hopes to give you the confidence to approach your organization's MDM issues with a solid knowledge of how to implement and manage an MDM solution by using SQL Server 2008 R2 Master Data Services.

Chapter 1: Introduction to Master Data Services

This chapter introduces the field of master data management and discusses its history. It explores the variety of popular MDM solutions and compares them to the Microsoft Master Data Services solution.

Chapter 2: Installation and Configuration

This chapter helps you consider the scope of your MDS implementation, and then gives you the steps to install and configure MDS. This chapter has a list of the Windows features and roles you must install before you can configure the Master Data Manager web application. This chapter also provides information about service packs and cumulative updates. Because this is the first version of the MDS product, it's important to install these updates and ensure you're working with the latest and greatest version of the product.

Chapter 3: Starting an MDS Project

This chapter gives you more in-depth ideas about how MDS will fit into your organization. Before you begin working with the product, it is important to spend quality time determining your organization's master data management needs. This chapter also includes information about how to deal with duplicate records and data cleansing.

Chapter 4: Creating Your Model

In this chapter, you start building a model. This chapter explains how to deploy the sample models that are included when you install MDS. This chapter also provides a start-to-finish walkthrough for creating the primary model objects. At the end of this chapter, you will have created a complete product model and should be able to understand the relationships between the MDS model objects.

Chapter 5: Integrating Master Data Services with Other Systems

This chapter explains how to load master data into MDS so that users can begin to manage it. This chapter introduces the database staging tables and the format required for importing data into the tables. It presents sample data, as well as procedures for loading the data and initiating the staging process, which imports the data into the correct tables in the MDS database.

Chapter 6: Working with Hierarchies and Collections

This chapter introduces the different types of MDS hierarchies: explicit and derived. After a brief introduction, you are led through the creation of some sample hierarchies. This chapter also shows variations on these hierarchies, which address specific business cases. This chapter also introduces the concept of collections and shows you how to create one. Finally, code samples show you how to use the web service to work with hierarchies.

Chapter 7: Working with Master Data

This chapter is intended for users who need to work with master data on a daily basis. This chapter shows you how to filter data to find what you need, how to edit your data, and how to work with data in hierarchies. In addition, you learn how to review and reverse the transactions that are recorded whenever a user changes data. You also learn how to annotate transactions and data, which can be useful for change tracking. Finally, this chapter includes samples for using the web service to retrieve and update data.

Chapter 8: Using Business Rules

This chapter shows you how to create and configure business rules, and then how to publish them and apply them to data. You are shown how to configure e-mail notifications, how to use business rules to create internal workflows, and how to use business rules to trigger external workflows. Finally, code samples show how to use web services to interact with business rules.

Chapter 9: Creating Versions of Data

In this chapter, you learn how to change a version name and description. You learn about saving versions of your data (rather than your model structure), and about what it means to lock and commit a version. This chapter explains how to validate a version against business rules, how to flag a version of your data for subscribing systems or users, and how to determine where a version of data came from. And like all chapters, web service examples are provided.

Chapter 10: Using Metadata

This chapter introduces the concept of *metadata*, which in MDS means data that describes your data. This chapter shows where your users can view metadata within the web application. It shows you how to add and update metadata, and how to extend the Metadata model, which all metadata is based on. Finally, web services examples are given.

Chapter 11: Implementing Security

This chapter covers how to configure the granular level of security provided by MDS. This chapter explains how to add users and groups, how to configure administrators to have more permissions than the average user, and how to test permissions to ensure you've configured them correctly. This chapter explains the difference between functional area permissions, model object permissions, and hierarchy member permissions. It also explains which permissions apply when overlapping assignments are made. Finally, web service examples show how to set security.

Chapter 12: Publishing Data to External Systems

This chapter explains the concept of subscription views, which are standard SQL views that you create from within MDS. This chapter shows how to use these SQL views to export data to systems outside of MDS.

Chapter 13: Extending MDS with Web Services

This chapter shows you how to enable the web service. It includes a summary of all operations and gives you a basic idea of the use of each. It also includes additional code samples that weren't provided in other chapters, including how to search for members, return member counts, validate data, get and reverse transactions, and handle errors.

About the Sample Company

Throughout this book we use a fictional company called "Main Street Clothing Company." We envision this company to be a small clothing retailer, just large enough to have a corporate office and manage its own IT. We thought that using one single continuous example would be the most successful way to demonstrate MDS concepts to the uninitiated. MDS was built and priced to provide a solution that can truly solve MDM issues for companies of all sizes, and we wanted to provide a complete example for this new emerging market. No matter the size of your business, many if not all of the concepts explained using Main Street Clothing Company should be applicable to your situation.

About the Sample Data

In many chapters of the book, we mention www.mdsuser.com. We created this site to give you sample data to use as you go through the chapters in the book. Our intention was to give you two common models—Product and Finance—that you could experiment with while reading the book, and then modify in any way you want. These models are not meant to be taken too seriously—they are samples that we put together with the hope that it is easier to learn something when you can see a real-world example. MDS can be used for any domain you care to manage; it's not restricted to lists of customers or products, but these domains provide you with a frame of reference.

You should always feel free to deploy these models, update them to your heart's content, and then delete them and start over. In the writing of this book, we've created and deleted our model dozens of times, and the only recourse is that we lost track of what we were doing from time to time. Until you've seriously solidified your MDS solution, you should feel free to push MDS to its limits and seek help when you're stuck. There is a community of committed users on the MDS forums on MSDN; the forums are often a good place to start when you're troubleshooting.

In this book we also provide code samples that illustrate the more common procedures described in each chapter. Chapter 13 is devoted completely to how to programmatically interact with MDS. All of the code samples in the book are available electronically at www.MHProfessional.com/computingdownload and at www.mdsmodeler.com. These samples are free and are meant to be used in support of the book. We truly hope you find the samples and this book useful and that you achieve success with your MDM implementation.

Chapter 1

Introduction to
Master Data Services

In This Chapter

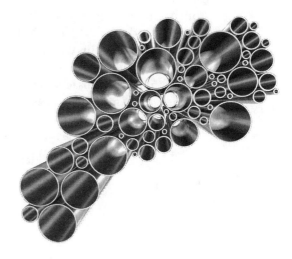

I n this chapter, we talk about the field of master data management and its history. We discuss how other solutions have attempted to tackle master data management, and explain how Microsoft has approached master data management as part of SQL Server 2008 R2. Finally, we introduce the sample company we'll be using throughout the rest of the book and describe some of its business problems that a master data management solution is meant to solve.

What Is Master Data Management?

Master data management (MDM) is the management of the nontransactional data within an organization. The definition of "master" data varies by organization, but can be loosely defined as the nouns that describe all business processes. These nouns might be organization-specific data, like your list of products or employees. Or they might be common reference data provided by an external service provider or government agency, like address information or a Dunn & Bradstreet (D-U-N-S®) number. Although customer and product are the two most commonly managed domains, many businesses find value in managing additional domains, such as wells and fields at big oil companies and recipes at food manufacturers.

When we discuss master data management, we often use the word *domain*. We use this overloaded word to mean a group of related business data that is an area of focus for a master data management solution—for example, accounts or customers.

In most businesses, customers buy products or services. Because customer relationships are essential, each time a customer buys a product or service, the transaction is recorded. After the transaction is recorded and coded properly, the details of the transaction will never change. MDM is about managing the relationships between these static transactions, rather than the transactions themselves. For example, for a retail chain, each store has a certain group of employees and a manager. That Sally is the manager of Store #1 is master data. That Sally worked four hours on Friday is a transaction.

The more often this data is required for a transaction, the greater its importance to your organization. Central management of this data helps identify data discrepancies between multiple transactional systems and helps your organization run more efficiently.

Master data management is composed of the following:

▶   The business policies (who owns the data, where the data lives, and so forth)

▶   The processes (how the data is updated)

▶   The technological tools that facilitate these processes

By definition, all companies must be completing some form of MDM, although the term generally refers to the implementation of formalized processes and specifically designed tools.

History of Master Data Management

When companies began using computer applications to manage information, in order to perform tasks and generate results, all pertinent data had to be loaded into each application directly. Over time, companies adopted more applications and had to enter the same dataset into each of them. As a response to this, developers began to employ the technique of creating master files that stored key, reusable data for use within each application. These initial master files were the first master data management systems.

Once the master data was loaded into each application, new records would be added in the application or to the master list, and the two sets of data were no longer in sync. Early data reconciliation efforts were time consuming and costly. Very few tools existed that could identify differences and manage duplicate records.

Enterprise resource planning (ERP) systems were then created to help combine the data in these systems and to solve the constant need for integration between systems. ERP systems were meant to be single software suites that managed standard business processes within an organization. Each module in an ERP system could leverage the common master data tables required for the associated business process. Many organizations today consider the master data tables within their ERP systems to be the "master" data within their organization.

As more and more organizations adopted ERP systems, they realized that using these single systems in isolation was unrealistic. They then adopted multiple ERP systems, and their master data problems re-emerged. Specialized systems designed to manage the most problematic domains became major implementations in the larger organizations. Now there is a push in the industry to provide solutions that can solve master data issues across a wide variety of domains.

An Overview of Master Data Management Solutions

All organizations must deal with their master data management issues. Whether managing domains in Excel spreadsheets or purchasing a specialized solution, providing process around managing master data and integrating across all systems in any size organization is a central IT problem being addressed today.

ERP solutions can have drawbacks as MDM solutions, other specialized solutions can prove to be too specialized, and often MDM solutions cater to only the biggest organizations. Microsoft hopes to provide an adaptable solution that can cater to organizations of all sizes.

Shortcomings of ERP Systems as MDM Solutions

While ERP systems are a significant consumer of master data, using these systems by themselves to manage master data has major drawbacks. Also the initial concept that a single ERP system would handle all of the computing needs of an organization was shortsighted.

ERP Systems Are Not Specialized or Innovative

While many ERP systems contain modules for most common business processes, a specific industry need or the need for more innovative software leads businesses to implement additional systems. Integration of these new systems with current IT infrastructure and business processes becomes a major implementation cost of any new system.

ERP Systems Do Not Play Well with Others

As companies merge with or acquire their competitors, companies inherit additional ERP systems. Since these systems are highly customized and not initially designed for easy integration, additional processes must be created to ensure that these systems are synchronized across the organization. The complexities of these software systems and the underlying data models make successful integration, or even effective synchronization, impossible for large organizations. When Tyler moved across the country for work, it was impossible for his electronic bank accounts at a nationwide bank to move with him because each of the bank's regions was on its own system. Imagine, it was easier to move the contents of a house 3000 miles than to move a set of data and transactions that would fit on a thumb drive.

ERP Systems Do Not Manage Analytical Dimensions Effectively

The need for complex modeling and analysis of transactional data to determine statistics and trends has led companies to create advanced online analytical processing (OLAP) systems and associated data warehouses to go along with them. These systems have added new, complex data modeling needs that were just not supported in legacy applications. Hierarchies and other consolidations are not natively managed by ERP systems.

ERP Systems Are Not Designed to Manage Attributes

Many ERP system vendors realize that users will want to store additional attributes in their master tables. To accommodate this, they provide a few custom fields for customers to use as they see fit. These custom fields get overloaded with information without providing any validation of appropriate use.

Specialized Master Data Management Solutions

As you would suspect, the most common domains for management are those domains most troublesome to large organizations. Specialized systems have been created to manage these domains, with many features designed directly for them. These systems were designed to manage a single domain and don't translate well to other master data problems. The first two solutions designed to manage master data were customer data integration and product information management.

Customer Data Integration

Customer data integration (CDI) is a solution designed to provide a standard view of customers across an organization. Some CDI solutions accomplish this as a single system that centralizes customer data across an enterprise. Other solutions manage the integration of multiple ERP systems and additional systems through a registry approach. These solutions manage customer IDs from multiple systems to ensure synchronization and provide a consistent view of each customer.

A central feature of CDI solutions is the ability to identify and manage duplicate customer records. Other common features include address correction and standardization and the ability to integrate with service organizations to further enrich business-specific customer knowledge. CDI implementations tend to incorporate most systems within an enterprise and focus on a relatively small subset of attributes.

Companies with customer management problems will certainly benefit from a CDI implementation. Unfortunately, these features do not translate well to managing other domains across the enterprise such as organization or product.

Product Information Management

Product information management (PIM) solutions are designed for the product domain. There are fewer PIM solutions than CDI solutions and PIM solutions tend to focus on specific industries. Most PIM solutions centralize product data management and provide integration to many distribution systems. These solutions tend to be implemented in large retailers and wholesalers that need to manage multiple sales channels for large product catalogs. Management of online catalogs and integration with standardized product channels are some specialized features of PIM solutions.

Again, these systems are highly effective to solve a narrow band of problems. These systems do not translate well to additional domains. Very few providers have solutions in both the CDI and PIM spaces.

Catering to the Titans

Historically, vendors of MDM solutions have catered to the needs of Fortune 500 companies. Until recently, the MDM market was dominated by complex and expensive applications that generate large amounts of consulting dollars to trained implementers. These companies generally have the means and the budget to pay for the consulting time and tools that comprise an MDM solution. These solutions were tied to either a specific domain or a feature set that supported one domain better than others. These solutions are expensive and are built to solve a unique set of issues in large organizations. The size and complexity of these engagements has led many of these projects to end in failure.

The MDM market's focus on Fortune 500 companies doesn't mean that small and midsize companies don't face similar issues with managing their data. Any organization that's attempting to store critical data in multiple systems or spreadsheets and having trouble determining a true version of its master data is in need of an MDM solution.

The costs associated with MDM solutions and the high risk of failure in self-deploying such solutions leave a large portion of the small and midsize business market underserved. Out of necessity, many of these businesses are using Excel spreadsheets or internally designed systems to manage master data. These systems typically neglect the need for security, central management, and versioning.

Microsoft's Solution to Master Data Management

In the spring of 2006, Microsoft acquired Stratature in an effort to jump-start its master data management strategy. Already a customer of Stratature, Microsoft had been impressed with the rapid time to value and the ease of customization that Stratature's +EDM product provided.

Microsoft initially planned to ship its MDM solution as part of SharePoint, because information workers are the primary consumers of master data. However, because IT plays a significant role in managing MDM solutions, MDS moved to the Server and Tools division and became a feature of SQL Server 2008 R2.

What Master Data Services Delivers

Master Data Services (MDS) provides a number of features that facilitate central management of master data while providing greater access to the editors and consumers of this information.

Domain Agnostic

MDS is not designed for a specific domain. Any data type and virtually any data schema can be supported by the MDS system. Chapter 3 discusses how to map your organization's systems and determine how MDS might best suit your needs. Chapter 4 shows you how to create your model, entities, and attributes, which are the core MDS objects.

Hierarchy Management

Excel- and IT-developed applications are notoriously bad at representing hierarchical data. Specialized controls and multiple hierarchy types in MDS provide effective and flexible management of business hierarchies. Chapter 6 shows you how to create hierarchies and collections.

Web-Based UI

A web-based user interface (UI) provides access to a large user base without the need for installing software on numerous machines. As intranet access becomes more portable, mobile device access can be integrated into the master data management story. Chapter 7 provides instructions for business users to help them work with data in the Master Data Manager web application, which is the primary place where business users will interact with the data.

Transaction Logging

Even with a robust security model, it is essential to provide an audit trail of changes. MDS provides a filterable transaction log to ensure a manageable history of changes. Chapter 7 explains how to view and reverse transactions. It also explains how to annotate transactions so users can explain why they made changes to the master data.

Versioning

Many domains require snapshots of different points in time to be maintained. With MDS, each model can be versioned, which allows users to tag specific versions for subscribing systems. Chapter 9 shows you how to create versions of a model and how to flag versions for subscribing systems.

Security

The ability to control access at entity, attribute, and record levels allows IT to empower business stewards to update data in a single centralized tool without risking unauthorized changes. Chapter 11 shows you how to implement security.

The Value Proposition

The MDS system is built to be rapidly deployed for any domain within an organization. Once deployed, all models support additional customization without complex coding or reconfiguration. The intent is to make master data management software more accessible to small and midsize businesses, and to aid departments of large companies in creating solutions for themselves. While Master Data Services provides a rich web services platform for system integration and you can use web services to create your own custom user interface, you do not need to use web services to take advantage of what MDS has to offer. An MDS implementation can be completed successfully by business users with no knowledge of coding.

About the Sample Company

In an effort to provide context to the features of MDS, all of our examples are based on a fictitious children's clothing company called Main Street Clothing Company. This company is a regional retailer with stores in three states.

For the past ten years the company has been in an expansion phase; it has a novel store layout and, with the bankruptcy of a competitor, it has grown to 13 locations. As the economic environment has cooled, the company is looking to manage costs and understand its business better.

An IT study early in the year determined that a new ERP implementation would be cost prohibitive and that the company would be best served by committing to its current IT infrastructure for a minimum of five years. Figure 1-1 shows the overall IT infrastructure.

In the ERP study, a number of inefficiencies and poor business processes were identified:

▶   While the purchasing department was able to track merchandise purchases through purchase orders added to the financial system, contacts and specifics were being managed in a number of Excel spreadsheets. When the purchasing manager was in the hospital unexpectedly for two weeks, the employees who filled in didn't understand much of the process.

▶   The addition of a new website sales channel in 2007 led to the explosion in both product and customer lists that had not been managed well. Customer information was inconsistent and difficult to manage. Many products online were drop shipped, leading to some confusion with the current warehouse process because logistics personnel could not readily identify these items and spent time looking for the items or attempting to request additional inventory from the purchasing department.

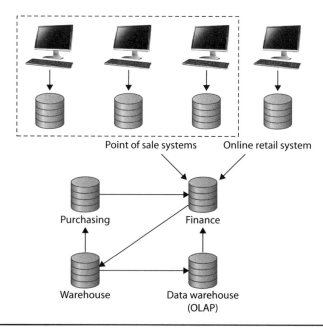

Point of sale systems   Online retail system

Purchasing   Finance

Warehouse   Data warehouse
                         (OLAP)

Figure 1-1   *System architecture for Main Street Clothing Company*

▶   Management has been complaining about the speed at which reports have been
    provided at month end. Complexity of the organization and the constant changes
    to its hierarchies has led to almost a week of cleanup and reconciliation effort with
    each month's end.

    By using the implementation of Master Data Services in the Main Street Clothing
Company, we hope to provide continuity to the procedures and give context to the
business problems and processes being solved in our implementation.

Summary

Master data management issues are pervasive within organizations and have existed since
the beginning of the electronic age. Solutions have evolved over time to address these
issues, and Master Data Services is another phase of that evolution. Traditionally, MDM
solutions have tended to cater to larger corporations that can afford customized solutions
for specific domains. Master Data Services provides an accessible and affordable solution
for organizations of all sizes. Throughout this book we will incorporate samples designed
around a small company that is tackling common MDM challenges.

Chapter 2

Installation and Configuration

In This Chapter

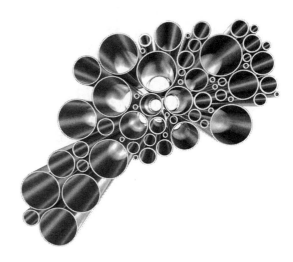

The first step in any software application is to deploy the software, and Master Data Services in no exception. In this chapter, we begin with a quick discussion of project size and scope. This should help you determine your needs, including whether you need any external assistance. We then discuss installing the application to a server. As MDS is a web-based application, the deployment and configuration can be extensive. At the end of the chapter, we discuss options to secure your data and some steps to extend the application.

Determining the Initial Scope of Your Project

Before installing Master Data Services, it is important to determine your short- and medium-term goals for the application. MDS was designed as a web application to provide a simple deployment model for a wide range of organizations. This is also a good time to make sure you have the necessary information to deploy and configure the application successfully, and to determine whether your project requires external expertise. There are a number of questions to be considered before installing MDS:

▶ *Which domains will I manage in MDS?* While this book addresses how to organize this data in later chapters, it is important to take an initial assessment of what data must be stored to create a functional MDS solution.

▶ *How many attributes will I need to manage?* For each domain that will be managed in MDS, it is valuable to understand the number of attributes that are relevant to the organization. A central benefit of MDS is the ability to modify your model at any time, so a complete list is not essential. A rough estimate of the number of attributes provides one of the best metrics of the scope of the management problem and can provide insight into the owners, editors, and consumers of the records to be managed.

▶ *How many employees will edit the data?* To provide an effective long-term solution and to see the largest return on investment (ROI) for any master data solution, it is imperative to empower the owners of the data to make changes directly within the system. Whether this is accomplished directly in the Master Data Manager web application or in some external entry system that is integrated with MDS, empowering the business owners reduces IT effort and eliminates the communication breakdowns that occur when routing data changes through IT.

▶ *How many employees will consume the data?* Ideally, completed implementations should give everyone with a business need in the organization the access to the cleanest and most accurate data at all times. In most MDM projects, reaching this ideal state is a work in progress and data consumers should be prioritized based on business need and the costs associated with providing access.

▶ *How many systems do I need to integrate?* Depending on the size of the organization, identifying all systems that rely on a specific domain may not be feasible this early in a project. Most small and medium-sized businesses should identify all systems that consume the domain to be mastered and determine the primary owner of each system.

Based on the preliminary data that you discover from answering the preceding questions, you can determine the relative complexity of your MDM project. The table shown in Figure 2-1 should help you to enumerate the complexity of your project.

The complexity of your project should affect both the scope of the implementation and the amount of ongoing effort required to maintain the MDS project. Small projects should be manageable by novice individuals with sufficient business knowledge and the aid of this book. These projects should be functional and productive within a week's worth of effort.

Many small projects revolve around finding a home for "homeless" data within the organization. This data is critical to regular business processes, but not important enough to be managed in any standard process system. Much of this homeless data tends to live in unmanaged Excel spreadsheets. The transition of this homeless data into MDS can provide structure and control over it. If IT personnel were previously responsible for

	Small	Medium	Large
Entities	Fewer than 20	Fewer than 50 per model	More than 50 per model
Attributes	Fewer than 20	Fewer than 50 per model	More than 50 per model
Hierarchies	Fewer than 5	Fewer than 4 per model	More than 4 per model
Source systems	Fewer than 3	Fewer than 3 per model	More than 3 per model
Subscribing systems	Fewer than 5	Fewer than 5 per model	More than 5 per model
Simple workflows	Fewer than 5	Fewer than 5 per model	More than 5 per model
Complex workflows	0	Fewer than 3 per model	More than 3 per model

Simple   Complex

Figure 2-1 *Project scope*

managing changes provided by business users, they can now provide users with access to the appropriate data directly. No formal roles or duties need to be created.

A wide range of projects fall into the intermediate range. These projects can be handled internally, but require resources to be fully committed to the implementation effort. Most small and medium-sized business implementations will be intermediate-sized projects. As these projects become more complex, bringing in outside expertise for the implementation should be considered seriously. Making the decision to do so does not diminish the need for internal knowledge and education; although these consultants will aid in the implementation of the solution initially, internal staff will be needed to maintain the MDM system and processes going forward. Most of these projects can be managed in a single phase, requiring approximately 30 to 200 hours to be successfully implemented. Identification of at least one data steward within the organization is essential to long-term success.

Data steward is a common role found in MDM projects. These individuals tend to be technically savvy while still understanding the nuances of the business domains. A data steward must be a champion of data governance and must help create sustainable data maintenance processes within the organization. Many times, data stewards find themselves acting as referees in how data is maintained, caught between competing business processes and applications. Systems may maintain different rules regarding the quality and timeliness of data that must be managed by the data steward. The ability to find efficient compromises will determine how effective a data steward is for an organization.

Once projects reach a certain level of complexity, they become too large to manage in a single phase. The cost and complexity of these large projects requires engaging external expertise that can provide the guidance and resources necessary to implement enterprise-wide MDM solutions. These large projects may span multiple years and locations, and breaking these projects into multiple milestones and ROI checkpoints is advisable. If these projects can be broken down into more manageable intermediate projects, lessons learned from preceding projects can be applied to later implementations.

About the Main Street Clothing Company Implementation

Main Street Clothing Company will be managing two models within MDS. Within these models, the company plans to maintain fewer than ten entities. Initially, the number of systems to integrate will be limited to three process systems. Based on this information, IT feels comfortable providing a single internal resource to build and deploy MDS. Billy Jean, an IT-savvy assistant to the controller, has been identified to manage the Finance model. The Product model will be managed by a designee of the VP of Purchasing. This person has not yet been identified.

Preparing the Web Server

Master Data Services requires a 64-bit machine and runs only on the following operating systems:

- ▶ Windows Server 2008
- ▶ Windows Server 2008 R2
- ▶ Windows Vista Business, Enterprise, and Ultimate
- ▶ Windows 7 Professional, Enterprise, and Ultimate

While MDS needs to create (or attach) a backend database to a SQL Server 2008 R2 instance, this instance does not need to be located on the same machine. MDS does not support SQL Server Standard or Express editions for the database backend.

In preparation for installing the MDS application, you must enable a number of Windows features to support the web-based UI.

Windows 7 Web Application Requirements

Figure 2-2 lists the minimum features that must be installed for MDS to function properly in Windows 7. These features can be found by opening Control Panel, clicking Programs, and then clicking "Turn Windows features on or off."

Windows Server 2008 R2 Web Application Requirements

In Windows Server 2008 R2, use Server Manager to configure the following role services and features.

First, install the Application Server role services by completing the following steps:

1. Open Server Manager.
2. In the left pane, expand Roles.
3. Click Application Server.
4. In the Summary section, Role Services subsection, click "Add Role Services" on the right.

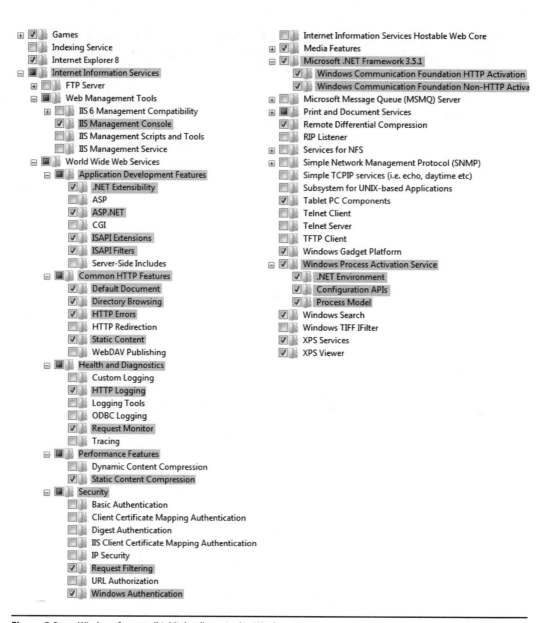

Figure 2-2 *Windows features (highlighted) required in Windows 7*

5.   Select the following role services:

   ▶   .NET Framework 3.5.1

   ▶   Web Server (IIS) Support

   ▶   HTTP Activation (under Windows Process Activation Service Support)

6.   Click Install.

Now, install the Web Server role services by completing the following steps:

1.   Open Server Manager.
2.   In the left pane, expand Roles.
3.   Click Web Server (IIS).
4.   In the Summary section, Role Services subsection, click "Add Role Services" on the right.

Select the following role services:

Role Service	Setting
Common HTTP Features	Static Content Default Document Directory Browsing HTTP Errors
Application Development	ASP.NET .NET Extensibility ISAPI Extensions ISAPI Filters
Health and Diagnostics	HTTP Logging Request Monitor
Security	Windows Authentication Request Filtering
Performance	Static Content Compression
Management Tools	IIS Management Console

Now install the following features by completing the following steps:

1.   Open Server Manager.
2.   In the left pane, click Features.
3.   In the right pane, click Add Features.

Select the following features:

Feature	Setting
.NET Framework 3.5.1 Features	.NET Framework 3.5.1 WCF Activation HTTP Activation Non-HTTP Activation
Windows PowerShell Integrated Scripting Environment	
Windows Process Activation Service	Process Model .NET Environment Configuration APIs

Installing Master Data Services

Installing MDS is a relatively simple process and is only responsible for dropping the bits onto the machine. Any machine that will implement the Master Data Manager web application or the web services needs to run the installation package. In SQL Server 2008 R2, the MDS feature is not a part of the standard SQL Server setup. The stand-alone msi file to install MDS is located in the Master Data Services folder at the root of the installation media.

Procedure: Install Master Data Services

To install Master Data Services, complete the following steps:

1. On the SQL Server installation media, open MasterDataServices\x64\<language> (for example, MaterDataServices\x64\1033_ENU_LP\).
2. Double-click MasterDataServices.msi. The Welcome page is displayed.

3. Click Next.

4. Accept the terms of the license agreement and click Next.

5. Enter your name and/or company and click Next.

6. Optional. On the Feature Selection page, click Browse to change the location where the files will be installed. Unless there is some technical reason to change this location, you should leave the standard location alone.

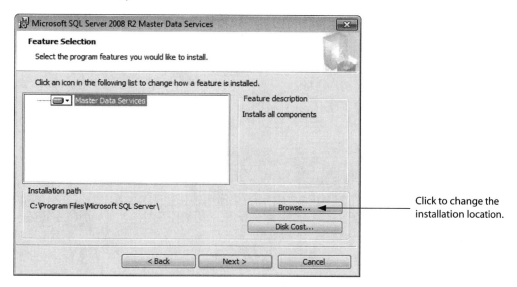

Click to change the installation location.

7. Click Next.

8. On the Ready to Install Program page, click Install.

9. You may be prompted to allow the installation to proceed. If you are, click Yes.

10. When the installation completes, click Finish.

11. You may be prompted to allow the installation to proceed. If you are, click Yes.

After successful installation, Master Data Services Configuration Manager is displayed on your screen, and you can now use it to create your database and web site and to enable web services.

About MDS Configuration Manager

Once the bits are installed, MDS Configuration Manager will assist you in the process of configuring MDS for first use. MDS Configuration Manager, shown in Figure 2-3, can be broken into two sections: Databases and Web Configuration. If valid versions of Windows PowerShell or Internet Information Services cannot be found, the initial screen will provide that status. If applicable, you will need to resolve these issues before continuing with configuration of MDS.

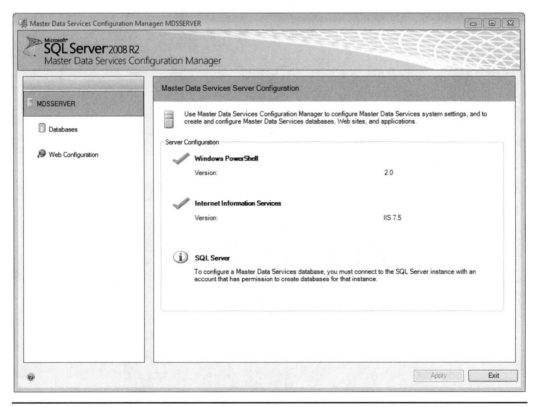

Figure 2-3   *Master Data Services Configuration Manager*

Creating an MDS Database

The initial step in configuring Master Data Services is to create a new MDS database. The database can only be created on a SQL Server 2008 R2 database server. Whether this is a local instance or an instance that exists on another database server, MDS Configuration Manager will perform a check to ensure that the database server is Enterprise, Developer, or DataCenter. Once this check is successful, an "empty" MDS database will be created on the database server. This empty database will contain all of the tables, views, and stored procedures that make up the architecture of MDS.

You must first determine whether to install the MDS database locally or on another machine. There are two major factors that should influence this decision:

▶ *Do you already have access to a database farm or server running SQL Server 2008 R2?* Although not always available, this would provide the most economical way to split the two roles of MDS onto separate machines. Please be aware that MDS licensing requires that all machines that have any component of MDS installed must be licensed for Enterprise Edition SQL Server 2008 R2.

▶ *Does your organization have any restrictions about having the database server and web server roles on the same machine?* Although this is an antiquated philosophy born in older, less secure versions of both products, some companies still insist that the database server and web server not be on the same box.

A lesser concern for most companies should be the application's performance. Although it is true that MDS will use processor capacity for both stored procedures on the database server and handling requests on the web server, in most implementations these burdens should be handled by standard hardware that is available on the market today. Microsoft does not provide minimum hardware requirements for MDS, but due to the cost of the license, we suggest a minimum of 8GB of RAM on a quad-core machine. With this configuration, an implementation that must support 20 concurrent users would be fine.

Procedure: Create an MDS Database

The Master Data Services database is where your master data will be stored. To create an MDS database, complete the following steps:

1. If Master Data Services Configuration Manager is not open, launch it from Programs | Microsoft SQL Server 2008 R2 | Master Data Services | Configuration Manager.

2. In the left pane, click Databases.

3. In the right pane, click the Create Database button.

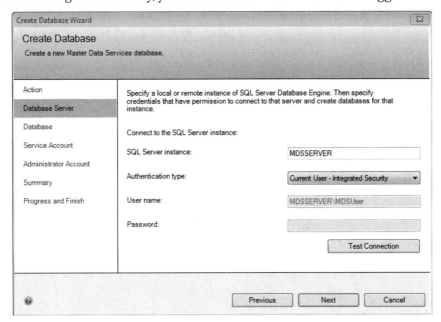

The Create Database wizard is displayed.

4. Click Next.

5. On the Database Server page, leave the defaults unless you want to connect to a remote instance of SQL Server or use a different type of authentication. If you choose Integrated Security, you must use the credentials of the logged-in user.

NOTE

In this example we specify a local account but you can use a domain account instead.

6.   Click Test Connection to ensure you can connect successfully.

7.   Click OK to close the dialog box.
8.   Click Next.
9.   On the Database page, enter a name for your database. Depending on the collation and regional settings for your database, searches you do in the Master Data Manager web application may or may not be case sensitive.

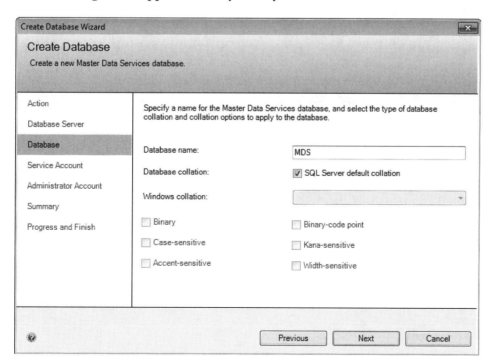

10. Click Next.

11. On the Service Account page, type the name of the account that the web sites use to connect to the database. Later, you will designate the same account if you create an associated web site.

12. Click Next.

13. On the Administrator Account page, type the name of a user who you want to have the ability to edit all data and to view and update all models. This user is more likely to be a business owner than to be an IT person.

14. Click Next.

15. On the Summary page, click Next.

16. A progress message is displayed while the database is created. When it's done, you should see a success message.

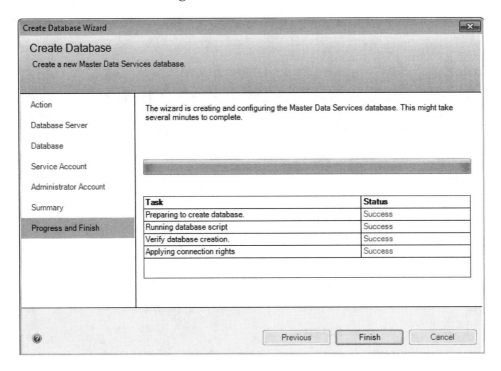

17.   Click Finish to close the wizard.

MDS Configuration Manager opens and displays the default settings.

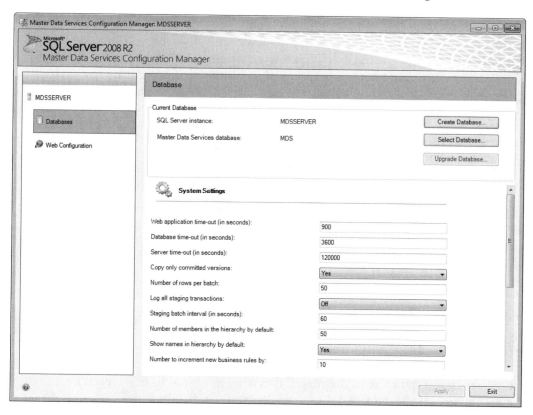

About System Settings

System settings displayed on the Database page of MDS Configuration Manager
are stored in your MDS database in the tblSystemSetting table. These settings apply
to the database, the web site, and web services. Many of the system settings are self-
explanatory, but we will discuss them in the chapters that explain the features they
apply to. For now, you can leave the default values.

Creating the Master Data Manager Web Application

Throughout much of this book, we will talk about Master Data Services as a platform. MDM applications need the capability to integrate with all of the systems and business processes within an organization. Unlike other platforms that Microsoft creates, MDS comes with a complete user-facing, web-based UI. Configuring this web application on a web server will allow any user to access MDS through their browser.

NOTE

MDS officially supports Internet Explorer 7 and 8. While users can access the site using other browsers, those other browsers may display screens incorrectly, with menus that behave poorly or not at all. Unless you are extremely adventurous and vehemently opposed to IE, always access MDS with IE 7 or 8.

When creating the Master Data Manager web application, there are two possible workflows: either you select the default web site and create the web application, or you create a new site and the web application is automatically created. Later in this chapter, we discuss how to secure your web site. If you plan to secure MDS to require SSL connections, it is advisable to create a new site now.

Changes to any of this configuration information at any time will not affect the underlying MDS implementation. All MDS implementation-specific data is stored in the database. This allows you to back up and restore MDS on any number of servers or configurations without any potential for loss of data.

If your server is part of a server farm where the default site has been removed or you cannot use it, you can create a site now. Otherwise, you can skip this procedure, select the default web site, and go straight to creating your application.

Procedure: Create a Master Data Manager Web Site (Optional)

To create a Master Data Manager web site, complete the following steps:

> **NOTE**
>
> *If you create a new site, the web application is automatically created. You can skip the procedure for creating a web application and continue with associating the site to the database.*

1. Open Master Data Services Configuration Manager.
2. In the left pane, click Web Configuration.
3. Click the Create Site button.

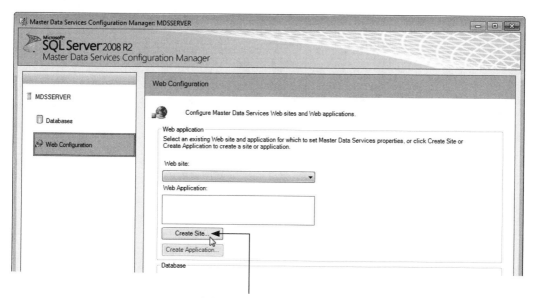

Click to create a web site.

4. In the Create Web Site dialog box, enter a name for your web site.

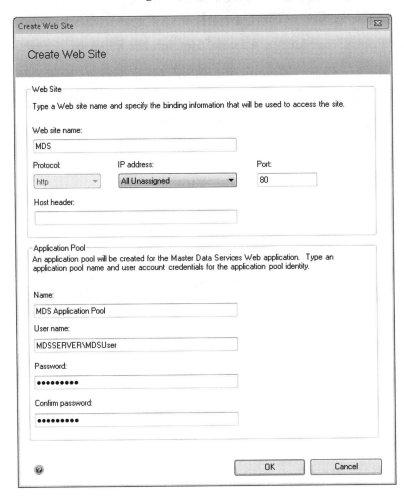

5. In the Protocol list, leave the default setting of http. If you need to use HTTPS, you will have to use IIS to configure the site after it is installed.

6. In the IP Address and Port fields, leave the default values or enter new values. A default installation in Windows 7 already uses port 80, so you must select a different port, like 8080, or you will get an error.

7. In the Host Header field, if your site is going to be on an intranet, leave it blank. If your site will be available on the Internet or you want to create multiple host names for your site, enter the host name.

8. In the Application Pool section, leave the name of the site or enter your own. An application pool with this name will be created in IIS.

9. In the User Name field, enter the same username you used as the service account when you created the database.

10. In the Password and Confirm Password fields, enter the user account password.

11. Click OK.

12. A note about HTTPS is displayed. Click OK.

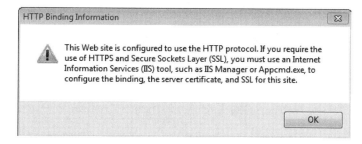

For more information about securing your web site, see the "Securing Your Web Application" section later in this chapter.

Procedure: Create a Master Data Manager Web Application

If you chose to use the default web site, you can create the Master Data Manager web application by completing the following steps:

1. In the Web Site list, select "Default Web Site" and click the Create Application button.

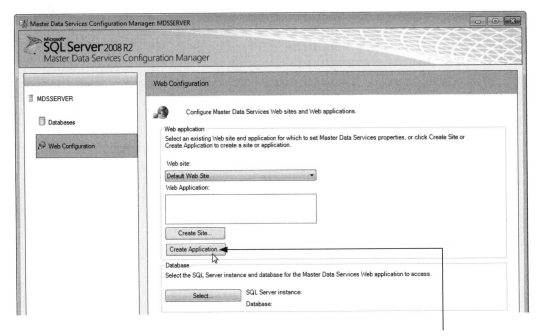

Click to create a web application.

2. In the Create Web Application dialog box, you can change the default alias or application pool names or leave them alone. The alias determines your URL. In this example, the URL will be http://MDSServer/MDS.

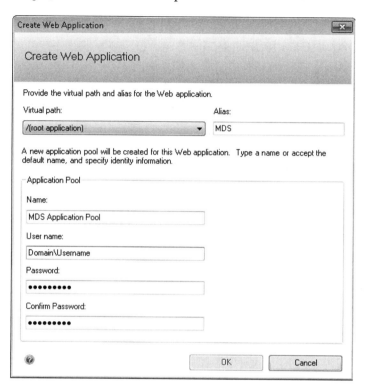

3. In the User Name field, type the name of the user you used for the service account when creating the MDS database. This user is the application pool identity in IIS.

4. Click OK to save.

Procedure: Associate the MDS Database with the Web Application

You must now associate a database with the web application you just created.

1.   In the Web Configuration dialog box, in the Database section, click the Select button.

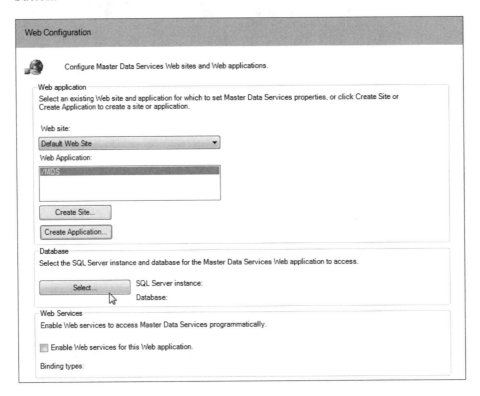

2.   In the Connect to a Master Data Services Database dialog box, click Connect.

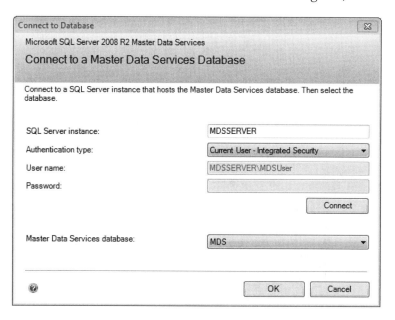

3. In the Master Data Services Database list, your database is automatically selected. Click OK to close the window. You can now view the association between your web site and its database.

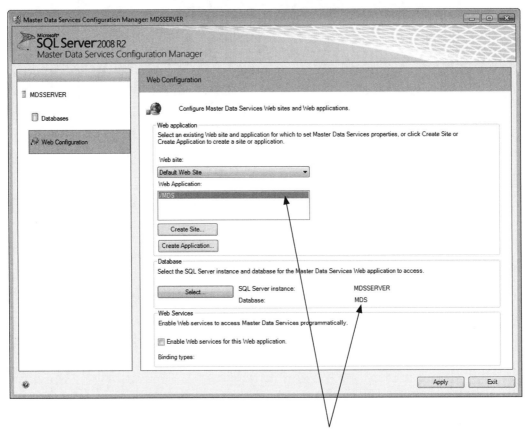

The SQL Server instance associated with your web application is displayed.

4. To enable web services, select the "Enable Web services for this Web application" check box. (More details about configuring web services are provided in Chapter 1.)
5. Click Apply to save your changes.

After you associate your web application with your MDS database, you are prompted to launch the web application. If you can successfully open the Master Data Manager home page from the local machine and from others on the intranet, your installation has been successful.

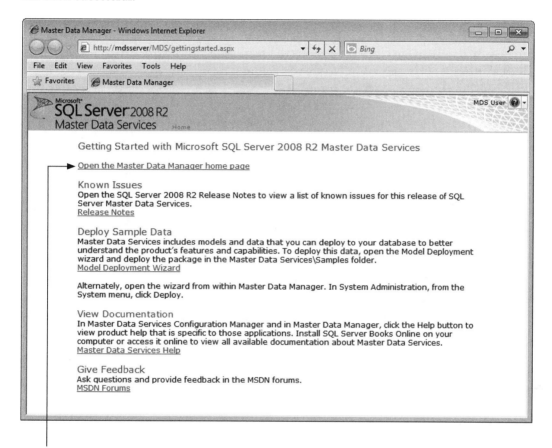

Click to open the Master Data Manager web application.

If Internet Explorer prompts you for your username and password, enter the credentials you used for the Administrator Account when creating the database. Other users do not have permission to access the Master Data Manager web application until the administrator gives them permission.

Securing Your Web Application

MDS Configuration Manager will create an unsecured web site only. This means that data traveling over the wire (between the web server and the client's browser) is unencrypted and readable by anyone. Since this site will not be publicly available and the master data stored is not highly sensitive, these settings should be fine for most organizations. If you are concerned about the security of your master data or if sensitive internal information is stored in MDS, you can require SSL for your web site.

This requires three steps to be completed: create or download a certificate, apply the certificate to the default web site, and require SSL.

First, you must download a certificate for your web site. To do so, complete the following steps:

1. Open Internet Information Services (IIS). You can do this by right-clicking My Computer and choosing Manage. IIS is listed under Services and Applications.
2. In the Connections pane, click the server name.
3. In the center pane, double-click Server Certificates.
4. In the Actions pane, click the action preferred by your organization. Since every company has a different policy for getting and managing certificates, we will leave the acquisition of your certificate up to you.

After you have a valid certificate, you must apply the certificate to the web site. To do so, complete the following steps:

1. In IIS, click Default Web Site (or other site you created).
2. In the Actions pane, click Bindings.
3. Click the Add button.
4. From the Type list, select https.
5. Select the SSL certificate you created.
6. Click OK.
7. Click Close.

Now require SSL by completing the following steps:

1. In the Connections pane, click the web site.
2. In the center pane, double-click SSL Settings.

3. Select the Require SSL check box and indicate whether you want to ignore, accept, or require client certificates.

4. In the Actions pane, click Apply.

Getting the Latest Version of MDS

Microsoft issues hotfixes in response to customer requests. These hotfixes are periodically compiled into cumulative updates. And eventually, these cumulative updates are released as service packs, roughly a year after the initial release.

In the case of Master Data Services, some significant updates have been made as part of these releases, so you want to make sure you've downloaded them. Microsoft began releasing cumulative updates for MDS in June of 2010. These cumulative updates are released approximately every two months. Currently these updates are complete installations of MDS, which means installing the latest cumulative update will install all of the fixes supplied in previous updates. While many companies have policies against installing anything lower than a service pack without specific requirements, because MDS is a version 1 product, we suggest that you install the latest cumulative update before starting your project. We also recommend that you seriously review each subsequent cumulative update for any fixes that will affect your implementation positively.

To install the June 2010 cumulative update, complete the following steps. You should follow a similar process to install any future cumulative updates. The steps are slightly complicated, so we thought we'd walk you through them. Before you install the cumulative update, it is important to note the following:

▶ The update will work only once and it must be run on a 64-bit machine.

▶ The update should be downloaded by using Internet Explorer, rather than other browsers.

▶ If you're running Windows 7, make sure you always right-click the msi file and choose "Run as administrator."

▶ You should stop IIS before installing the update.

▶ If you already have MDS installed, you must have the SQL Server 2008 R2 version, rather than a customer preview version.

To install the cumulative update, complete the following steps.

1. Go to http://support.microsoft.com/kb/2143880.
2. Click the "View and request hotfix downloads" link.

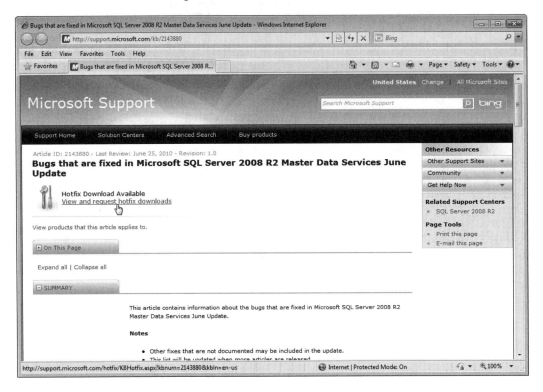

3. Accept the terms and conditions.

4. Select the first hotfix that's listed. It should have MD_Services or something similar as part of the filename. The other update is for SQL Server 2008 R2 but is not specific to Master Data Services.

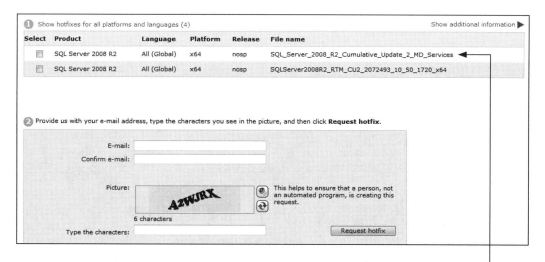

Select the Master Data Services update

5. Enter your e-mail address and type the characters provided in the Picture box.

6. Click the Request Hotfix button.

7. Within a few minutes you will receive an e-mail. Click the link at the bottom of the e-mail.

8. To unzip the files, you must enter a password that was included in the e-mail.

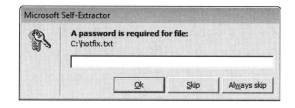

9. The files are unzipped, and you can now double-click the MasterDataServices
    .msi file to start the installation.

10. When the installation is complete, MDS Configuration Manager opens. Select
    your database by clicking the Select Database button. You are then prompted to
    upgrade the database.

11. Click the Upgrade Database button.

12. A wizard walks you through the upgrade. When it's finished, the updates have
    been successfully installed.

Summary

In this chapter, you have successfully installed Master Data Services. After determining
the scope of your application, you were able to determine the best architecture for your
system. You then explored the configuration options available in MDS and deployed
the web application.

Chapter 3

Starting an MDS Project

In This Chapter

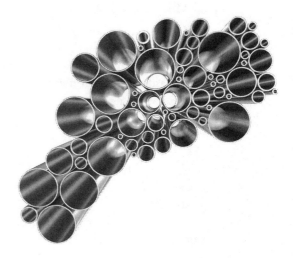

Before you build a model in MDS or any master data management (MDM) system, it is essential to have a basic understanding of your data and current processes. In this chapter, we provide deeper insight into what is and what is not master data, and we provide some simple labels for your current business systems. Toward the end of the chapter, we discuss some tips and tricks for modeling your data, with the goal of helping you to free your enterprise from many of the data restrictions that have plagued it for so long. We then apply these lessons to the Main Street Clothing Company example.

How Do I Know Master Data When I See It?

Over the past year, one of the questions most commonly asked by customers has been, "Is there a definitive line between master data and other important data in my company?" The truth is, there isn't one and there shouldn't be. In most companies, master data management is used only for business-critical domains like product or customer. This limitation is necessary simply because the implementation of MDM solutions throughout these organizations is so prohibitively expensive. If an accessible solution with a rapid time to value were available, other important domains could benefit from MDM tools as well.

We've already talked about a couple of the key differentiators between master data and transactional data within an enterprise, but they are worth repeating: Data that you wish to store in MDS should not relate to a single event in time because it is transactional data. In MDS, you should store information that has a state or continues to have a state for some specific period of time. This information is master data.

Business Process Models

Before you build your model in MDS or any MDM system, it is imperative to understand the flow of data through your enterprise. Where do new accounts, customers, or products originate? What is the process that turns a concept into a product? What is the process to onboard a new customer? How does the data flow from inception to all systems across the organization?

Business process modeling can provide decision makers with the information that they need to prioritize and plan the creation of their MDS implementation. Modeling all processes related to the creation and maintenance of domains you are interested in managing is the most logical place to start. Although you could employ skilled business process managers to interview employees and provide detailed designs of their findings, most projects can get by with a do-it-yourself approach.

Your first step should be a quick inventory of any existing documentation of current processes, like the example shown in Figure 3-1. Much of what you require might

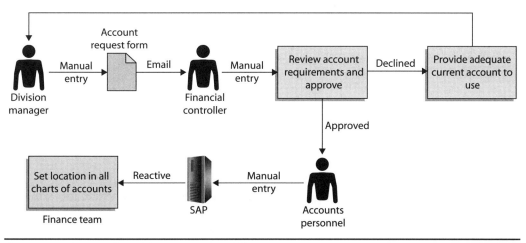

Figure 3-1 *Diagram of sample business process model*

already exist. Be sure to review any existing documents with current employees in the modeled roles. It is astounding how quickly reality can diverge from the documentation given a little bit of time. The more manual the processes, the more easily these processes can change or be abandoned.

When you conduct the interviews required to create a business process model yourself, you should complete the following two steps in sequence. Each step provides insight into the investigated domain. Make sure to record the actors, activity, and length of time required for each business process.

1. Determine how new data members are created in the organization. Make sure to investigate any alternative methods that may lead to the creation of a new member. Lead the interview with questions like "How does this system interact with other systems?" or "Are there any emergency processes?" These can lead to important discoveries. As you begin to integrate systems across organizations, it may be pertinent to ask about any automated systems that may generate new members.

2. For each of the methods discovered in the previous step, drill into any workflow or process to enrich the data member before you consider it complete and ready for use in any systems within the scope of the project. Each system that will be reliant on this information may have different requirements, so it is best to address each system's needs. This step is also the best time to identify the primary owner for each business process or system. Primary owners will have a vested interest in their processes and will require assurances that most if not all of their current domain needs will be addressed in any business refactoring.

All of the information you collect will result in a diagram or set of diagrams similar to Figure 3-1. These diagrams will help you to determine the most palatable flow of master data through the organization. You will need to review each system within the scope of the project to decide what type of role it will play for data of each domain type. Determining the role played by each system is the next step in determining how MDS fits into your organization.

System Roles

Systems can be categorized into three different roles. As different domains have significantly different origination points, it is common for the same system to perform separate roles for different domains within a company.

System of Entry

A system of entry (SOE) is a system where data is first entered in a business. These systems typically have all of the users who are able to create new data. Generally, these are the systems that are used daily by the owners of the type of data being investigated. Many systems of entry require that rules be enforced before data can fully be entered. Oftentimes these rules force much of the accumulated information about the member record to be managed outside of the system.

Think of a new product being created. Often, the inception of a new product is scribbled on a napkin or sketched on a whiteboard. Many of the details of the product will be discussed and decided via e-mail format. It is important to capture and manage this process, because creating a workflow and roles around product creation can provide many benefits, like online collaboration and a tracked history of the creative process. The lack of resources to manage this process often impedes the implementation of a new product.

System of Record

A system of record (SOR) is any system within the organization that is considered the source for other systems. Typically, the enterprise resource planning (ERP) system is the system of record within an organization, but oftentimes many other systems can be considered sources for downstream systems. Many data inconsistencies are created on multiple SORs within an organization. While MDS strives to be an adequate SOE for organizations, it is imperative that many if not all SORs are moved onto the MDS platform. This is where much of the value of master data management is derived.

Subscribing System

As your MDS implementation matures, the most common type of system should be a subscribing system. Subscribing systems are those systems that consume data from another system with no direct user changes to the managed domain. Some larger companies use an intermediate store to pass data to multiple systems. As long as direct changes are not made in any of these systems, all these systems can be considered downstream subscribing systems.

Mapping the Data

The next phase in the project plan is to determine data sizes and types within the Master Data Services system. Analysis of all source systems' main tables and their columns to determine the best data type for storing that data can provide an initial roadmap for MDS. There are two main questions that must be asked during this phase: What kinds of internal constraints are placed on this column? Are there any downstream constraints in the organization that require further data cleansing to be performed?

You should start the mapping process by identifying those columns within the source system that you will manage in MDS. For each of these columns, determine a rudimentary data type. In Chapter 4, we discuss the different data types available in MDS, but for now just identify data as date, number, or string.

If you identify a date field, be very careful that this field provides information across multiple systems and is a state of the mapped domain. Oftentimes, date fields are red flags that you have mistaken a system-specific field such as "entry date" for a more important field like "start date" or "discontinued date." You should be extra wary of any column that requires the storage of a specific date or time. These fields generally signal that the information stored is most likely transactional in nature.

Columns that you identify as numeric should be reviewed as well. Is this column storing a valid state on a record? We have seen many projects in which the designers have been tempted to map in fields such as account balances or sales figures. These numbers are subject to daily change and are best handled as part of a business intelligence (BI) solution. Master Data Services does not support simple math functions or consolidations, in an effort to dissuade users from storing inappropriate data. This does not mean all numbers should not be stored. MSRP, safety stock levels, standard terms, and credit limits are all valid information for MDS. When identifying numeric columns, you should log the precision, or number of decimal places, each column will require. While many systems may not limit this on the backend, the actual required precision should be easy to determine for the primary system owner.

When mapping a source system to MDS, it may be advisable to create additional entities to store choices for certain fields. Some of these relationships are easy to see. If there is a foreign key relationship within the source system that displays options for one field to another, you should continue to preserve this relationship. For instance, if a customer has a relationship to an address table that stores addresses available to the customer, this relationship can be modeled in MDS.

Some relationships are not quite as evident, though. For instance, a source system may only store specific attributes as text fields, yet valid values for those text fields may be constrained by the business process. If those values are better managed in a separate table, and a foreign key relationship between those tables would be advisable, you want to highlight those relationships now. Determine if any of these relationships may be reused. For instance, within many data sources, there will be a number of fields that map to a choice of either Yes or No. In these cases, you may want to create a single entity to store those valid choices.

Determining What to Do with Duplicate Records

Data quality is a major concern for corporations, and the identification and management of duplicate records is a central task in the effort to ensure data quality. Duplicate records exist within organizations for a variety of reasons. One of the biggest reasons employees duplicate records is that they are unaware that records already exist in a separate system, because the systems are not integrated effectively. These records should be merged wherever possible.

Some companies intentionally duplicate records within systems for a specific purpose, typically to work around limitations within current applications to support necessary business processes. In most cases, these duplicates must remain within the business application to continue to provide the workaround they were designed for.

Determining Which Attributes to Manage

To determine whether an attribute should be managed in MDS, data stewards must decide on the nature of the attribute. Is this a state of the domain? Is this information useful for multiple systems? All numeric and date fields should be evaluated closely. Tracking information should not be managed if it is specific to an application in the organization. Calculated values or balances should not be managed in an MDS system because these values will change over time. Make sure that attributes that store a product's age are not managed as such but that you manage the product's date of creation instead.

The Main Street Clothing Company Example

Before the Main Street Clothing Company can build anything in Master Data Services, it is critical that it examine its current processes. All of the following chapters of this book will leverage information collected in the following pages. Although building an MDM solution can be an iterative process, early understanding of the problem space and employees' roles in the process can lead to rapid satisfaction and effective adoption of the new system. An early successful implementation can lead to additional requests for new domains.

Finding a Data Steward

Once Main Street Clothing Company had determined that an MDS implementation would be beneficial to its organization, it needed to find a project manager. Since there were a number of important sets of data to manage and some amount of ongoing responsibility would be required post-implementation, Anthony Green was identified as the best candidate for the position. Anthony has been with Main Street Clothing Company for a number of years in a business analyst role. He has some limited database experience and was involved in a number of prior system implementations. Main Street plans to have Anthony remain as the owner of the MDS server and serve as the *de facto* data steward for the organization.

Leveraging the Business Process Models

During the implementation of SAP, the implementation team created detailed maps of the business process for creating new products and accounts. Anthony can use these maps to determine the best way to integrate MDS into the current process. A portion of this is shown in Figure 3-2.

Anthony is able to leverage this information to investigate how much time is required to create a new account and he finds very little inefficiency in this process. The major issue with accounts is the difficulty the accounting department has when managing multiple consolidations for the chart of accounts. These issues tend to be related to legal and taxation requirements. Figure 3-3 shows Main Street Clothing Company's process for processing accounts.

Despite his best efforts, Anthony was unable to find any process maps that detailed the location data for the company. Although it has been over a year since Main Street Clothing Company has opened a new store location, everyone agrees that the workflow for opening a new store is disorganized and reactive.

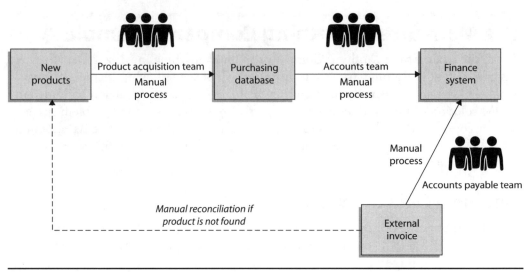

Figure 3-2   *Product business process map*

Filling in the Gaps

In reviewing the existing business process models, Anthony determined that the system of entry for products in his company was first created in a custom Access database run by the product acquisition team. This team consists of a manager and two buyers who work with a number of manufacturers and suppliers.

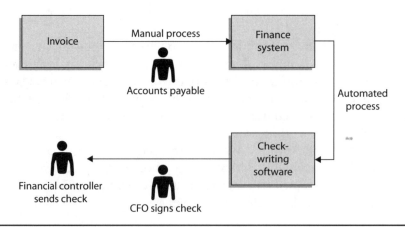

Figure 3-3   *Account business process map*

The product acquisition team enters the products that they wish to purchase into their homegrown system. They also use this system to keep track of notes such as expected demand and types of offers they are considering. After the manager has agreed with their findings, the buyers e-mail a spreadsheet of new product purchases to the accounts team.

The accounts team then manually codes new products into the system and ties them to a supplier code. When an invoice arrives from the supplier, new product inventory is added into the ERP system for those products. Any products that are absent on the initial entry must be entered at this time. An attempt will be made to contact the appropriate buyer to determine whether the new product is accurate, but if the buyer is unavailable, much of the product information will be left blank for later input. Many of these inconsistencies are not found until month-end reports are run and data is blank. Sometimes, additional merchandise is accepted and placed in the store even though it was not intended to be purchased by the buyer. In these cases, the product acquisition team must scramble to determine if this is a happy mistake or if they need to pull the inventory from the shelves. The product acquisition team estimates that this happens two to three times each year.

Anthony then reviews the business process models for location. He determines that much of the information in the SAP system is in one large entry as the location is conceived. Because the creation of a new store is a long process with many people involved, there is no standard process for collecting all the required information, such as square footage, lease type, and other information that is negotiated or decided upon. Anthony determines a larger problem for location is that the parties responsible for managing renewal of leases or other location management do not have access to the system where this data is stored. They are managing this information in files and folders and have very few electronic warnings before these things require attention. This creates the unwelcome situation where lease negotiations or other decisions are triggered by third parties who call headquarters.

Investigation of the employee process shows Anthony that, in many cases, starting dates and ending dates are incorrect in the source system because the accounts team has been incorrectly coding the hire date as the start date for the last six months. One store manager was aware of the issue but had been unable to get the accounting department to fix the problem. The accounts team, which was in the middle of month- and year-end close, felt this problem could wait to be resolved and just forgot to return to the problem once those times of high stress had concluded. Anthony would like to address these inconsistencies as part of the MDS implementation.

Determining System Types

Now that Anthony has reviewed the current processes, he needs to determine the role each system will play when MDS is added into the process. As each business process treats systems differently, he recognizes that he should look at the matrix of each system for each domain within the organization.

Domain	Product Mgmt. System	ERP	Data Warehouse	Warehouse Tracking System
Product	SOE	SOR	Subscribing	Subscribing
Location	No data	SOR	Subscribing	Subscribing
Employee	Subscribing	SOR	Subscribing	Subscribing
Account	No data	SOR	Subscribing	Subscribing

Once MDS is implemented in the organization, many of the systems will perform a different role within the organization. The following table shows the revised system model.

Domain	MDS	ERP	Data Warehouse	Warehouse Tracking System
Product	SOE, SOR	Subscribing	Subscribing	Subscribing
Location	SOE/SOR	Subscribing	Subscribing	Subscribing
Employee	SOE	SOR	Subscribing	Subscribing
Account	SOE/SOR (hierarchy only)	SOE, SOR	Subscribing	Subscribing

For each domain to be managed in MDS, Anthony builds a new business process model to show what the proposed process will look like once his implementation is complete. He will use these diagrams to socialize the new process and ensure that all participants feel their interests will be met when the new MDS implementation is complete. It is important that all stakeholders feel that the implementation team is aware of their specific needs and that the new process will not be an obstacle to their daily jobs.

In the model shown in Figure 3-4, Anthony proposes the product management database be replaced with a model that includes MDS. All of the functionality that was supported in this system can be replicated within MDS.

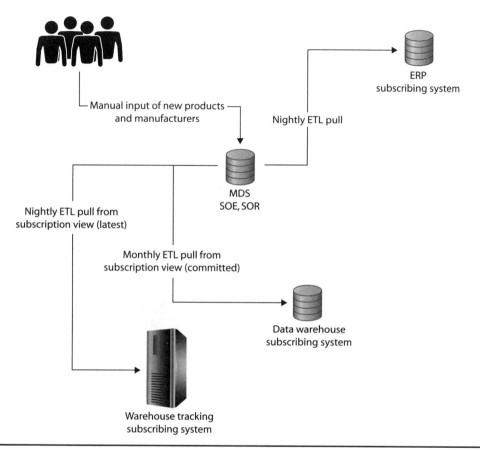

Figure 3-4 *New product management process with MDS*

Anthony suspects that the distributed nature of locations management makes MDS a natural place to manage this domain. In the model shown in Figure 3-5, Anthony shows the location management process where MDS is now used to manage the location workflow process.

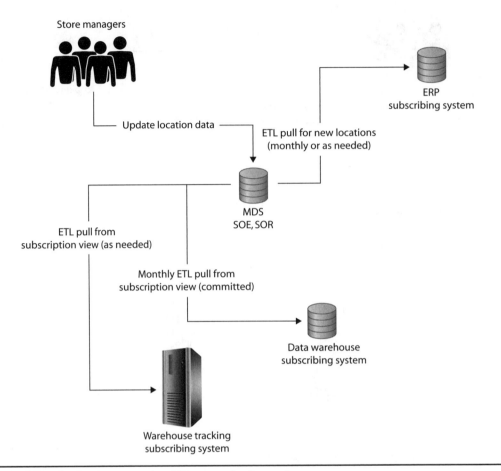

Figure 3-5   *New location process where MDS manages location creation process*

Cleansing Data for Initial Import into MDS

Now that Anthony has socialized the proposed process for managing products in MDS, he must create a clean list of products to initially load into MDS. In many organizations, producing a clean list of products can be a large project; due to the size of Main Street Clothing Company, Anthony will take an export from the product management database as a starting point. He will enhance this export by adding any products that exist in the ERP system. These additional products may have been added if they were part of an invoice received from a supplier.

Very little de-duplication will be required for managing any domains at Main Street Clothing Company. One of the benefits of implementing an MDM solution while a company is small is that you can get a handle on your data before the complexity and size of the processes and data make cleansing a major project for the organization. For each domain, Anthony will create an Excel spreadsheet listing all of the records and their managed attributes.

Summary

It is important to understand the flow of data within an organization before implementing an MDM system. Any MDM system that does not match the natural flow of data through an organization is doomed to fail, as busy users work in the easiest, most natural manner. All systems within an organization can be classified as either systems of entry, systems of record, or subscribing systems.

Many systems within the organization will have data-cleansing needs. It is important to determine what remediation will be acceptable if duplicate records are found. If history must be maintained for duplicate members, a mapping between the MDS source and the system should be maintained. In the next chapter, we discuss how to create our models in MDS.

Chapter 4

Creating Your Model

In This Chapter

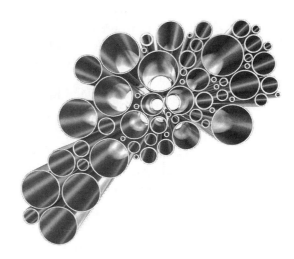

I n this chapter, we discuss the creation and customization of MDS models. In MDS, models are the central work surface that will be exposed to the master data editors and consumers once your project goes live. The success of your project will depend mainly on how well you build your model.

We begin with a discussion of modeling concepts. Then we show you how to deploy prebuilt models. We load the sample company's Finance model and then spend the remainder of the chapter creating a Product model from scratch. Finally, we give examples of how to use web services to perform some of the procedures we've already performed in the UI. (From now on, we will use "Master Data Manager web application" and "web UI" synonymously.)

MDS Modeling Concepts

Master Data Services is made up of a relatively simple group of concepts. These concepts are encapsulated as data containers and services exposed in MDS. While these concepts are simple to understand by themselves, it is the varied and complex data schemas that these concepts support that provide both the power and complexity of MDS. Before we delve into the implementation of the model objects, let's review general definitions of these MDS concepts. Each of these concepts is described in more detail later in the chapter.

- ▶ **Models**   Models are the highest level of organization within MDS. Models are nothing but containers of related entities. Only entities within the same model can be related within MDS. Models are the first concept discussed in this chapter.

- ▶ **Entities**   Entities are the base containers for data in MDS. In their simplest form, entities can be thought of as tables in a database. Users control the attributes (columns) that are managed for each entity. If explicit hierarchies are enabled for an entity, the entity becomes far more complex, managing parent members and their consolidations as well as collections, their attributes, and the members associated with those collections. Most of this chapter is devoted to discussing how to create the structures of entities.

- ▶ **Members**   Members are the records that populate all the entities created in MDS. Members can be either leaf or consolidated. Leaf members are the primary members of an entity. If an entity is enabled for explicit hierarchies and collections, then consolidated members can be created, and can have their own attributes. Members will be discussed in this chapter as well as in Chapter 7.

- ▶ **Attributes**   Attributes describe members. Attributes can be loosely thought of as columns in a table. Entities contain members and their attribute values. Attributes can be free-form or domain-based.

▶ **Domain-based Attributes**   Domain-based attributes are attributes in which the available values are restricted to the members stored in a related entity.

▶ **Hierarchies**   Hierarchies are consolidations or groupings of members that aid in reporting and analysis. There are two management types for hierarchies in MDS: explicit and derived. Hierarchies enforce rules for member inclusion to ensure consolidations do not lose or double count values in connected applications. Hierarchies will be discussed in detail in Chapter 6.

▶ **Collections**   Collections provide member grouping flexibility that is not supported in hierarchies. Collections will be discussed in detail in Chapter 6.

Building a Model

Master Data Services begins as a blank canvas, allowing you to create your data models within the product in any way you choose. The model structure is created in the System Administration functional area of the Master Data Manager web application, or by using the web services. As you create the structure, you can open the Explorer functional area of the UI to see the results of your work. The Explorer functional area is where users will go day to day to manage their master data.

Opening the System Administration area of the Master Data Manager web UI for the first time can be a daunting experience. The initial screen, shown in Figure 4-1, displays a model called Metadata. This is the only system model within Master Data Services and its use will be explained in Chapter 10.

Notice that the menu bar and page title of the System Administration functional area both contain the word "Explorer." If you go back to the home page, you'll see that there is an Explorer functional area, where you will manage master data. This is not the same as the System Administration area, where you use the Explorer page to manage your model structure. Most of the time, when we mention Explorer, we mean the functional area that you access from the home page.

If you are a new user of MDS, you have two avenues for creating your first useful model within the product. You can load a model deployment package into your database and modify the model from there, or you can build your model from scratch.

Starting with a predefined model can be the easiest way to get started with SQL Server MDS. Over the course of this book, we are going to work with Finance and Product models for our fictional company, Main Street Clothing Company. In this chapter, we are going to deploy the Finance model and create the Product model from scratch. You can find the complete packages of our models, both with and without sample data, at our web site: www.mdsuser.com.

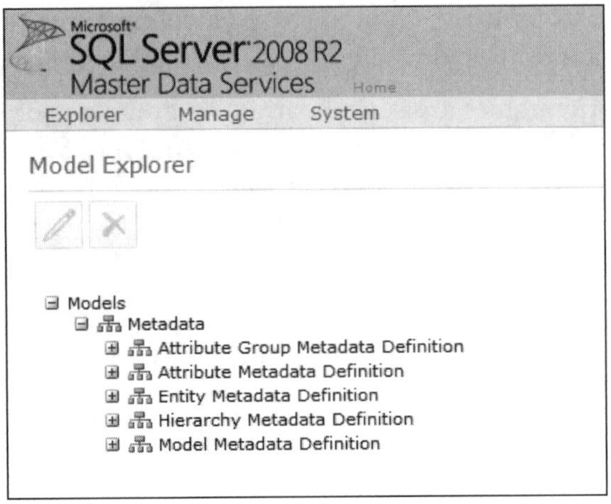

Figure 4-1 *The default Metadata model that is created during installation*

MDS also includes three sample models in the installation. These samples are very basic Customer, Product, and Account models, located in Program Files\Microsoft SQL Server\Master Data Services\Samples\Packages. You can take a look at them to get a better idea of some of the more common features of the application.

While these packages provide some data and attributes and support the documentation provided in SQL Server Books Online, they are relatively limited in their functionality and do not provide adequate coverage for the exercises listed in this book. However, these models include sample data, hierarchies, business rules, and versioning, so you can see what the end result of all your upcoming work might look like.

In the next exercise, we will walk through how to deploy our sample Finance model.

Deploying a Model

A model deployment package is an XML file saved with a .pkg extension. It includes the model structure, the business rules (Chapter 8), and version flags (Chapter 9). It does not include metadata (Chapter 10), file attributes (Chapter 4), and user and group permissions (Chapter 11). Model packages can contain the data from a version of the model, but they do not have to.

Model deployment in MDS was designed to provide organizations with two very important capabilities related to managing data models in MDS. The first is the capability to develop, test, and deploy a model within three separate implementations of MDS, while limiting the number of objects that need to be re-created in each environment. This enables IT management to roll out changes en masse and to ensure the production environment remains operational throughout the process.

The second capability enables organizations to share their model schemas with others. There are a number of efforts across a host of industries to standardize object models. Previously, most organizations would develop data models in a vacuum, creating schemas that solved their current problem most efficiently. They integrated only those applications owned by the organization and central to the solution. IT departments at all of their competitors were doing the same. This led to a wide variety of data models among competitors in the same industry. Some organizations built data models that were flexible, stable, and scalable, but many did not. When consolidation within an industry occurred, acquiring companies discovered similar business processes were hard to integrate due to the vastly different data models that had been developed in isolation.

Following are a couple of advantages to employing common data models within an industry:

▶ **Benefit of experience**   Civilization wouldn't get very far if each new generation needed to reinvent the wheel. By leveraging a common data model developed by industry experts, companies are able to avoid issues that they might otherwise experience personally.

▶ **Standardization**   Standards help companies and software providers by limiting the amount of variation that must be managed. Standards allow companies to better manage acquisitions and new integration projects. Software can focus on enhancing business value as opposed to compatibility.

MDS supports these efforts in two ways. By not enforcing its own model, MDS ensures there is one less data model to be managed. Model deployment empowers industry leaders to quickly build master data–centric versions of these industry models, providing efficient deployment across their industry. Any customization that needs be made to these standardized models is still supported in MDS.

Procedure: How to Deploy a Model

To deploy a sample model, complete the following steps:

> **NOTE**
>
> *If you want to deploy the sample Finance model we refer to in this book, get it from www.mdsuser.com before you start this procedure.*

1. On the Master Data Manager home page, click System Administration.
2. On the menu bar, choose System | Deployment.
3. On the Model Deployment wizard screen, click Deploy.
4. Click Browse to find the sample package file.

5. In the Windows "Choose File to Upload" dialog box, select your package (.pkg) file and click Open.

6. The wizard shows the path to your model. Click Next.

7. A success message tells you that the model was successfully loaded. This means that the model and its data are ready to be imported, not that the import has taken place.

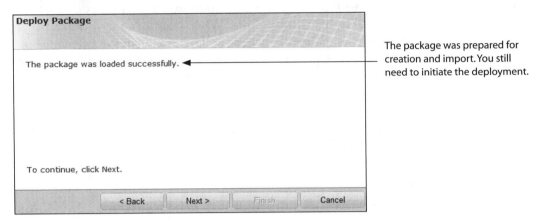

The package was prepared for creation and import. You still need to initiate the deployment.

8. Click Next. At this point, the Finish button is available, but don't be tempted to click it. You cannot exit the wizard while the package is being deployed, though you can minimize it if you want. Wait until you see the success screen before you click Finish.

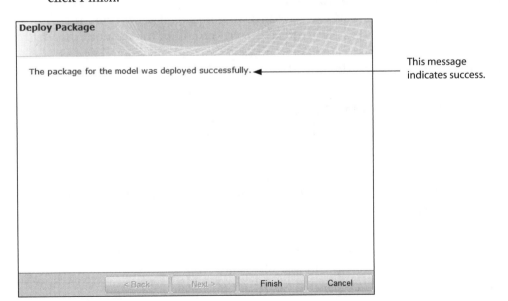

This message indicates success.

You can confirm that the model was deployed successfully by going to the home page and looking in the drop-down list of available models.

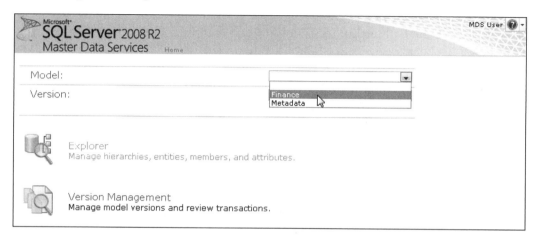

To view the Finance model in more detail, select VERSION_1 from the Version list and then click Explorer. Your business users will manage master data in the Explorer functional area. When you configure security, you will be able to give users access to specific data within the Explorer functional area.

All other functional areas of the web UI are intended for administrators. Let's take a moment to discuss the other four functional areas.

▶ **Version Management**   Use this area to validate full versions of your model against business rules. You can also create versions of your models and their data, and assign version flags, which indicate to subscribing systems which version of a model to use. More details about versioning can be found in Chapter 9.

▶ **Integration Management**   Use this area to import data into the proper MDS database tables. You can also use this area to create subscription views, which are SQL views used by subscribing systems to retrieve data from MDS. More information about staging data can be found in Chapter 5. See Chapter 12 for information on exporting data by using subscription views.

▶ **System Administration**   Use this area to build your models, entities, attributes, attribute groups, and derived hierarchies. You also use this area to manage business rules and create and deploy models. You will use System Administration extensively in this chapter and in Chapter 8 when we discuss business rules.

▶ **User and Group Permissions**   Use this area to give users access to specific functional areas and to specific data within those areas. More information about security is provided in Chapter 11.

About Models

As discussed previously, models are the highest level of organization within Master Data Services. Models are nothing but containers of related entities. Only entities within the same model can be related within MDS. This supports a simplified versioning model where all entities within a model are versioned simultaneously. Although many models revolve around a single domain such as customer or product, this is not a requirement. You can combine major entities into a single model if this makes business sense.

When determining whether or not to include an entity in a model, there are a number of factors to consider:

► Do the entities in the model have a relationship to one another?

► Is this relationship master data? Many entities have relationships that are transactional in nature. Only those relationships that are states that change over time and are not discreet instances should be managed in the MDS system. If the two entities have a natural affinity to be versioned at separate times, you may need to manage them in separate models.

► Does an entity only relate to a subset of another entity? If only a subset of the members participate in the relationship between the two entities, ensuring accurate selection may be compromised. Business rules can be used to ensure only the valid members are selected; business rules will be discussed in greater detail in Chapter 8.

About Main Street Clothing Company's Models

After performing all of the analysis discussed in the last chapter, Anthony Green has determined that he will require two models to be created in the organization's Master Data Services instance. The Product model will revolve around a central Product entity. This entity will not require an explicit hierarchy, so Anthony creates only product leaf members to begin. Due to the interconnected nature of all other managed entities, Anthony will create an additional model called Finance. Since there is no central entity or an entity called Finance, he will create the model only.

Procedure: How to Create a Model

To create a model, complete the following steps:

1. On the Master Data Manager home page, click System Administration.
2. On the menu bar, choose Manage | Models.
3. On the Model Maintenance page, click the Add model button.

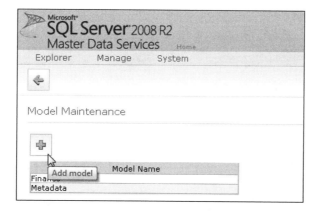

4. In the Model name field, type a name for your model. For this example, we'll call the model **Product**.

    The three check boxes on this page can be confusing if you've never done this before:

    ▶ **Create entity with same name as model**   Leave this box selected. This check box does just what it says—it creates an entity called Product. This option is here because, in many cases, a model revolves around a central entity.

    ▶ **Create explicit hierarchy with same name as model**   Briefly, an explicit hierarchy is a free-form hierarchy in which you can specify any number of levels, with a leaf member being allowed at any level and consolidated members being used for grouping. If you think you might want a hierarchy like this, you can select this check box. Because we don't discuss explicit hierarchies until Chapter 6, clear this check box for now. You can always enable this later.

    ▶ **Include all leaf members in mandatory hierarchy**   When you clear the preceding "Create explicit hierarchy" check box, this option is disabled.

5. Click Save.

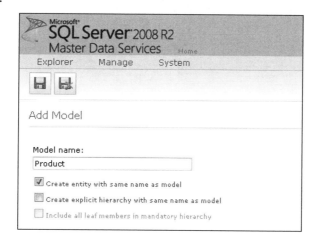

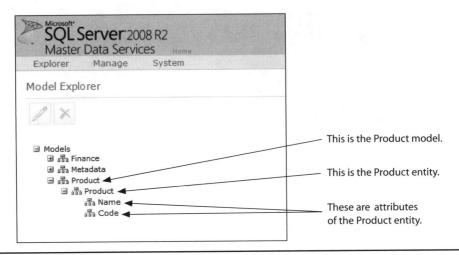

Figure 4-2 *Models in the System Administration functional area*

The Product model is now displayed as a hierarchy in System Administration, as shown in Figure 4-2. If it's not displayed already, click Explorer on the menu bar in System Administration to view it.

The hierarchical structure that is displayed here is meant to give you a quick look at the models you have permission to view and to the entities in each. This structure is not meant to represent levels of importance the way a typical hierarchy would. As you learn more about entities and attributes, we will provide more details about this structure.

Viewing the Results in Explorer

Now let's look at the model in the Explorer functional area. Go back to the Master Data Manager home page by clicking the logo or the Home link.

Click the logo or link to return to the home page.

TIP

If you are running Internet Explorer 8, you should choose Compatibility Mode before viewing data in the Explorer functional area of Master Data Manager. From the IE Tools menu, choose Compatibility Mode.

Select the Product model from the list. Select the version, which was automatically created as VERSION_1. Now click Explorer.

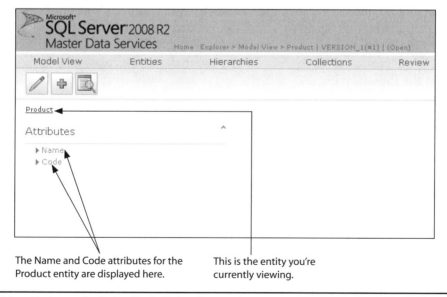

The base entity is displayed by default.

A *base entity* is the entity that is displayed by default when you open the Explorer functional area of the UI. As shown in Figure 4-3, the base entity is at the top of the hierarchy structure. After you create more entities, you will be able to drag-and-drop

Figure 4-3   *The base entity displayed in the Explorer functional area*

items in the hierarchy to move a different entity into the "base" position. More than one entity can be listed as a base entity within a model. If multiple entities are listed as base entities, all base entities will display when Explorer opens. You do not need to have a base entity in your model, though. If you don't, when Explorer opens, the screen will be largely blank, which is not a problem; all actions can be done from the menu bar.

Now you're ready to learn more about entities and practice creating a few.

About Entities

In MDS, all data that is managed by the system is stored in entities. Entities can be loosely thought of as tables in SQL. The data within entities are called members.

MDS's entities can also support explicit hierarchies. Once explicit hierarchies have been enabled for an entity, an entity becomes far more than a single table. The entity can then support parent and collection members, as well as hierarchy and collection relationships. Hierarchies and collections are discussed in detail in Chapter 6.

About Main Street Clothing Company's Entities

Within the Product model, the Product entity has already been created. We now need to create all of the supporting entities that will be used as options for attributes of members in the Product entity. While most of these entities will be used to populate a single domain-based attribute only, some entities can be used to populate multiple entities within the model. Entities such as Neck Style, Color, and Size can only be used for a single purpose, but multiple entities can use attributes with constraints such as "Yes" and "No."

First we will create the Yes No Picklist entity; then we will create all other entities needed in the Product model.

Procedure: How to Create an Entity

To create the Yes No Picklist entity, complete the following steps:

1. On the Master Data Manager home page, click System Administration.
2. On the menu bar, choose Manage | Entities.
3. On the Entity Maintenance page, click Add entity.

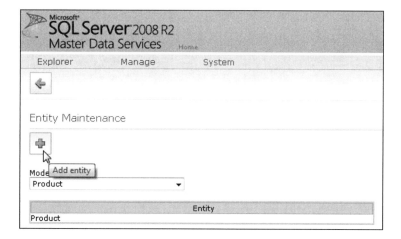

4. On the Add Entity page, in the Entity name box, type **Yes No Picklist**.
5. In the "Enable explicit hierarchies and collections" list, select No. Again, you can enable this later if you need to.

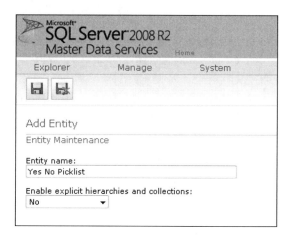

6. Click Save.

NOTE

Sometimes when you save an entity, you have to wait a long time for the page to refresh. You know the entity has been created when the Add Entity page closes and you're returned to the Entity Maintenance page.

The Yes No Picklist entity is now displayed on the Entity Maintenance page.

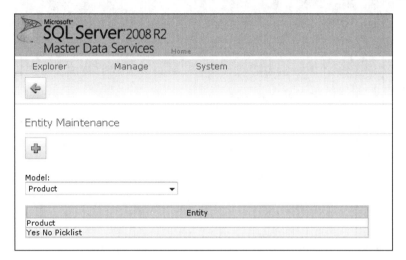

NOTE

To continue following along with the examples in this chapter, create the following entities: Type, Fabric, Neck Style, Gender, Color, and Size. These entities will contain lists of values that will be used to describe products, as you will soon learn.

When you are done, your Entity Maintenance page should look like Figure 4-4. Your entities are automatically alphabetized here.

Viewing the Results in Explorer

Now let's look at the entities in Explorer. Go back to the home page by clicking the logo in the top left or by clicking the Home link.

1. Select the Product model, VERSION_1, and click Explorer.
2. Now on the menu bar when you choose Entities, you see a list of available entities, as shown in the adjacent illustration.

Figure 4-4   *Completed Entity Maintenance page*

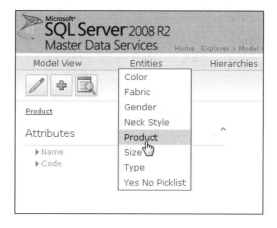

If you select an entity to view it in more detail, you can see that there is no master data in the entity yet. If there were, a grid would be displayed.

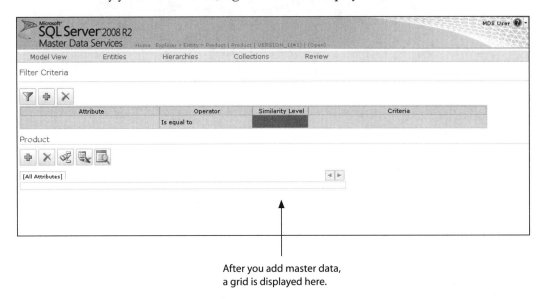

After you add master data,
a grid is displayed here.

Let's stop creating the model for a moment and talk about the members that will populate the grid.

About Members

Members are the individual records stored in Master Data Services. Members are uniquely identified by the required Code attribute. There are two types of members in MDS: leaf members and consolidated members.

Leaf members are the most granular level of records in an entity and usually represent physical objects within your business. For example, in a Product entity, a leaf member might be Men's Shirt #602. A leaf member in an Employee entity might be John Smith. A leaf member in a Warehouse entity might be Warehouse-98101.

One notable exception to this rule of thumb applies to any entities managed within the Finance domain. When managing entities associated with Finance, leaf members typically represent those low-level identifiers that transactions can be coded to. If transactions are coded with a store, account, employee, and product, you can be assured that the available values for each of these attributes should be stored as leaf member records in the associated entities.

Consolidated members are used only in explicit hierarchies, and will be discussed in more detail in Chapter 6.

About Main Street Clothing Company's Members

When implementing MDS, most entities will need to be populated from an initial data source. In the last chapter we retrieved and cleansed an extract file of the current products. In the next chapter we will discuss how to use staging tables to populate all of the current members into the proper entities. Before this staging can be completed, Main Street Clothing Company must ensure that all of the entity containers have been properly configured to accept the staged data.

Some entities that are used as domain-based attributes have so many members that loading them through staging at the same time as the product members makes the most sense. In the case of simple entities with very few members, however, the effort to stage the members would exceed the effort needed to create them through the UI. These members need to be created before we attempt to stage any product data.

Procedure: How to Add a Member

To add a leaf member, complete the following steps:

1. On the Master Data Manager home page, select the Product model and VERSION_1 from the drop-down lists.
2. Click Explorer.
3. On the menu bar, choose Entities | Product.
4. Under the word "Product," click Add member.

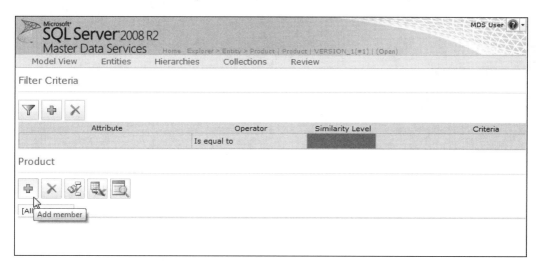

5. On the Member Information page, enter a name and code for your product. When we use the staging process to import the majority of our products, the name will be a concatenation of many fields. If you want to continue using our example, complete the fields as follows:

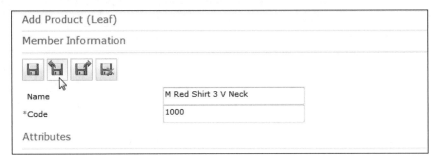

6. Click "Save and go back," which is the second button from the left. If you were to click the "Save and add another" button, you would be prompted to create a new member. If you click Save, you remain on this page, where you can edit the member's attributes.

The member is now displayed in the grid.

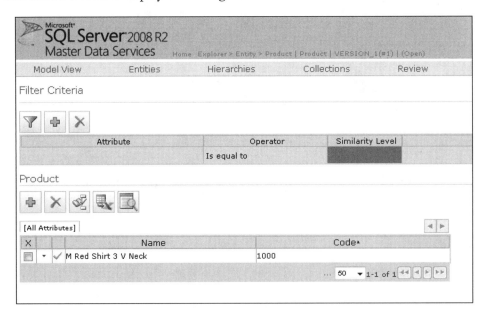

Now add a few members to the Yes No Picklist entity:

1.   On the menu bar, choose Entities | Yes No Picklist.
2.   Above the grid, click Add member.
3.   On the Member Information page, populate the fields as follows:

4.   Click "Save and add another" (the third button from the left).
5.   On the Member Information page, enter **No** for the name and **N** for the code.
6.   Click the "Save and go back" button.

The members are now displayed in the grid.

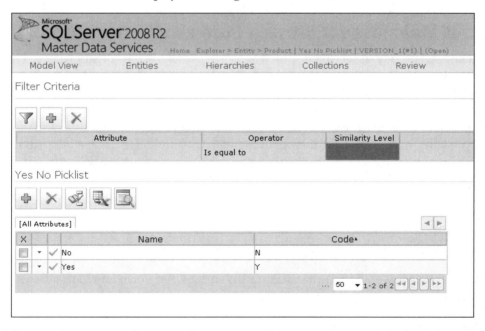

After you learn more about attributes, you will create a domain-based attribute that will use the Yes No Picklist values as the source.

About Attributes

All entities within Master Data Services can be enriched by the creation of additional attributes. MDS supports a subset of the attributes supported in SQL Server. MDS supports four specific types of free-form attributes for leaf and consolidated entity members: text, datetime, number, and link. Text and link are essentially string fields, with link providing one-click support for hypertext links. Number supports as many as seven decimals and datetime allows you to specify the mask for how the data will be input.

In order to relate two entities and ensure that values are constrained to specific values, MDS gives users the ability to create domain-based attributes. These attributes limit available values to the list of active members within the related entity.

The last type of attribute available to entities is the file attribute. Within a master data entity, it may be advisable to manage some files associated with each member. For instance, there may be instruction documents, specifications, blueprints, or photos that need to be associated with a Product entity within an organization. However, the file attribute has a number of limitations that make it less attractive to use for file management than SharePoint. First, to limit database sizes of MDS, file attributes will not be versioned. Only the last loaded file will be available within the MDS system. The transaction log will display information related to new files that have been loaded, but these will not be reversible.

About Main Street Clothing Company's Attributes

In order for Anthony to successfully load all of the current products into Master Data Services, he must complete the creation of a Product entity. This includes creation of all free-form attributes to the proper specifications identified in the last chapter. All product attributes that have currently been identified need to be created in MDS.

It is quite possible that during the attribute creation process or subsequent data loads, new information will be uncovered that changes the shape or type of attribute in MDS. Creating models in MDS should be an organic process. As new column needs are discovered at Main Street Clothing Company, Anthony will determine the best process for integrating these columns into Main Street's daily processes, ensuring that no process requirements are overlooked.

Procedure: How to Create an Attribute

Let's start by creating a free-form attribute. To create a free-form attribute, complete the following steps:

1. On the Master Data Manager home page, click System Administration.
2. On the menu bar, choose Manage | Entities.

3. On the Entity Maintenance page, select Product from the list of entities.
4. On the toolbar that is displayed, click the "Edit selected entity" button.

NOTE

The button does not appear until after you click the entity in the list.

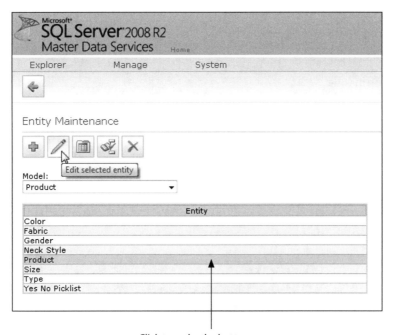

Click to make the buttons appear.

On the Edit Entity page, you can see that two attributes are listed: Name and Code. When you create an entity, these attributes are automatically created. You cannot delete them.

5. Click the "Add leaf attribute" button.

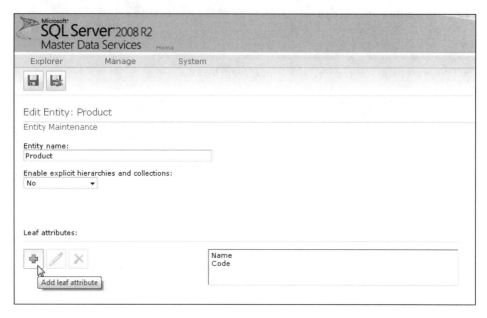

6. On the Add Attribute page, select Free-form and complete the fields as shown here:

► The value of the "Display pixel width" field determines how wide the column will be when it's displayed in the Explorer area of the UI.

► The Input mask field lets you decide if you want to show negative numbers in parentheses or if you want to show a minus sign instead.

► For now, don't enable change tracking. You will use this later, along with business rules, to notify someone when an attribute value changes.

7. Click Save.

On the Edit Entity page, the new attribute is displayed.

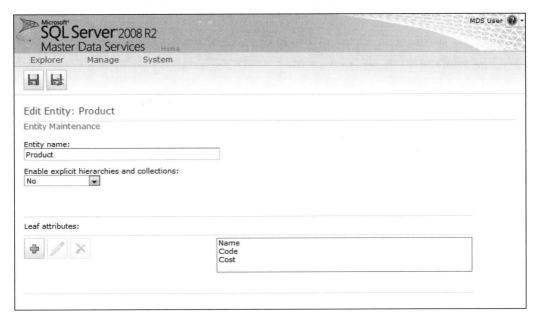

You can click either Save or Cancel to leave this page. Either way, your attribute is saved.

NOTE

To continue following along with the examples in this chapter, create the following free-form attributes: Retail Price (number with two decimal places), Safety Stock Level (number with no decimal places), Reorder Point (number, also with no decimal places), and Design (text).

If you make a mistake, you can delete the attribute and create a new one, or you can edit the attribute and change the editable fields. At this point you might also want to edit the Name and Code attributes to set the "Display pixel width" field to a smaller number.

TIP

If you want to hide an attribute without using security, set the "Display pixel width" field to 0.

Procedure: How to Create a Domain-Based Attribute

Each domain-based attribute has two parts:

▶ The entity that contains the members that will be used as a picklist.

▶ The attribute that refers to the entity.

You have already created an entity called Yes No Picklist and populated it with two members. Now you need to create a domain-based attribute that uses the members from the entity as attribute values.

To create a domain-based attribute, complete the following steps:

1. On the Master Data Manager home page, click System Administration.
2. On the menu bar, choose Manage | Entities.
3. On the Entity Maintenance page, select Product from the list of entities.
4. On the toolbar that is displayed, click the "Edit selected entity" button.

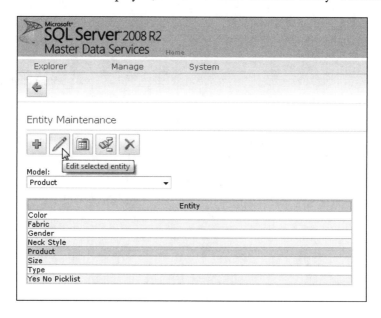

5. On the Edit Entity page, in the Leaf attributes section, click the "Add leaf attribute" button.

6. On the Add Attribute page, select Domain-based and complete the fields as shown here:

7. The attribute is going to be called "Discontinued." For each product, we want to know whether or not it has been discontinued. So type **Discontinued** as the attribute name and select Yes No Picklist as the entity that provides the members to use as attribute values.

8. Click Save.

Viewing the Results in Explorer

Now let's go back to Explorer and look at the Discontinued attribute:

1. On the Master Data Manager home page, select Product and VERSION_1 from the lists and then click Explorer.

2. On the menu bar, choose Entities | Product.

3. Scroll all the way to the right until you see the Discontinued column.

4.   Double-click the cell until it becomes a drop-down list.

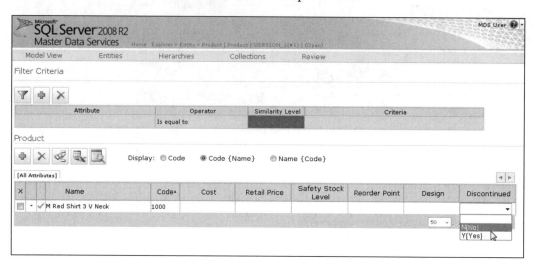

5.   Select N(No) for the attribute value.

6.   Press TAB, press ENTER, or double-click any other cell to save.

TIP

You can click the radio buttons above the grid to show the name and code of each attribute value, or to show the code only.

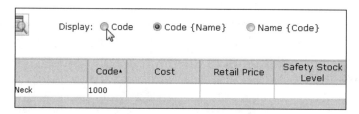

Now create other domain-based attributes:

1.   Based on the entity Yes No Picklist, create a domain-based attribute named **Available to Outlet**.

2.   Based on the entity named Type, create a domain-based attribute named **Type**.

You can use the same name for the domain-based attribute that you already used for the entity.

3.   Do the same with Fabric, Neck Style, Gender, Size, and Color.

Viewing the Results in System Administration

If you go back into the System Administration functional area (or if you are in System Administration already and on the menu bar you click Explorer), you can view your model structure in a hierarchical format, as shown in Figure 4-5.

The domain-based attributes can be expanded to show that they are entities with their own Name and Code attributes. The free-form attributes do not have attributes; they are just attributes of the Product model.

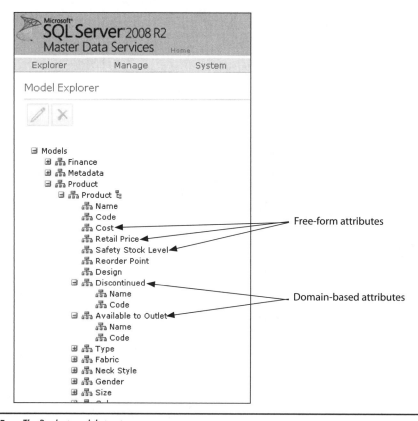

Figure 4-5   *The Product model structure*

About Attribute Groups

Master Data Services can contain every attribute associated with an entity in a business. Because of this, some entities can become unwieldy when viewed as a single table in the web UI. In a large organization, it is not uncommon for a major entity to contain over 400 attributes. Very few if any system users are interested in viewing all attributes simultaneously. Most users are interested only in specific, related attributes at any one time. MDS provides the ability to group attributes into multiple tabs in the Master Data Manager web application. MDS calls these groupings *attribute groups*. Any attribute can be added to any attribute group.

Typically attribute groups are created for each role consuming data within an entity. Different functional areas of the organization will be concerned with different groups of attributes for each entity stored in the application. Access to attribute groups can be managed by applying security for different users or groups at the attribute group level. This will be covered in more detail in Chapter 11.

About Main Street Clothing Company's Attribute Groups

Main Street Clothing Company has determined that the best approach to grouping attributes in Master Data Services is to group attributes by role. Because multiple roles are interested in the same attribute values, some attributes will appear in multiple attribute groups. In many cases, the same individuals perform the duties of multiple roles. Managers of these groups saw value in splitting these roles early in the design phase in an effort to prepare for future employee growth. Anthony reviewed all proposed consumers of MDS and determined the following roles:

▶ **Logistics**   In the past year, the company has leased warehouse space in two central locations to manage back inventory and take advantage of bulk discounts. To manage these warehouses, information related to reordering stock and product status is provided in a single group.

▶ **Marketing**   The Marketing role includes the VP of marketing and the individual store managers. All of these individuals need access to information about the variety of products and their costs in order to make informed decisions about incentives and discounts.

▶ **Pricing**   Within the company, multiple groups are interested in pricing. To aid in the management of these attributes, a separate attribute group was created to display only the cost and suggested retail price of each product.

Procedure: How to Create an Attribute Group

CAUTION

As soon as you create one attribute group, any new attributes must be added to an attribute group or they won't be displayed in Explorer.

1. On the Master Data Manager home page, click System Administration.
2. On the menu bar, choose Manage | Attribute Groups.

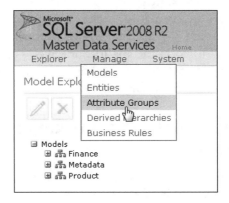

3. Select a model and entity from the lists and click Leaf Groups.

4.   Buttons are displayed, and you can now click the "Add attribute group" button.

5.   In the "Leaf group name" box, type **Logistics**. This will be the first tab displayed in Explorer on the grid that displays members in the Product entity.

6.   Click Save. The group is displayed as a folder on the Attribute Group Maintenance page.

7.   Expand the Logistics folder by clicking the plus sign to the left of it.

8.   Click the Attributes label. The "Edit selected item" button is displayed.

9. Click the "Edit selected item" button.

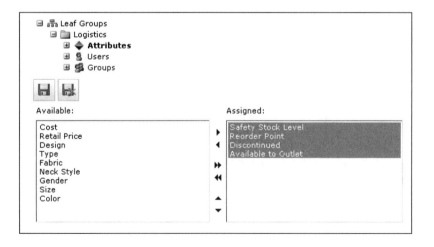

10. A list of available attributes is displayed. Assign attributes to the group by selecting them and then clicking the right-pointing arrow. In this example, we're going to add Safety Stock Level, Reorder Point, Discontinued, and Available to Outlet.

TIP

You can use CTRL-click to select multiple attributes and then add them all at the same time by clicking the arrow.

11.   Click Save. The attributes are now displayed beneath the Logistics group.

Before looking at the results in Explorer, create a few more groups:

Group	Attributes
Marketing	Color, Type, Fabric, Design, Gender, Size, Neck Style
Pricing	Cost, Retail Price

You can include attributes in multiple groups, or in none. Name and Code are automatically included in all groups.

> **NOTE**
>
> *To rename a group, click the name of the group and then click the "Edit selected item" button.*

Viewing the Results in Explorer

Let's take a few minutes to view the attribute groups in Explorer.

On the Master Data Manager home page, ensure that the Product model and VERSION_1 are selected. Click Explorer. Then, on the menu bar, choose Entities | Product. The tabs are displayed, and each tab has the columns you selected, in addition to the Name and Code columns.

TIP

If you create a new attribute and you don't want people to see it in Explorer, don't add it to an attribute group.

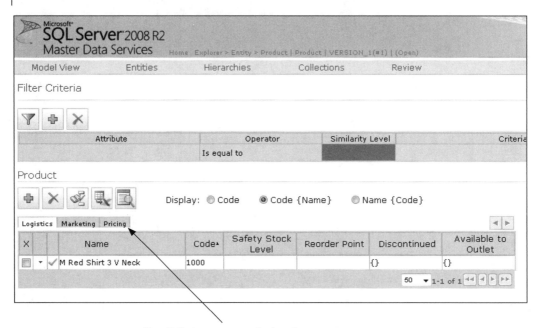

The attribute groups are displayed.

If you decide you want to change the order of your tabs, complete the next procedure.

Procedure: How to Reorder Attribute Groups

You can change the order of your tabs by completing the following steps:

1. On the Master Data Manager home page, click System Administration.
2. On the menu bar, choose Manage | Attribute Groups.

3. Click the Leaf Groups label.
4. Click the "Edit selected item" button.

The list of attributes in the group is displayed.

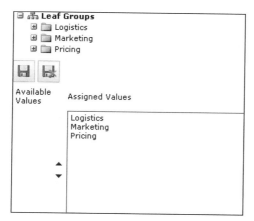

5. Click the attribute group you want to move and use the arrows to move it up and down. The topmost group will be the leftmost tab in Explorer.
6. When you're done, click Save.

Using Web Services

Creating and retrieving any of the Master Data Services objects explored in this chapter are completed using the same MDS web service operations, MetadataCreate and MetadataGet, respectively. While these two calls can be extremely powerful, they require users to create an array of different objects to successfully create and get data from the web service. In the examples in this section, the encapsulation allows developers using these calls to ignore internal IDs and work with only common object names when coding against the MDS web service. Throughout the rest of the book, we will provide examples of calls to encapsulate common coding scenarios.

Creating a Model

The first object that must be created in the Master Data Services system is a model. We can create a new model with a minimum of information from the user.

```
public void CreateModel(string newModelName)
{

    // Create the request object
    MetadataCreateRequest request = new MetadataCreateRequest();

    //Create new model container and give it a name
    Model newModel = new Model();
    newModel.Identifier = new Identifier { Name = newModelName };

    //Create Metadata container on the request object and
    //add model to models collection
    request.Metadata = new Metadata();
    request.Metadata.Models = new Collection<Model>();
    request.Metadata.Models.Add(newModel);

    // Make the service request to create
    MetadataCreateResponse response = mds_Proxy.MetadataCreate(request);

    // Make the service request to create
    response = mds_Proxy.MetadataCreate(request);

    //ErrorHandling will be discussed in Chapter 13
    HandleErrors(response.OperationResult);
}
```

Creating an Entity

In this example, we encapsulate the call to create a new entity for a given model. This example only creates an entity that is not hierarchy enabled. The web service requires us to create the model objects to hold the new entity object. More complex examples can be found in Chapter 13.

```
public void CreateLeafEntity(string ModelName, string newEntityName)
{

    // Create the request and response objects
    MetadataCreateRequest request = new MetadataCreateRequest();

    //Create Metadata container on the request object
    request.Metadata = new Metadata();

    //Initialize the entities collection
    request.Metadata.Entities = new Collection<Entity>();

    //Create new entity in the Metadata and set model
    request.Metadata.Entities.Add(new Entity
    {
        IsFlat = true,
        Identifier = new ModelContextIdentifier
        {
            Name = newEntityName,
            ModelId = new Identifier { Name = ModelName }
        }

    });


    // Make the service request to create
    MetadataCreateResponse response =
mds_Proxy.MetadataCreate(request);
    HandleErrors(response.OperationResult);
}
```

Creating an Attribute

Attributes can be created on a variety of object types in MDS. Attributes can be created on leaf and consolidated entities as well as collections. The following example creates a new attribute of a specified type on the entity and model that has been passed in.

Similar to the entity creation example, this procedure builds on the creation of an entity object and adds the attribute.

```
        public void CreateFreeFormAttribute(string ModelName,
string EntityName, string newAttributeName, MemberType pMemberType,
AttributeDataType pAttrType, int DisplayWidth)
{
    // Create the request and response objects
    MetadataCreateRequest request = new MetadataCreateRequest();

    //Create the Metadata object
    request.Metadata = new Metadata();

    //Initialize the attributes collection
    request.Metadata.Attributes = new Collection<MetadataAttribute>();

    //Add the new attribute (all of the attribute property settings
    //are included inside required identifier)
    request.Metadata.Attributes.Add(new MetadataAttribute
    {
        Identifier = new MemberTypeContextIdentifier
        {
            Name = newAttributeName,
            MemberType = pMemberType,
            ModelId = new Identifier { Name = ModelName },
            EntityId = new Identifier{ Name = EntityName }

        },
        DataType = pAttrType
    });
}
```

Summary

In this chapter we created the initial structure of our Master Data Services solution. We created models, entities, and attributes. Attribute groups provide the ability to display attributes for each role or process that consumes the data stored. Unlike the example in this book, implementing a model in MDS at your company can and should be an iterative process. The customizability and speed of structural changes in this application allows organizations to quickly react to changing business processes or discovered inefficiencies. Often, changes to the data model are identified as we load data into the model, which will be the focus of the next chapter.

Chapter 5

Integrating Master Data Services with Other Systems

In This Chapter

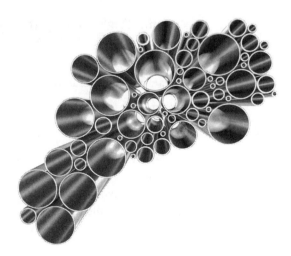

While master data management requires extensive integration with other systems within your enterprise, Master Data Services does not provide any features around extract, transform, and load (ETL). MDS is designed to leverage SQL Server Integration Services (SSIS), but it also works well with other ETL solutions such as Informatica, InfoSphere DataStage, or any other product in this space.

To get data into and out of the system and communicate with other applications, Master Data Services uses staging tables for the incoming data flow and subscription views for the outgoing data flow. In this chapter, we describe these staging areas of the application and discuss common methods to integrate systems with MDS. We also discuss some tips and tricks for integrating using SSIS and T-SQL jobs. This chapter is not meant to be a substitute for other SSIS books that may be available; for more complex operations, such as complex data flows and manipulations, you should look at *Hands-On Microsoft SQL Server 2008 Integration Services, Second Edition* by Ashwani Nanda for assistance.

Staging Architecture

The current staging architecture of Master Data Services is a generic architecture that supports any possible data model. MDS accomplishes this feat through three separate tables designed to support the loading of leaf members, consolidated members, attributes, and hierarchy relationships. Staging records across these three tables can be managed in batches based on users or systems. A fourth table is used to track summary information. The four tables are as follows:

- ▶ **mdm.tblStgMember**   Use to create new leaf members, consolidated members, and collections

- ▶ **mdm.tblStgMemberAttribute**   Use to update the attributes of existing members and collections

- ▶ **mdm.tblStgRelationship**   Use to add members to a collection or move members in an explicit hierarchy

- ▶ **mdm.tblStgBatch**   A summary table used to store batch information

In this chapter, we show you how to load members and their attributes into the appropriate MDS tables. We also show you how to create and edit collections and how to move members in explicit hierarchies. Because we haven't introduced the concepts of collections and explicit hierarchies yet, you may have to return to this chapter after you understand how collections and explicit hierarchies work.

Preparing Data for Import

To import data into MDS, you must first put your data into the format required by the MDS staging tables. Then you import the data into the staging tables in the MDS database. Finally, you initiate a batch process that takes the data from the staging tables and puts it into the appropriate MDS tables.

For example, your original data might be in a format similar to that shown in Figure 5-1. To get the data into the MDS staging tables, it must be in a format similar to that shown in Figure 5-2. Your columns can be in any order, but certain columns are required and others are not. In this example, we didn't include the name because it isn't required, but we did include the code because it is required.

You can run the staging process more than once. Each time you do, it attempts to overwrite the values in the database. If it cannot overwrite the values, it will produce an error message. You can run staging as often as you need to and clear staging batches when done.

Security in Staging

While MDS is a feature of SQL Server, MDS does not rely on the SQL Server security model to secure data within the system. In Chapter 11 we will go into the details of the MDS security model, but in this chapter it is important to be aware that giving access to SQL objects within the MDS database must be handled with care. Ensure that rights to specific tables and procedures are maintained and that any user who is provided full access to the MDS database recognizes that only specific tables discussed in this chapter are appropriate for manual manipulation.

Staging and subscription views are separate from the web-based security model that is enforced in the web UI. Subscription views are SQL views used by subscribing systems to get data from MDS. These views are described in detail in Chapter 12.

The use of the staging tables and consumption of subscription views are intended for advanced system batch integration. To ensure that these processes can be completed as quickly as possible, database objects lie outside of the security model and rely on

	A	B	C	D	E	F	G
1	Name	Code	Gender	Type	Color	Size	Fabric
2	M Red Shirt 3 V Neck	1000	Male	Shirt	Red	3	Cotton
3	M Red Shirt 4 V Neck	1001	Male	Shirt	Red	4	Cotton
4	M Red Shirt 5 V Neck	1002	Male	Shirt	Red	5	Cotton
5	M Red Shirt 6 V Neck	1003	Male	Shirt	Red	6	Cotton
6	M Red Shirt 7 V Neck	1004	Male	Shirt	Red	7	Cotton

Figure 5-1   *Sample data provided by the organization*

	A	B	C	D	E
1	MemberType_ID	MemberCode	ModelName	EntityName	UserName
2	1	1000	Product	Product	Domain\tyler
3	1	1001	Product	Product	Domain\tyler
4	1	1002	Product	Product	Domain\tyler
5	1	1003	Product	Product	Domain\tyler
6	1	1004	Product	Product	Domain\tyler

Figure 5-2   *Sample data in a format accepted by the MDS staging tables*

database administrators to restrict access using SQL Server security roles to limit access to any sensitive information stored in MDS. We will discuss the securing of these database objects in Chapter 11.

NOTE

All of the procedures in this chapter require that you be a model administrator. For more information about model administrators, see Chapter 11.

System Settings

Before you do load data into the staging tables, confirm the staging system settings that are set in Master Data Services Configuration Manager. You launch it from Programs | Microsoft SQL Server 2008 R2 | Master Data Services | Configuration Manager.

Log All Staging Transactions

Set this setting to On to have transactions logged when the staged records are loaded into the appropriate Master Data Services database tables.

Staging Batch Interval

When you set the staging process to start, this setting determines the number of seconds afterward that your batch is processed. The default setting is 60 seconds (1 minute).

Loading Members

tblStgMember is the first staging table you need to become familiar with. This table is used to import new members into any entity within the Master Data Services system. The only two attributes that can be loaded into the MDS system through the member staging table are Name and Code. As always in MDS, the Name field is optional.

Staging tables can be broken down into three distinct areas:

▶ **The context information required to load the record**   In all three staging tables, the context fields provide enough information to identify the location for the data to be stored in MDS. The context information will at least include the model, entity, and MemberType_ID of the record. When loading information related to a specific hierarchy, you must specify the name of the hierarchy.

▶ **The name–value pairs of the information to be loaded or updated in MDS**   Only the name and code of the new member to be created are provided in this area of member staging.

▶ **The status columns**   The Status_ID provides the current status of each row, and the ErrorCode provides the last error encountered for this member. This can be frustrating, as it may take several iterations to correct all of the issues with a record you are attempting to import.

While it may be obvious that you need to load member records before you load their corresponding attributes, you may not recognize that all of the related members for the domain-based attributes must be entered into MDS as well. Staging is the most expedient way to load large numbers of records into an entity. The additional cost of formatting the records to the shape of the staging table is far less than the amount of effort to add these records manually. When loading domain-based attribute values, a little more analysis is required. Generally, if an attribute includes fewer than ten values, it is more efficient to create the attributes manually by using the Master Data Manager web application. With more than ten attribute values, you might want to consider using staging.

The exception to the preceding rule is when you are creating repeatable processes for loading data into MDS. When building staging processes that will be scheduled to run on a regular basis, it is best to include all domain-based attributes that may change to include additional values. This will ensure that the staging process is more robust and does not fail when the first new product color is added to the system.

About Main Street Clothing Company's Staging Process

Main Street Clothing Company has created what it believes to be a basic, functional model structure. Now Anthony Green needs to ensure that all the requisite information is loaded, to ensure that all products can be staged into the system.

Anthony determines that the best method for addressing new attribute values will be a manual process managed by the Product Procurement team. This process will be managed though the use of business rules, as discussed in Chapter 8.

Anthony compiles a summary of the attribute values that need to be loaded before the company's current product list can be loaded. He reviews each attribute to determine if there are any important attributes associated with these values that should be managed as well. For each attribute, he will need to create or load several members to be used as domain-based attribute values.

Attribute	Number of Members
Color	15
Gender	2
Neck Style	4
Type	7
Fabric	4
Size	14

Since none of these attribute values requires advanced management nor has over 15 values, Anthony determines that loading these records manually is the most efficient method. A few of the more technical manufacturers have discussed system integrations to provide electronic access to new product lines. As these systems become available, Anthony will review the necessary ETL processes to automatically load new products and their requisite domain-based values.

If Anthony had decided to use the staging process, he could create a spreadsheet similar to those available at www.mdsuser.com.

tblStgMember Fields

Use tblStgMember to create leaf members, consolidated members, and collections. After you create the members and/or collections, you can proceed with updating the members' or collections' attributes.

The following table describes the columns in tblStgMember.

Column Name	Required?	Description
Batch_ID	No	Leave this field blank. When the batch is processed, an ID for the batch will populate this field. This value is also added to the ID field in the mdm.tblStgBatch table when the batch is processed.
UserName	No	Each user who is logged in to Master Data Manager can view his or her own records and those with no username assigned.

Column Name	Required?	Description
ModelName	Yes	The name of the model. *Note: This value is case sensitive.*
HierarchyName	Sometimes	The name of the hierarchy. Required only when you are adding consolidated members (MemberType_ID = 2). Leave this field blank when adding leaf members and collections.
EntityName	Yes	The name of the entity.
MemberType_ID	Yes	The type of member you want to create. 1 is for leaf members, 2 is for consolidated members, and 3 is for collections.
MemberName	No	A name for the member or collection.
MemberCode	Yes	A unique code for the member or collection. *Note: Members with duplicate codes will not be imported.*
Status_ID	Yes	The status of the import process. Enter 0 for records that are ready for staging. The system updates this value to 1 if the record is successfully loaded and to 2 if the record is not successfully loaded.
ErrorCode	No	An error code for all records that have a Status_ID of 2. You can view the errors in more detail in Master Data Manager.

Member Staging Examples

You can populate the tblStgMember table by using T-SQL statements or by using SQL Server Integration Services. In our SSIS examples, we'll import a CSV file, but there are a variety of options available, including SQL Server, Access, Excel, and others.

The examples in this section are meant to illustrate the staging process, but they do not necessarily build on the Product model that we've laid out so far. You can visit www.mdsuser.com to download the CSV files you need to stage in all of the members, attributes, and collections for the Product and Finance models. You can get those files now and compare them to the examples, or try creating your own sample products.

Use the following examples to create a leaf member, a consolidated member (needed only for explicit hierarchies), and a collection (a different type of grouping that your organization may or may not use). When using a CSV file to stage members, the first row in the file should contain the column names.

Create a Leaf Member

In this example, we are going to specify the member code required to create a leaf member. We are not going to specify the member name, because the name is not required. In Chapter 8, we'll show you how to use business rules to create a concatenated member name.

Also in these examples, we're going to specify a username of "tyler." When Tyler opens the Master Data Manager web application, all the members assigned to this username and all the members with no username assigned will be counted in the number of records available for staging.

T-SQL	
| | ```
INSERT INTO mdm.tblStgMember
(UserName, ModelName, EntityName, MemberType_ID,
MemberCode) VALUES
(N'Domain\tyler',N'Product', N'Product', 1, N'1001')
``` |
| CSV File | UserName,ModelName,EntityName,MemberType_ID,MemberCode
Domain\tyler,Product,Product,1,1001 |

Create a Consolidated Member

This example shows you how to create a consolidated member with the name Short Term Assets and the code STA.

T-SQL	
| | ```
INSERT INTO mdm.tblStgMember
(ModelName, HierarchyName, EntityName, MemberType_ID,
MemberName, MemberCode) VALUES
(N'Finance', N'Chart of Accounts', N'Accounts', 2,
N'Short Term Assets', N'STA')
``` |
| CSV File | ModelName,HierarchyName,EntityName,MemberType_ID,MemberName,MemberCode
Finance,Chart of Accounts,Accounts,2,Short Term Assets,STA |

Create a Collection

This example shows you how to create a collection with the name Boys Winter Set and the code BWS. This collection won't have any members in it. It is simply creating a collection with this name and code. To add members to collections, you can use the relationships staging table.

T-SQL	`INSERT INTO mdm.tblStgMember (UserName, ModelName, EntityName, MemberType_ID, MemberName, MemberCode) VALUES (N'Domain\suzanne', N'Product', N'Product', 3, N'Boys Winter Set', N'BWS')`
CSV File	UserName,ModelName,EntityName,MemberType_ID,MemberName,MemberCode Domain\suzanne,Product,Product,3,Boys Winter Set,BWS

Loading Attributes

Use tblStgMemberAttribute to update attribute values for existing members and collections. You can also use this table to delete or reactivate existing members or collections.

If your original data was like that shown in Figure 5-2, and you have successfully created your members, you can update the member attributes by using a data format similar to that shown in Figure 5-3. In this format, you import all attributes for one member at a time. Column E in the spreadsheet contains all the attributes for member 1000.

Or you might prefer to stage a single attribute for all members at the same time, as shown in Figure 5-4. In this example, for all members (1000–1004), you're staging the values for the Gender attribute.

	A	B	C	D	E	F
1	ModelName	EntityName	MemberType_ID	MemberCode	AttributeName	AttributeValue
2	Product	Product	1	1000	Gender	M
3	Product	Product	1	1000	Type	Shirt
4	Product	Product	1	1000	Color	Red
5	Product	Product	1	1000	Size	3
6	Product	Product	1	1000	Fabric	Cotton

Figure 5-3   *Staging attributes: one member at a time*

	A	B	C	D	E	F
1	ModelName	EntityName	MemberType_ID	MemberCode	AttributeName	AttributeValue
2	Product	Product	1	1000	Gender	M
3	Product	Product	1	1001	Gender	M
4	Product	Product	1	1002	Gender	M
5	Product	Product	1	1003	Gender	M
6	Product	Product	1	1004	Gender	M

Figure 5-4   *Staging attributes: one attribute at a time*

tblStgMemberAttribute Fields

The following table describes the fields in tblStgMemberAttribute.

Column Name	Required?	Description
Batch_ID	No	Leave this field blank. When the batch is processed, an ID for the batch will populate this field. This value is also added to the ID field in the mdm.tblStgBatch table when the batch is processed.
UserName	No	Each user who is logged in to Master Data Manager can view his or her own records and those with no username assigned.
ModelName	Yes	The name of the model. *Note: This value is case sensitive.*
EntityName	Yes	The name of the entity.
MemberType_ID	Yes	The type of member you want to update. 1 is for leaf members, 2 is for consolidated members, and 3 is for collections.
MemberCode	Yes	A unique code for the member or collection.
AttributeName	Yes	The attribute name. To deactivate or reactivate a member, use MDMMemberStatus. For more information, see "Using Staging to Deactivate and Reactivate Members" later in this chapter.
AttributeValue	Yes	For free-form attributes, the attribute value. For domain-based attributes, the member code. To deactivate or reactivate a member, use De-Activated or Active. Leave this blank to designate a blank value for an attribute. *Note: Numbers, dates, and the Name attribute cannot be assigned a blank value this way.*
Status_ID	Yes	The status of the import process. Enter 0 for records that are ready for staging. The system updates this value to 1 if the record is successfully loaded and to 2 if the record is not successfully loaded.
ErrorCode	No	An error code for all records that have a Status_ID of 2. You can view the errors in more detail in Master Data Manager.

Attribute Staging Examples

These examples will show you how to populate the tblStgMemberAttribute table by using T-SQL statements or by using SQL Server Integration Services to import a CSV file. Again, many of the members referred to in these examples do not exist yet in the samples we've provided, and you will get errors if you try to update a member or collection that doesn't exist. Use these examples to get ideas for how to stage your own data, or use the staging spreadsheets we've provided at www.mdsuser.com.

Update a Leaf Member's Attribute

This example updates member code 1001's Gender attribute to Male (M). Because Gender is a domain-based attribute, you must use the code (M) rather than the name (Male) for the attribute value.

T-SQL	```INSERT INTO mdm.tblStgMemberAttribute (ModelName, EntityName, MemberType_ID, MemberCode, AttributeName, AttributeValue) VALUES (N'Product', N'Product', 1, N'1001', N'Gender', N'M')```
CSV File	ModelName,EntityName,MemberType_ID,MemberCode,AttributeName,AttributeValue Product,Product,1,1001,Gender,M

Update a Consolidated Member's Attribute

This example updates the Name attribute of the Short Term Assets (STA) consolidated member.

T-SQL	```INSERT INTO mdm.tblStgMemberAttribute (ModelName, EntityName, MemberType_ID, MemberCode, AttributeName, AttributeValue) VALUES (N'Finance', N'Finance', 2, N'STA', N'Name', N'Short Term Assets')```
CSV File	ModelName,EntityName,MemberType_ID,MemberCode,AttributeName,AttributeValue Finance,Finance,2,STA,Name,Short Term Assets

Update a Collection's Attribute

This example updates the Description attribute of the Boys Winter Set (BWS) collection to read "Boys 2011 Winter Set." If you have not defined additional attributes for your collections, the only attributes you can update are Owner_ID, Description, Name, and Code.

T-SQL	
	``INSERT INTO mdm.tblStgMemberAttribute (ModelName,
EntityName,
MemberType_ID, MemberCode, AttributeName, AttributeValue)
VALUES
(N'Product', N'Product', 3, N'BWS', N'Description',
N'Boys 2011 Winter Set')```
CSV File	ModelName,EntityName,MemberType_ID,MemberCode,AttributeName,AttributeValue
Product,Product,3,BWS,Description,Boys 2011 Winter Set

Using Staging to Deactivate and Reactivate Members

You can use the Attributes staging table to update the status of a member; the two possible statuses are Active and De-Activated. When you deactivate a member, the member code changes to a 32-character GUID, thus removing it from the UI. You can also use staging to reactivate the member. This can be useful if you want to restore a member's attributes and its membership in hierarchies and collections. If you were to delete the member and create a new one, you lose these relationships.

These procedures require that you look in database tables for information, and you should use care and ensure you're comfortable working in the database if you decide to do this. In Chapter 7 we will show you how to delete and reactivate members in the Master Data Manager web application. Using the web UI is simpler than using staging and leaves less room for error.

Example: Deactivate a Member

This example shows how to deactivate member 1001.

T-SQL	
	``INSERT INTO mdm.tblStgMemberAttribute (ModelName,
EntityName,
MemberType_ID, MemberCode, AttributeName, AttributeValue)
VALUES
(N'Product', N'Product', 1, N'1001', N'MDMMemberStatus',
N'De-Activated')```
CSV File	ModelName,EntityName,MemberType_ID,MemberCode,AttributeName,AttributeValue
Product,Product,1,1001,MDMMemberStatus,De-Activated

Example: Reactivate a Member

This example shows how to reactivate a member that was deactivated. Note that the member code is now a 32-character GUID.

To find this GUID, open your MDS database. In the view_SYSTEM_SCHEMA_ENTITY view, find the name of the entity that contains the deactivated member or collection. The value in the EntityTable column tells you which table to look in to find the GUID of the deactivated member. Now open that table and find the GUID of the deactivated member.

T-SQL	`INSERT INTO mdm.tblStgMemberAttribute (ModelName,`
	`EntityName,`
	`MemberType_ID, MemberCode, AttributeName, AttributeValue)`
	`VALUES`
	`(N'Product', N'Product', 1, N'12345678912345678912345678`
	`912345',`
	`N'MDMMemberStatus',N'Active')`

CSV File	ModelName,EntityName,MemberType_ID,MemberCode,AttributeName,AttributeValue Product,Product,1,12345678912345678912345678912345,MDMMemberStatus,Active

Loading Relationships

The third staging table within MDS is the relationship table. You will use the tblStgRelationship table to load both explicit hierarchy relationships and collection relationships. Explicit hierarchy relationships can be entered in one of two ways. You can load data as a parent relationship or you can load data as sibling relationships.

In most cases, the easiest way to load data into MDS is to load it in parent-child format. Many systems do not care about the order of members within the hierarchy, only the consolidations themselves; in these cases, parent-child format will be the easiest way to load records through staging. When parent-child records are loaded through staging in this manner, the sort order will be triggered in a standard way. Any new children of a consolidated member in the system will be placed as the last sibling in the tree, similar to how birth order works in people.

If sort order matters and you cannot control the order of data within your staging load, you can load records into MDS using the sibling type. Using sibling as the target type, new relationships will be created at the same level of the hierarchy as the next sibling to the target code specified. This will allow you to directly set the order of records in an explicit hierarchy without reloading the entire hierarchy.

Creating a new record as the first sibling of any parent requires a two-step process. The first step is to load the new relationship as a sibling to the first child of the target parent. The second step is to set the first child as a sibling to the just loaded member. This will reverse the order of these two child members.

tblStgRelationship Fields

Use tblStgRelationship to move members in explicit hierarchies and add members to collections. You cannot use this table for updating derived hierarchies or removing members from collections. To update derived hierarchies, you must update the attribute values that determine the hierarchy. To remove members from collections, you must do it manually. For more information about hierarchies and collections, refer to Chapter 6.

The following table describes the fields in tblStgRelationship.

Column Name	Required?	Description
Batch_ID	No	Leave this field blank. When the batch is processed, an ID for the batch will populate this field. This value is also added to the ID field in the mdm.tblStgBatch table when the batch is processed.
VersionName	N/A	Do not use. This column is not evaluated in the staging process.
UserName	No	Each user who is logged in to Master Data Manager can view his or her own records and those with no username assigned.
ModelName	Yes	The name of the model. *Note: This value is case sensitive.*
EntityName	Yes	The name of the entity.
HierarchyName	Yes, if you are updating explicit hierarchy relationship	The explicit hierarchy name, if you are staging a relationship in an explicit hierarchy. If you are adding a member to a collection, leave this field blank.
MemberType_ID	Yes	4 is for explicit hierarchies and 5 is for collections.
MemberCode	Yes	A unique code for the member.
TargetCode	Yes	For collections, the code of the collection to add the member to. For explicit hierarchies: ▶ The code of the leaf member that will be a sibling or ▶ The code of the consolidated member that will be a parent or sibling If you have a nonmandatory explicit hierarchy, use MDMUNUSED to add a leaf member to the Unused node. To add members to the root of any explicit hierarchy, use ROOT.

Column Name	Required?	Description
TargetType_ID	Yes	For explicit hierarchies: ▶ 1 to make the target member the parent of the staged member ▶ 2 to make the target member a sibling of the staged member For collections, use 1.
SortOrder	No	For explicit hierarchies, an integer that indicates the order of the member in relation to the other members under the parent. Each member should have a unique number. If this is not populated, then the order of records in the staging table is used as the order.
Status_ID	Yes	The status of the import process. Enter 0 for records that are ready for staging. The system updates this value to 1 if the record is successfully loaded and to 2 if the record is not successfully loaded.
ErrorCode	No	An error code for all records that have a Status_ID of 2. You can view the errors in more detail in Master Data Manager.

Relationship Staging Examples

The following examples show how to populate the tblStgRelationship table by using T-SQL statements or by using SSIS to import a CSV file. Again, many of the members referred to in these examples do not exist yet in the samples we've provided, and you will get errors if you try to update a member or collection that doesn't exist. Use these examples to get ideas for how to stage your own data, or use the staging spreadsheets we've provided at www.mdsuser.com.

Set a Parent-Child Relationship in an Explicit Hierarchy

This example sets the Short Term Assets (STA) consolidated member as the parent of the Cash member in the Chart of Accounts explicit hierarchy.

TIP

If you want to specify the Unused node of an explicit hierarchy as the parent, use MDMUNUSED for the TargetCode. If you want to assign to the root, use ROOT.

T-SQL	`INSERT INTO mdm.tblStgRelationship (ModelName, EntityName, HierarchyName, MemberType_ID, MemberCode, TargetCode, TargetType_ID) VALUES (N'Finance', N'Finance', N'Chart of Accounts', 4, N'Cash', N'STA', 1)`
CSV File	ModelName,EntityName,HierarchyName,MemberType_ID,MemberCode,TargetCode,TargetType_ID Finance,Finance,Chart of Accounts,4,Cash,STA,1

Set a Sibling Relationship in an Explicit Hierarchy

This example sets Long Term Assets at the same level as Short Term Assets in the Chart of Accounts explicit hierarchy.

T-SQL	`INSERT INTO mdm.tblStgRelationship (ModelName, EntityName, HierarchyName, MemberType_ID, MemberCode, TargetCode, TargetType_ID) VALUES (N'Finance', N'Finance', N'Chart of Accounts', 4, N'LTA', N'STA', 2)`
CSV File	ModelName,EntityName,HierarchyName,MemberType_ID,MemberCode,TargetCode,TargetType_ID Finance,Finance,Chart of Accounts,4,LTA,STA,2

Add One Collection to Another

This example adds the Boys Winter Set (BWS) collection to the Fall and Winter Sets (FWS) collection.

T-SQL	`INSERT INTO mdm.tblStgRelationship (ModelName, EntityName, HierarchyName, MemberType_ID, MemberCode, TargetCode, TargetType_ID) VALUES (N'Product', N'Product', NULL, 5, N'BWS', N'FWS', 1)`
CSV File	ModelName,EntityName,HierarchyName,MemberType_ID,MemberCode,TargetCode,TargetType_ID Product,Product,NULL,5,BWS,FWS,1

Add a Leaf Member to a Collection

This example adds leaf member 1052 to the Boys Winter Set (BWS) collection.

| T-SQL | ```
INSERT INTO mdm.tblStgRelationship (ModelName, EntityName,
HierarchyName, MemberType_ID, MemberCode, TargetCode,
TargetType_ID) VALUES
(N'Product', N'Product', NULL, 5, N'1052', N'BWS', 1)
``` |
|---|---|
| CSV File | ModelName,EntityName,HierarchyName,MemberType_ID,MemberCode,TargetCode,TargetType_ID
Product,Product,NULL,5,1052,BWS,1 |

Add a Consolidated Member to a Collection

This example adds the Boys (B) consolidated member to the Fall and Winter Sets (FWS) collection.

| T-SQL | ```
INSERT INTO mdm.tblStgRelationship (ModelName, EntityName,
HierarchyName, MemberType_ID, MemberCode, TargetCode,
TargetType_ID) VALUES
(N'Product', N'Product', NULL, 5, N'B', N'FWS', 1)
``` |
|---|---|
| CSV File | ModelName,EntityName,HierarchyName,MemberType_ID,MemberCode,TargetCode,TargetType_ID
Product,Product,NULL,5,B,FWS,1 |

Importing Data into the Staging Tables

You may already have decided how to get your data into the MDS database's staging tables. If you haven't, we'll show you how to do it by using SQL Server Integration Services. After you import your data into the tables, you can proceed with running the import, which puts the data from the staging tables into the appropriate MDS database tables.

Procedure: How to Import Data into SQL Server by Using SSIS

In this procedure, we are going to use a flat CSV file with a header row that includes column names. To import a CSV file into the SQL Server MDS database staging tables by using SSIS, complete the following steps:

1. Open SQL Server Management Studio.
2. Right-click the MDS database.
3. On the submenu, select Tasks | Import Data.

4. On the Welcome page, click Next.
5. On the Choose a Data Source page, select Flat File Source as your data source.
6. Browse to the file. (You must select CSV as the file type to view your files. TXT is selected by default.)
7. Select the "Column names in the first data row" check box.

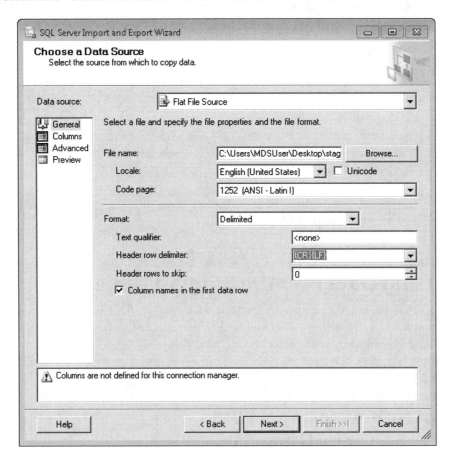

8. Click Next.
9. On the next Choose a Data Source page, confirm that the preview of your data looks accurate and click Next.
10. On the Choose a Destination page, confirm that your MDS database is selected and click Next.
11. On the Select Source Tables and Views page, ensure that you select [mdm] .[tblStgMember] or another appropriate staging table. You can also click the Preview button at the bottom of this page to preview your data.

CAUTION

The correct table is not selected by default. Be careful not to click Next without changing the destination table.

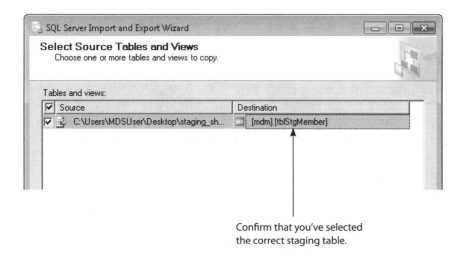

Confirm that you've selected
the correct staging table.

12. Click Next.
13. On the Review Data Type Mapping page, click Next.
14. On the Save and Run Package page, click Next.
15. On the Complete the Wizard page, click Finish.

When the process is complete, a message is displayed, stating that the execution was successful.

Initiating the Staging Process

After you have populated the staging tables with your data, you must run the batch process that loads the data from the staging tables into the MDS-specific tables. You will use this same process no matter what you are importing. To initiate the staging process, you can use

► The Master Data Manager web application

► A stored procedure in the MDS database

► Web services

Procedure: How to Use Master Data Manager to Initiate the Staging Process

To use the Master Data Manager web application to initiate the staging process after you've loaded data into the MDS staging tables in SQL Server, complete the following steps:

NOTE

Staging batches are processed in sequence, and processing begins at an interval determined by a setting in Master Data Services Configuration Manager. The staging tables are processed one after another. tblStgMember is processed first, followed by tblStgMemberAttribute, and then tblStgRelationship. You cannot initiate the processing of each table individually, so you should import only the records you intend to load.

1. On the Master Data Manager home page, click Integration Management.

    On the Staging Batches page, a batch is displayed for the Finance model if you deployed the sample Finance model in Chapter 2.

2. Scroll down to the Unbatched Staging Records section. Select the model and version. The total number of records to be imported should be displayed.

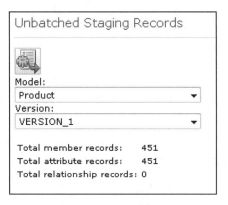

NOTES

Committed versions are not available in the list. If the number of records to be imported does not seem correct, ensure that your username was properly formatted, that the Batch_ID field for each record in the table is NULL, and that the Status_ID field for each record is 0. Also remember that the model name is case sensitive.

3. Above the Model list, click the "Process unbatched data" button.

The batch is added to the list of staging batches and assigned an ID, and the Status column is updated to Queued to Run.

ID	Name	Model	Version	Status	Started	Completed	Records	Errors
1		Finance	VERSION_1	Not Running	7/19/2010 9:16:45 PM	7/19/2010 9:16:59 PM	332	0
2	PRODUCT unbatched	Product	VERSION_1	Queued to run			902	0

Batch 2 is queued to run.

TIP

On the menu bar, click Import to refresh the page until the Status column is updated.

When the batch has finished processing, the Status column is updated to Not Running and errors are listed in the Errors column.

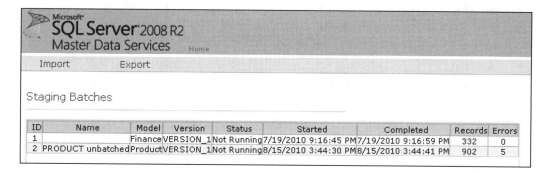

ID	Name	Model	Version	Status	Started	Completed	Records	Errors
1		Finance	VERSION_1	Not Running	7/19/2010 9:16:45 PM	7/19/2010 9:16:59 PM	332	0
2	PRODUCT unbatched	Product	VERSION_1	Not Running	8/15/2010 3:44:30 PM	8/15/2010 3:44:41 PM	902	5

You can go to Explorer to view your staged members, or open the Staging Batch Errors page to view the details of your errors.

Procedure: How to Use Stored Procedures to Initiate the Staging Process

After you have loaded data into the staging tables by using either T-SQL or SSIS, using the web UI or web services to trigger a staging load process can be inconvenient. While we do not recommend coding against stored procedures as a general rule, the benefits outweigh the risks in this case.

You can trigger logging of transactions or validation by using staging stored procedures. The stored procedures, described in the following section, provide access to additional functionality that is not exposed in the UI. These stored procedures are also more accessible when loading data through SSIS.

> **NOTE**
> *Microsoft does not guarantee these interfaces will remain constant or provide any backward compatibility at the stored procedure level.*

Staging Sweep

If you do not want to mess with managing the batch process, udpStagingSweep allows you to load any data that is not assigned to a batch. This can be a very useful procedure for initially loading MDS; however, this can be a risky procedure to use in a more mature solution. This stored procedure will load all unbatched data from all three staging tables for the User_ID specified. Using this method, the UserName column becomes mandatory, requiring the user to be a valid user in MDS.

Use the following execution script for calling udpStagingSweep.

```
EXEC mdm.udpStagingSweep @userID, @versionid, @process
```

Following is an explanation of the parameters required by the procedure.

▶ **userID** This corresponds to a User_ID in the system table tblUser. The user provided must be a model administrator to ensure successful operation of this stored procedure. For more information about model administrators, see Chapter 11.

▶ **versionID** The model and version are calculated by the provided value. Be careful not to use the version number, as this value needs to be populated from the tblModelVersion table.

▶ **process** Set this value to 1 to immediately trigger the staging process.

Creating Batches

The udpStagingBatchSave stored procedure allows you to add a row into the MDS batch table described in the "Viewing the Staging Batch Table" section later in this chapter. This procedure will return a BatchID that you can attach to all rows you want to load into MDS. With this BatchID, you can trigger the batch load directly using the triggering batch loads stored procedure described in the next section.

```
EXEC mdm.udpStagingBatchSave
@UserID,@VersionID,@BatchID,@OriginalBatchID,@BatchName,@ExternalSystemID,
@StatusID,@TotalMemberCount,@TotalMemberAttributeCount,
@TotalMemberRelationshipCount,@ErrorMemberCount,@ErrorMemberAttributeCount,
@ErrorMemberRelationshipCount,@BatchID output
```

Use the explanation of each parameter later in this chapter to load batch information properly into the tblStgBatch table.

Triggering Batch Loads

Batches can be triggered directly using the following MDS stored procedure. This procedure can log staged records as transactions and trigger validation after the completion of the staging of the records.

```
EXEC mdm.udpStagingProcess @UserId,@Version_ID,@StagingType_ID,
@LogFlag,@DoValidate,@Batch_ID
```

Using Web Services to Stage Data

There are a number of calls within the web service that leverage the staging tables and processes to load data into Master Data Services. Some of these calls provide support for bulk loading of data. These calls manage the entire process of populating the staging tables and triggering the staging process. The structure of these calls will be discussed in greater detail in Chapter 13.

The following operations provide the ability to trigger the staging process and to retrieve staging errors. These web service operations can be used within a larger integration framework to create automation around managing processes or exposing errors in a specialized user interface.

Creating Batches

The following code example will batch unbatched staging records into Master Data Services for the specified model and version. Without passing the unbatched criteria parameters, the StagingProcessRequest operation will trigger staging on all batches that are queued to run in the staging batch table.

```
//Triggering staging for a specific model and version
public string ProcessUnbatchedStaging(string ModelName, string
VersionName)
    {
        StagingProcessRequest request = new StagingProcessRequest();
        StagingProcessResponse response = new
StagingProcessResponse();
        request.Process = true;
        request.UnbatchedCriteria = new StagingUnbatchedCriteria();

        //You must set the model and the version to process unbatched
staging records
        request.UnbatchedCriteria.ModelId = new Identifier { Name =
ModelName };
        request.UnbatchedCriteria.VersionId = new Identifier { Name =
VersionName };

        //Call the web service and pass in the populated request
        response = mds_Proxy.StagingProcess(request);
        return response.OperationResult.Errors.Count.ToString();
    }
```

Initiating the Staging Process

The StagingGet operation will retrieve staging information related to the batches specified in the StagingGet request. All bulk calls will bring data into MDS using the staging tables, and the responses from these operations will provide staging batches.

```
//Get Information related to a staging batch
public collection<StagingBatch> StagingGet(Collection<Identifier>
stagingbatch, bool ReturnAllCriteria, bool ReturnMembers, bool
ReturnAttributes, bool ReturnRelationships )
    {

        //Create new request and response objects
        StagingGetRequest request = new StagingGetRequest();
        StagingGetResponse response = new StagingGetResponse();
```

```
            //Provide the Staging Batches to the search criteria
            request.StagingSearchCriteria = new StagingSearchCriteria()
                {
                    StagingBatches = stagingbatch
                };

            request.StagingResultCriteria = new StagingResultCriteria()
            {

                //Use this to return all staging information
                All = ReturnAllCriteria,

                //Each of the following return a specific staging table's
information
                Attributes = ReturnAttributes,
                Members = ReturnMembers,
                Relationships = ReturnRelationships
            };

            //Pass the populated request object to StagingGet operation
            response = mds_Proxy.StagingGet(request);

            //Return the staging batches to the caller
            return response.Batches;
        }
```

Clearing Batches

Once a batch has been successfully loaded and there are no more errors to correct, the batch should be cleared from the staging tables. Batch summaries will remain in the tblStgBatch table, but all the individual data elements will be deleted from the staging tables attached to the batches passed into the following call:

```
            //Clear data from staging tables by batch
            public int StagingClear(Collection <Identifier> Batch)
            {
                StagingClearRequest request = new StagingClearRequest();
                StagingClearResponse response = new StagingClearResponse();
                request.Batches = Batch;
                response = mds_Proxy.StagingClear(request);
                return response.BatchesQueuedToClearCount;
            }
```

Errors that Occur During Staging

Sometimes errors occur during the staging process. As each row in a staging table is processed, the Status_ID column is updated with a 1 if staging succeeded and a 2 if it failed. If staging failed, the ErrorCode column is updated with a number that can help you troubleshoot the issue.

You can see a translation of these error messages in the Master Data Manager web application; however, only the first 450–500 of these messages are displayed for each batch. We've included tables here to show you all possible errors that may be encountered when staging members into MDS.

Procedure: How to View Staging Errors in the Web Application

To view details of your staging errors in the Master Data Manager web application, complete the following steps:

1. On the Staging Batches page, click the row that lists the errors.
2. Click the "View details for selected batch" button.

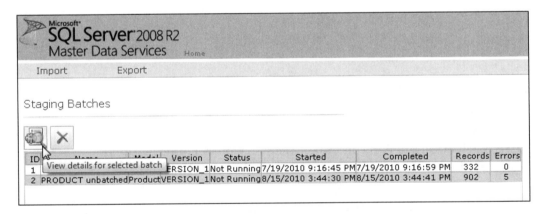

The Staging Batch Errors page is displayed with the details of your errors.

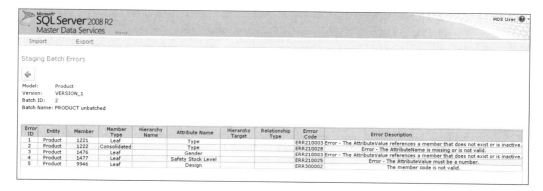

Member Staging Errors

The following table shows detailed information for all the errors that can be displayed in the ErrorCode column of tblStgMember.

Error Code	Description	Tips for Fixing the Issue
ERR210000	The record staged successfully.	None needed.
ERR210001	Error - The same MemberCode exists multiple times in the staging table.	Determine which member has the correct code and try again.
ERR210017	Error - The UserName is not valid.	View users in the User and Group Permissions functional area. Ensure that the user is listed there and that he or she has sufficient permissions. See Chapter 11 for more information.
ERR210018	Error - The ModelName is missing or not valid.	Confirm that the model name matches the model displayed in Master Data Manager exactly. *Note: Model name is case sensitive.*
ERR210019	Error - You must be a model administrator.	View users in the User and Group Permissions functional area. Ensure that the user is listed there and that he or she has sufficient permissions. See Chapter 11 for more information.
ERR210020	Error - The EntityName is missing or is not valid.	Confirm that the entity name matches the entity displayed in Master Data Manager exactly.
ERR210032	Error - The HierarchyName is required if MemberType_ID is 2.	Ensure you have a hierarchy name column and value specified.
ERR210033	Error - The entity is not enabled for collections.	In System Administration, click Manage | Entities, click the entity, and click the "Edit selected entity" button. In the "Enable explicit hierarchies and collections" list, select Yes.

Error Code	Description	Tips for Fixing the Issue
ERR210034	Error - The MemberCode is a reserved word and is not valid.	You cannot use Name or Code as a member code value. Other commonly used MDS words are also not allowed, such as Root and Unused.
ERR210035	Error - Because a code generation business rule does not exist, the MemberCode is required.	If a business rule existed to create the member code value automatically, MemberCode would not be required. If you are using business rules, ensure they are active. See Chapter 8 for more information.
ERR210036	Error - Because a code generation business rule exists, the MemberCode is not required.	Remove the value from the MemberCode column, or exclude or delete the business rule that generates the member code value.
ERR210037	Error - The MemberType_ID is not valid. Use 1 for leaf, 2 for consolidated (parent), or 3 for collection.	Ensure your MemberType_ID is 1, 2, or 3.
ERR210055	An unknown error occurred when staging member record.	If an unhandled exception occurs during the staging process, all records will be marked with this error. This error may have nothing to do with records that display this error.
ERR300003	Error - The MemberCode already exists.	You cannot stage the same member multiple times in the same batch.

Attribute Staging Errors

The following table shows detailed information for all the errors that can be displayed in the ErrorCode column of tblStgMemberAttribute.

Error Code	Description	Tips for Fixing the Issue
ERR210000	The record staged successfully.	None needed.
ERR210001	Error - The same MemberCode exists multiple times in the staging table.	Only the first member with this code is successfully imported. Determine which member should truly be imported.
ERR210003	Error - The AttributeValue references a member that does not exist or is inactive.	No attribute was updated. Ensure that the member code is correct and try again.
ERR210004	Error - The AttributeValue references a member that does not exist or is inactive.	No attribute was updated. Ensure that the member code is correct and try again.
ERR210006	Error - The MemberCode is inactive.	The member that you are attempting to update has been deleted in the current version. If this is an error, you can reverse the transaction and try again.
ERR210017	Error - The UserName is not valid.	View users in the User and Group Permissions functional area. Ensure that the user is listed there and that he or she has sufficient permissions. See Chapter 11 for more information.

Error Code	Description	Tips for Fixing the Issue
ERR210018	Error - The ModelName is missing or not valid.	Confirm that the model name matches the model displayed in Master Data Manager exactly. *Note: Model name is case sensitive.*
ERR210019	Error - You must be a model administrator.	View users in the User and Group Permissions functional area. Ensure that the user is listed there and that he or she has sufficient permissions. See Chapter 11 for more information.
ERR210020	Error - The EntityName is missing or is not valid.	Confirm that the entity name matches the entity displayed in Master Data Manager exactly.
ERR210021	Error - The MemberType_ID is not valid. Use 1 for leaf, 2 for consolidated (parent), or 3 for collection.	Ensure your MemberType_ID is 1, 2, or 3.
ERR210022	Error - You cannot update system attributes.	There are a number of system attributes for each entity, and these attributes cannot be updated through staging. These attributes are: ID Version_ID Status_ID ValidationStatus_ID EnterDTM EnterUserID EnterVersionID LastChgDTM LastChgUserID LastChgVersionID LastChgTS
ERR210023	Error - You cannot stage updates to file attributes.	The attribute you specified only allows files to be uploaded to it. You cannot do this through staging.
ERR210024	Error - The AttributeValue is too long.	The attribute value exceeds the allowed length set when the attribute was created. You can determine this length on the Attribute Edit screen in System Administration.
ERR210025	Error - The AttributeValue must be a number.	Domain-based attributes must use the code of the member from the source entity.
ERR210026	Error - The AttributeValue must be a date.	The attribute you are trying to update requires a date value.
ERR210027	Error - The AttributeValue must be an integer.	The attribute you are trying to update requires an integer.
ERR210028	Error - The AttributeName is missing or is not valid.	Ensure that you use a code for AttributeName if you are trying to update a domain-based attribute.

Error Code	Description	Tips for Fixing the Issue
ERR210029	Error - The AttributeValue is missing.	The AttributeValue column must contain a value when assigning a value to the code of an attribute.
ERR210030	Warning - The AttributeValue will be unassigned.	This is a warning that the attribute value is being unassigned.
ERR210031	Error - When you change the MDMMemberStatus attribute, the AttributeValue must be either "Active" or "De-Activated."	For more information, see "Using Staging to Deactivate and Reactivate Members," earlier in this chapter.
ERR210051	Error - The ObjectID cannot be updated because it is a system attribute.	You cannot update a system attribute.
ERR210052	Error - The MemberCode cannot be deactivated because it is used as a domain-based attribute value.	If a member is used as a domain-based attribute for another member, you cannot deactivate it.
ERR210054	An unknown error occurred when staging attribute value.	If an unhandled exception occurs during the staging process, all records will be marked with this error. This error may have nothing to do with records that display this error.
ERR300002	The MemberCode is not valid.	Ensure that the code matches that of an active member.
ERR300003	The MemberCode already exists.	You cannot stage the same member multiple times in the same batch.

Relationship Staging Errors

The following table shows detailed information for all the errors that can be displayed in the ErrorCode column of tblStgRelationship.

Error Code	Description	Tips for Fixing the Issue
ERR210000	The record staged successfully.	None needed.
ERR210006	Error - The MemberCode is inactive.	You cannot update the relationship for a member that is inactive. The member was deleted in the current version.
ERR210007	Warning - The transaction was not logged because the assignment already exists.	No action is needed. You attempted to set a relationship that has already been set.
ERR210008	Error - The TargetCode is inactive.	You cannot set a relationship based on a target member that is deleted in the version selected to load to.
ERR210009	Error - The MemberCode does not exist.	Ensure that the code matches that of an active member.
ERR210010	Error - The TargetCode does not exist.	The member specified by the TargetCode does not exist. Ensure that you're using the correct TargetType_ID.

Error Code	Description	Tips for Fixing the Issue
ERR210011	Error - When TargetType_ID is 1, the TargetCode cannot be a leaf member.	Set TargetType_ID to 1 only if you are staging a parent-child relationship. In this case, the TargetCode must be a consolidated member, because it is a parent.
ERR210012	A new non-mandatory explicit hierarchy relationship was created successfully.	None needed. This is a success message.
ERR210013	A new collection relationship was created.	None needed. This is a success message.
ERR210014	The member was assigned as a child of MDMUNUSED successfully.	None needed. This is a success message.
ERR210015	Error - For the non-mandatory hierarchy, the MemberCode exists multiple times in the staging table.	Ensure that each member is listed only once.
ERR210016	Error - The relationship could not be created because it would cause a circular reference.	This occurs when A is a parent of B, B is a parent of C, and you attempt to make C the parent of A. This relationship is not supported in MDS.
ERR210017	Error - The UserName is not valid.	The user could not be confirmed against the list of active users, which you'll find in the Master Data Manager web application in the User and Group Permissions functional area. For more information, see Chapter 11.
ERR210018	Error - The ModelName is missing or not valid.	Confirm that the model name matches the model displayed in Master Data Manager exactly. *Note: Model name is case sensitive.*
ERR210019	Error - You must be a model administrator.	View users in the User and Group Permissions functional area. Ensure that the user is listed there and that he or she has sufficient permissions. See Chapter 11 for more information.
ERR210020	Error - The EntityName is missing or is not valid.	Confirm that the entity name matches the model displayed in Master Data Manager exactly.
ERR210038	Error - The HierarchyName is required if the MemberType_ID is 4.	When updating explicit hierarchies, you must specify the explicit hierarchy name.
ERR210039	Error - MemberType_ID must be 4 (hierarchy) or 5 (collection).	The only possible values when staging relationships are 4 and 5.
ERR210040	Error - MemberCode is required.	A valid member code must be supplied for every row in the relationship staging table.
ERR210041	Error - "ROOT" is not valid for the MemberCode.	You can use this value for TargetCode only.
ERR210042	Error - "MDMUNUSED" is not valid for the MemberCode.	You can use this value for TargetCode only.
ERR210043	Error - TargetType_ID must be 1 (parent) or 2 (sibling).	If you are staging collections, you must use 1. If you are staging explicit hierarchy relationships, you must use 1 or 2.

Error Code	Description	Tips for Fixing the Issue
ERR210044	Error - TargetCode does not exist.	The TargetCode does not exist within the specified entity.
ERR210045	Error - "MDMUNUSED" is a reserved word and is not valid.	You can use this value for TargetCode only.
ERR210046	Error - The member cannot be a sibling of Root.	The Root node can contain children only.
ERR210047	Error - The member cannot be a sibling of Unused.	The Unused node can contain children only.
ERR210048	Error - MemberCode and TargetCode cannot be the same.	You cannot set a relationship of a member to itself.
ERR210049	Error - TargetType_ID must be 1 (parent) when staging collection relationships.	No other TargetType_IDs are allowed when adding members to collections.
ERR210050	Information - A hierarchy is not required for collections.	If you specified a hierarchy name while adding members to collections, the hierarchy name is ignored.

Viewing the Staging Batch Table

The last table specifically related to staging is the batch table, mdm.tblStgBatch. This table stores information related to each load of data into the MDS system. Summary information related to the success and failure of each record is stored in the batch table indefinitely.

Column Name	Required?	Description
OriginalBatch_ID	No	This is not currently implemented.
MUID	Yes	Unique identifier for the batch.
Version_ID	Yes	ID in the mdm.tblModelVersion table that identifies the model version that the data was or will be staged into.
ExternalSystem_ID	N/A	This column is not currently managed by the MDS system. The column was created to support the identification and tracking of staging records by external source system in concert with the mdm.tblExternalSystem table. Neither this column nor the table is currently used in the staging process.
Name	N/A	The name for the batch. When using the UI or the staging sweep stored procedure, this is populated with the model name and "unbatched." This value will be blank for system staging loads. You can set this value to anything when using the staging batch creation stored procedure, udpStagingBatchSave.

Column Name	Required?	Description
Status_ID	N/A	1 = "Queued to run"—The batch will be processed the next time the Service Broker queue is activated.* 2 = "Not Running"—The batch staging process has completed. 3 = "Running"—The batch is currently processing. 4= "Queued to clear"—The request to clear staging table records for this batch has been set and the staging tables will be cleared the next time the Service Broker queue is activated. 5= Batch has been cleared—All corresponding records for the batch have been cleared from the staging tables.
TotalMemberCount	N/A	The total number of members in tblStgMember that were associated with this Batch_ID.
ErrorMemberCount	N/A	The total number of members with errors in tblStgMember that were associated with this Batch_ID.
TotalMemberAttributeCount	No	The total number of attributes in the tblStgMemberAttribute staging table that were associated with this Batch_ID.
ErrorMemberAttributeCount	N/A	The total number of attributes with an error in tblStgMemberAttribute that were associated with this Batch_ID.
TotalMemberRelationshipCount	N/A	The total number of relationships in the relationship staging table that were associated with this Batch_ID.
ErrorMemberRelationshipCount	N/A	The total number of relationships with an error in tblStgRelationship that were associated with this Batch_ID.
LastRunStartDTM	No	The time that the staging batch process was initiated.
LastRunStartUserID	No	The user who ran the process that invoked the staging process.
LastRunEndDTM	No	The time that the staging batch process completes.
LastRunEndUserID	No	The user who ran the process that invoked the staging process.
LastClearedDTM	No	The date and time that this batch was cleared from the staging tables. Even though all the imported records are cleared, the summary data stored in this batch table remains.
LastClearedUserID	No	The user who initiated the batch clearing process.
EnterDTM	No	The date and time that the batch was "queued for processing."
EnterUserID	No	The user who ran the process to create the batch.

*The Service Broker queue is used only as an asynchronous timer. Generic staging messages are placed on the queue and staging batches are triggered by the Queued to Run status only.

Procedure: How to Clear the Staging Queue

To clear a batch from the staging queue, complete the following steps:

1. On the Master Data Manager home page, click Integration Management.
2. In the Staging Batches pane, click the row for the batch you want to clear.
3. Click the "Clear selected batch" button.

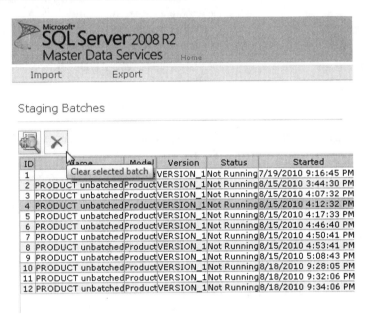

The value in the Status column changes to Queued to Clear. When it's done processing, the Status column changes to Not Running. This can be considered completed for any batch that is displayed.

Summary

In this chapter, we discussed techniques for using staging tables to load data into Master Data Services efficiently and effectively. We discussed the three types of staging tables and the kinds of data each table supports for staging. We reviewed examples of using SQL Server Integration Services or standard SQL calls to populate records into the staging tables. Within the discussion of staging tables, we also discussed types of errors that can occur during the data loading process from the staging into MDS, and provided likely solutions to these errors. In the next chapter, we will discuss hierarchy types in greater detail.

Chapter 6

Working with Hierarchies and Collections

In This Chapter

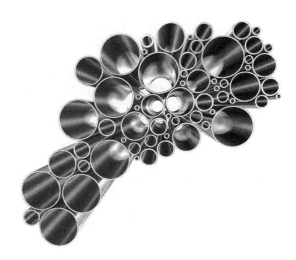

usinesses are not built only on lists; they require more complex structures for data. Dollars, units, and hours must all be calculated to produce consolidated views of a business. For many years, companies have been using business intelligence (BI) applications to better understand their businesses and discover opportunities for both cost savings and revenue growth. At the heart of these applications are the hierarchies that make consolidations possible.

When managing consolidations within a business, it is imperative that all values are accounted for once and only once. To ensure this, hierarchies in Master Data Services enforce that all leaf members have one and only one parent. This limits your ability to manage many-to-many relationships within MDS and display these relationships hierarchically.

In this chapter, we review the two primary types of hierarchies supported in MDS. We then create these derived and explicit hierarchies within our models. Finally, we create a number of special hierarchies and discuss the various uses for these special hierarchies.

Before you start this chapter, go to www.mdsuser.com and download the ZIP file for Chapter 6, called chapter6.zip. This ZIP file contains the following files:

File	When to Use	How to Use
Finance_data.pkg	Now	Go to System Administration, and on the menu bar, choose System	Deployment. Then deploy the package file. If you already have a model with this name, choose a new name.
Product_data.pkg	Now	Same as deploying the Finance package.
1line_members.csv	Procedure: How to Create a Three-Level Derived Hierarchy	Import this CSV file into the tblStgMember staging table. Then use Integration Management to import these members.
2manufacturer_members.csv	Procedure: How to Create a Three-Level Derived Hierarchy	Again, use tblStgMember and Integration Management to import these members.
3line_manufacturer_attributes.csv	Procedure: How to Create a Three-Level Derived Hierarchy	Use tblStgMemberAttribute and Integration Management to import these attribute values.
4account_consolidated_members.csv	Procedure: How to Create an Explicit Hierarchy	Use tblStgMember and Integration Management to import these consolidated members.
5account_relationships.csv	Procedure: How to Create an Explicit Hierarchy	Use tblStgRelationship and Integration Management to import these relationships.
6employee_manager_attributes.csv	Procedure: How to Create a Recursive Hierarchy	Use tblStgMemberAttribute and Integration Management to import these attribute values.

NOTE

If you rename the models when you deploy them, make sure you change the model names in each of the staging spreadsheets before you import them.

The Product model represents everything you created in Chapter 4, but it includes several hundred product members with their attributes already populated. This gives you a fair amount of data to work with and will help the samples in this chapter make more sense. The Finance model is similar insofar as it is fully populated with data and contains the structure you'll need to work with the hierarchies we create in this chapter.

Ragged vs. Level-Based Hierarchies

When you're working with hierarchies, it is important to understand some common terms used across applications. Any hierarchy can be either ragged or level based. *Ragged* describes hierarchies that support leaf members at multiple levels. A hierarchy is *level based* if leaf members always exist at the same level, regardless of the number of levels within the hierarchy.

Some business applications do not support ragged hierarchies, so it is important to know the limitations of downstream systems before you create hierarchies in MDS.

Derived Hierarchies

In MDS, derived hierarchies provide the ability to highlight preexisting data relationships within entities and display them hierarchically. Derived hierarchies are always level based. This means that every level within the hierarchy corresponds to a specific domain-based attribute within the entity–attribute chain (see Figure 6-1).

Explicit Hierarchies

Explicit hierarchies are multilevel hierarchies with very few restrictions. Explicit hierarchies are managed as name–value pairs, with consolidated members containing other consolidated or leaf members. Explicit hierarchies are created for one entity at a time. Derived hierarchies, in contrast, require multiple entities.

Consolidated members are almost always theoretical items, whereas leaf members represent physical items. Like leaf members, consolidated members can have attributes assigned to them. In the MDS database, a separate table exists to manage consolidated members and their associated attributes. Consolidated members are available only if an entity is enabled for explicit hierarchies. Each consolidated member can be associated with only a single hierarchy no matter how many explicit hierarchies have been created for the entity.

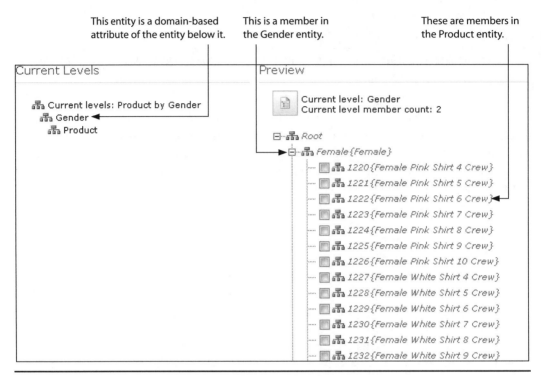

This entity is a domain-based attribute of the entity below it.

This is a member in the Gender entity.

These are members in the Product entity.

Figure 6-1   *A derived hierarchy, created by using a domain-based attribute*

Derived vs. Explicit: Which Hierarchy Is Best?

Derived hierarchies are determined by the structure of the model, and changes to the structure are rare. To illustrate the value of this rigor, consider the following scenario that organizations commonly encounter:

Our fictional company devises a regional hierarchy to manage sales. As with most of these hierarchies, this hierarchy begins as a level-based hierarchy, with each level within the hierarchy corresponding to a distinct type of attribute. To store the hierarchy, IT uses the parent-child format from its analysis system.

Over time, this hierarchy is modified by midlevel managers to help them manage their divisions better. Changes are not centrally managed, and new levels are added monthly. John is the manager of the Western region of the company. John has two managers who split duties managing the Southwest division for him: Bill and Margaret. Since Bill and Margaret are splitting the Southwest, John needs to split divisional data in the company's reports to measure this divisional structure. To do this, he creates two additional nodes within the hierarchy for the Southwest division, SWB (Southwest Bill) and SWM (Southwest Margaret).

Over time, Bill and Margaret move on to other jobs, either moving up in the company or on to other opportunities. Yet the Southwest division continues to be split into SWM and SWB. This is not an isolated occurrence, as many managers make isolated changes to the hierarchy structure. Some of these changes may not be warranted and others may have a short shelf life. Soon the initial hierarchy is unrecognizable and difficult to manage. The ability to provide managers with rigid derived hierarchies, malleable explicit hierarchies, and focused collections allows BI professionals to provide the perfect tool for each scenario.

Hierarchy Type	Description
Derived	Uses multiple entities. Based on domain-based attribute relationships. Level based. Hierarchy structure is designed in System Administration. Hierarchy members are updated in Explorer.
Explicit	Uses one entity only. Consolidated members are used to group other consolidated and leaf members. Ragged. Entity must be enabled for explicit hierarchies in System Administration. Hierarchy structure is designed in Explorer. Hierarchy members are maintained and updated in Explorer.

Creating Derived Hierarchies

Derived hierarchies require that you have one or more entities, each of which has a domain-based attribute that you want to group members by. In MDS, you cannot group members by more than one domain-based attribute at a time. This doesn't mean that your derived hierarchy can't have multiple levels, just that each level must be based on a domain-based attribute relationship.

Procedure: How to Create a Derived Hierarchy

In this example, you'll create a derived hierarchy that has two levels. You will roll up products by gender. Product will be at the lowest level in the hierarchy, and Gender will be one level higher.

To create a two-level derived hierarchy, complete the following steps:

1. On the Master Data Manager home page, click System Administration.
2. On the menu bar, choose Manage | Derived Hierarchies.
3. From the Model list, select the model if it isn't selected already. In this case, select Product.
4. Click the "Add derived hierarchy" button.
5. In the "Derived hierarchy name" field, type a descriptive name for your hierarchy. In this case, we're going to name the hierarchy **Product by Gender**.

6. Click the "Save derived hierarchy" button. The page that is displayed has three panes.

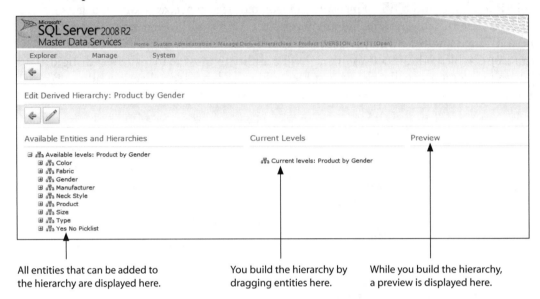

All entities that can be added to the hierarchy are displayed here.

You build the hierarchy by dragging entities here.

While you build the hierarchy, a preview is displayed here.

On the left are the entities that can be added to the current level in the hierarchy. In the center are all the entities in the derived hierarchy; right now there are none because you haven't added any yet. Each time you drag an entity from the left pane to the center pane, the left pane refreshes with the list of entities that remain available to add.

You should always drag the lowest-level entity first. In this case, we want a hierarchy with products at the lowest level.

7. In the left pane, click and drag Product to the "Current levels" label in the middle pane. Release the mouse button and the screen refreshes, with Product displayed in the Current Levels pane.

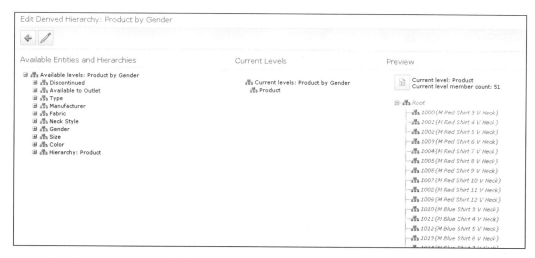

The Preview pane refreshes to show a list of products.

8. Now you can drag the entity you want to group by. In this case it's Gender, so click Gender in the left pane and drag it to the Current Levels pane.

The page refreshes and the Preview pane shows all products grouped by gender.

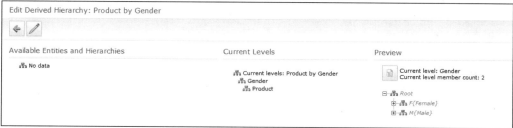

NOTE

The hierarchy is saved as you build it. No Save button is available on this page.

If you decide you do not want to group by gender, click Gender in the Current Levels pane and then click the Delete button that's displayed at the bottom of the pane. If you decide you want to rename your hierarchy, click the "Edit derived hierarchy name" button on the top left of this page.

The real value of a derived hierarchy occurs when new products are created. You can configure a business rule so that each time a new product is added, if the Gender attribute is not populated, an e-mail notifies all interested parties. Business rules will be covered in more detail in Chapter 8.

Procedure: How to Create a Three-Level Derived Hierarchy

Now you are going to create a derived hierarchy with three levels. After completing this procedure, you should be able to build your own multilevel hierarchies.

In the Product model you have built so far, you don't have the ability to create a three-level derived hierarchy. This is because the Product entity is the only entity that has domain-based attributes. To create a hierarchy with multiple levels, each entity in the hierarchy must be used as a domain-based attribute of another entity.

For example, right now you can roll up products by Gender, Size, Type—any of Product's domain-based attributes. But you can't roll up products by size and *then* by gender. You have to choose one or the other.

In this example, you will create a derived hierarchy that rolls up products first by product line, then by manufacturer. This will require two relationships:

▶ The Product entity must have a Line domain-based attribute.

▶ The Line entity must have a Manufacturer domain-based attribute.

When you're done creating the structure, you will be able to roll up Product by Line by Manufacturer. The Product model doesn't have this structure right now, so let's create it.

Create a Line Entity

Create an entity called Line and populate it with 14 members. (Note: It does not need to have explicit hierarchies enabled.) You can get these members from chapter6.zip on www.mdsuser.com. Import 1line_members.csv into tblStgMember and use the Integration Management functional area to start the staging process. Alternately, create the members manually by referring to the following table. Remember, you create the entity in System Administration and add members in Explorer.

Line Name	Line Code
Boys Fall	Boys Fall
Boys Summer	Boys Summer
Boys Spring	Boys Spring
Boys Activewear	Boys Activewear
Girls Activewear	Girls Activewear
Springtime Collection	Springtime Collection

Line Name	Line Code
Summer Boys	Summer Boys
Summer Girls	Summer Girls
Fall Boys	Fall Boys
Fall Girls	Fall Girls
Spring Girls	Spring Girls
Boys Active	Boys Active
Summer Collection	Summer Collection
Accessories	Accessories

Create a Manufacturer Entity

Create an entity called Manufacturer and populate it with six members. (Note: It does not need to have explicit hierarchies enabled.) You can get these members from chapter6.zip on www.mdsuser.com. Import 2manufacturer_members.csv into tblStgMember and use Integration Management to start the staging process. Or, create these members manually in Explorer.

Name	Code
Pish Posh	Pish Posh
Hipsters	Hipsters
Rings with Rosie	Rings with Rosie
TumbleJacks	TumbleJacks
TumbleJills	TumbleJills
Candy Canes	Candy Canes

For the Product Entity, Create a Line Domain-Based Attribute

Now, for the Product entity, you're going to create a domain-based attribute that's based on the Line entity.

1. In Master Data Manager, click System Administration.
2. On the menu bar, choose Manage | Entities.
3. From the Model list, select Product.
4. Click the Product entity and then the "Edit selected entity" button.

5. In the Leaf attributes section, click the "Add leaf attribute" button.

6. Choose Domain-based, type **Line** for the name, and select Line for the source entity.

7. Click the Save attribute button.

For the Line Entity, Create a Manufacturer Domain-Based Attribute

Now in System Administration, perform the same steps as you just did, but edit the Line entity instead. Add a leaf attribute, domain-based, called Manufacturer, based on the Manufacturer entity.

Assign a Line to Each Product, and a Manufacturer to Each Line

You can use 3line_manufacturer_attributes.csv from www.mdsuser.com to assign a Line attribute to each product, and then a Manufacturer attribute to each Line. Remember that attributes are imported into tblStgMemberAttribute and you use Integration Management to start the staging import process. Or, you can assign attributes manually in Explorer.

If you decide to do this manually, here are a few things to consider:

▶ The Line attribute is not part of an attribute group yet, so it will not be displayed in Explorer. Add it to the Marketing tab if you want to edit it.

▶ In the Explorer grid, you can click the X at the top of the leftmost column to select all members displayed on the page. Then double-click any cell in the Line column. When you press TAB or ENTER, all selected members are updated.

You are now ready to create your three-level derived hierarchy.

Create the Derived Hierarchy

Creating the hierarchy should be the easiest part of the process:

1. In System Administration, on the menu bar, choose Manage | Derived Hierarchies.

2. Ensure Product is selected in the Model list and click the "Add derived hierarchy" button.

3. For the name, type **Product by Line by Manufacturer**.

4. Click and drag Product to the Current Levels pane. A list of products is displayed in the Preview pane.

5. Click and drag Line to the Current Levels pane and drop it on Product.

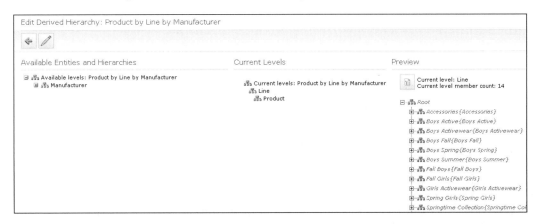

6. Manufacturer is the only entity available to add to the hierarchy. Click and drag it to Line in the Current Levels pane. When you release the mouse button, the full hierarchy is displayed in the Preview pane.

You can now expand and collapse nodes in the hierarchy to get an idea of the structure.

Hiding Levels

If you click any of the levels in the Current Levels pane, you can hide the level from users by selecting No from the Visible list. This can be useful when you have a multilevel hierarchy structure and users don't need to see many of the middle-tier levels when working with the hierarchy.

You can also change the name of a hierarchy level by updating the value in the Column name field.

System Settings for Hierarchies

There are two settings in Master Data Services Configuration Manager that apply to hierarchies and collections. Now that you know more about what hierarchies look like, you might want to change these.

Number of Members in the Hierarchy by Default

This setting determines how many members are displayed in a hierarchy node before a label named …more… is displayed. The default setting is to show 50 members.

Show Names in Hierarchy by Default

This setting determines whether the name and code of each member are displayed or only the code is displayed. The default setting is to show both name and code.

Creating Explicit Hierarchies

There are two types of explicit hierarchies in MDS: mandatory and non-mandatory. Before you create an explicit hierarchy, you should determine which type you'll need.

Non-mandatory Explicit Hierarchies

When you create a non-mandatory explicit hierarchy, all children are located in a node named Unused, as shown in Figure 6-2. Leaf members in the Unused node do not show up in subscription views based on the explicit hierarchy. This means that when you use subscription views as source data for subscribing systems, all the members in the Unused node are excluded. For more information on subscription views, see Chapter 12.

Non-mandatory explicit hierarchies are easier to work with when you have large numbers of leaf members. To build an explicit hierarchy, you must create consolidated members, which are displayed at the root by default. You can then move leaf members from the Unused node to the consolidated members that live at the root.

Mandatory Explicit Hierarchies

When you create a mandatory explicit hierarchy, all leaf members are initially located at the root of the hierarchy. As you create consolidated members, they are also added to the root, but they are displayed at the end of the list. To find them, you must search or scroll to the end of the hierarchy. Figure 6-3 shows a mandatory explicit hierarchy where consolidated members exist but are not displayed because they follow hundreds of leaf members.

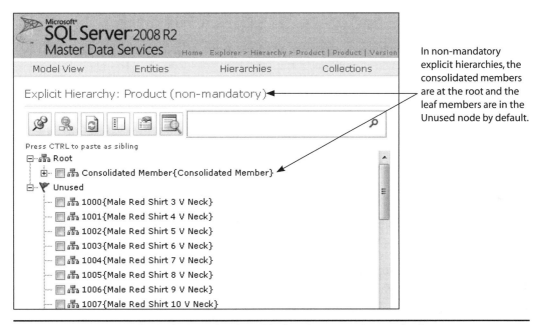

Figure 6-2   *A non-mandatory explicit hierarchy, where all leaf members start in the Unused node*

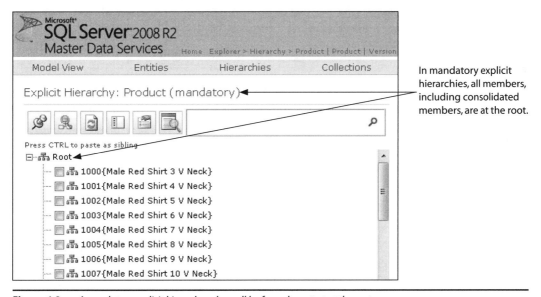

Figure 6-3   *A mandatory explicit hierarchy, where all leaf members start at the root*

Procedure: How to Create an Explicit Hierarchy

To create an explicit hierarchy, you are going to use the Finance model, which, if you deployed it from the web site, includes a full list of sample accounts. To create an explicit hierarchy, you complete the following tasks:

1. Enable the Account entity for hierarchies and collections.
2. Create consolidated members to be used to group leaf and other consolidated members.
3. Create the explicit hierarchy.

Enable the Entity for Hierarchies and Collections

Before you can create explicit hierarchies, you must always enable the entity for explicit hierarchies by completing the following steps:

1. In Master Data Manager, click System Administration.
2. On the menu bar, choose Manage | Entities.
3. From the Model list, select Finance.
4. Click Account and then click the "Edit selected entity" button.
5. From the "Enable explicit hierarchies and collections" list, select Yes.
6. In the "Explicit hierarchy name" field, type **Chart of Accounts**.
7. You are going to create a non-mandatory explicit hierarchy where all leaf members start in an Unused node, so clear the "Include all leaf members in mandatory hierarchy" check box.

8. Click the Save entity button.

If you decide you want additional explicit hierarchies in the future, edit the Account entity. You can now add explicit hierarchies, attributes for consolidated members, and attributes for collections from this page.

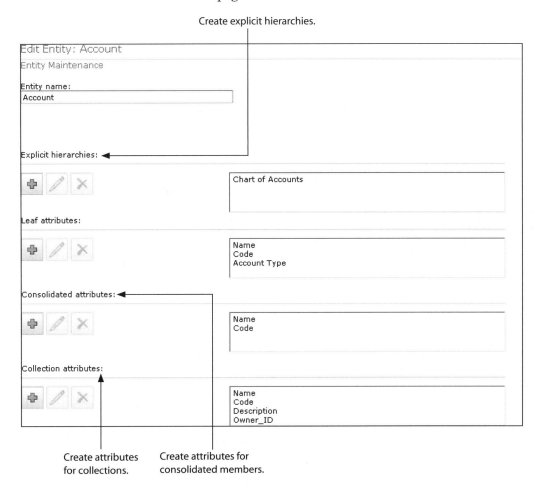

Create explicit hierarchies.

Create attributes for collections.

Create attributes for consolidated members.

Populate the Consolidated Members for the Account Entity

You can use 4account_consolidated_members.csv from www.mdsuser.com to populate the consolidated members (by using tblStgMember), or you can complete the following steps in the Master Data Manager web UI:

1. On the home page, select Finance and VERSION_1 from the lists and click Explorer.
2. On the menu bar, choose Entities | Account.

3.   Above the grid, select the Consolidated option.

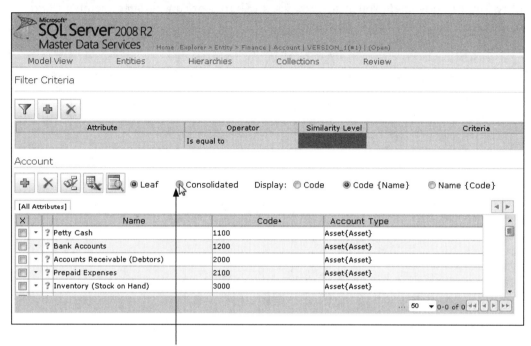

Select the Consolidated option.

4.   The list is blank. Now, by clicking the Add button above the grid, add the
      following consolidated members or create your own.

Name	Code
Cash	Cash
Cost of Goods Sold	Cost of Goods Sold
Fixed Expenses	Fixed Expenses
Long Term Assets	Long Term Assets
Long Term Liabilities	Long Term Liabilities
Marketing Expenses	Marketing Expenses
Revenue	Revenue
Salary Expense	Salary Expense

Name	Code
Shareholder's Equity	Shareholder's Equity
Short Term Assets	Short Term Assets
Short Term Liabilities	Short Term Liabilities
Variable Expenses	Variable Expenses
Revenue - Real	Revenue - Real
Revenue - Contra	Revenue - Contra
Revenue - INT	Revenue - INT
Expense	Expense
Assets	Assets
Liabilities	Liabilities
Profit and Loss Accounts	PL Accounts

Create the Explicit Hierarchy

The hierarchy structure was created when you enabled explicit hierarchies for the Account entity. Open Explorer to view it in more detail.

1. On the home page, select Finance and VERSION_1 from the lists and click Explorer.
2. On the menu bar, choose Hierarchies | Explicit:Chart of Accounts.

When you first open the hierarchy, only Root and Unused are displayed. If you expand Unused, all of the Account leaf members are displayed. If you click Unused, the grid on the right refreshes to display all of the Account leaf members.

You can now use 5account_relationships.csv with tblStgRelationship to move members in the hierarchy, or use the procedures in Chapter 7 that explain how to move hierarchy members. Figure 6-4 shows part of the hierarchy that will be created if you use the spreadsheet from www.mdsuser.com.

Figure 6-4   *An explicit hierarchy that shows a chart of accounts*

Recursive Hierarchies

A recursive hierarchy is a special type of derived hierarchy. In a typical derived hierarchy, the members in an entity are grouped by a domain-based attribute. In a recursive hierarchy, the members are still grouped by a domain-based attribute; however, this domain-based attribute is based on the entity itself. For example, each employee in an organization has a manager. And the manager can be any one of the employees. The following procedures show how to use this employee-manager relationship to create a recursive hierarchy that shows Main Street Clothing Company's organizational structure.

Procedure: How to Create a Recursive Hierarchy

To create a recursive hierarchy, you are going to use the Finance model, which, if you deployed it from the web site, includes a full list of sample employees. To create a recursive hierarchy, you are going to complete the following tasks:

1.   Create a domain-based attribute for the Employee entity. This attribute will be named Manager and will be based on the Employee entity.

2.   Assign a manager for each employee or load a list of Manager attributes.

3.   Create the recursive hierarchy.

For the Employee Entity, Create a
Manager Domain-Based Attribute

The Finance model has an entity called Employee. You need to create a domain-based attribute for the Employee entity:

1.   In Master Data Manager, click System Administration.

2.   On the menu bar, choose Manage | Entities.

3.   From the Model list, select Finance.

4.   Click the Employee entity and then the "Edit selected entity" button.

5.   In the Leaf attributes section, click the "Add leaf attribute" button.

6.   Choose Domain-based, type **Manager** for the name, and select Employee for the source entity.

7.   Click the Save attribute button.

Populate the Manager Attribute for Each Employee

You can use 6employee_manager_attributes.csv (from www.mdsuser.com) and tblStgMemberAttribute to populate each employee's Manager attribute.

If you choose not to use the staging process, you can populate each employee's Manager attribute value manually by entering it in Explorer. Keep in mind that you should not populate a manager for the CEO. As long as you have one employee without a manager, you will have someone at the top of your organizational structure. If you used the Finance model provided, each employee's title is already populated in Explorer.

Create the Recursive Hierarchy

After every employee has a manager (or even just a few, if you want to quickly see how this works), you can create the recursive hierarchy by completing the following steps.

1. In Master Data Manager, click System Administration.
2. On the menu bar, choose Manage | Derived Hierarchies.
3. From the Model list, select Finance.
4. Click the "Add derived hierarchy" button.
5. In the "Derived hierarchy name" field, type **Org Structure**.
6. Click the "Save derived hierarchy" button.
7. In the leftmost pane, click Employee and drag it to the Current Levels pane. When you release the mouse button, the Preview pane shows an alphabetical list of employees.

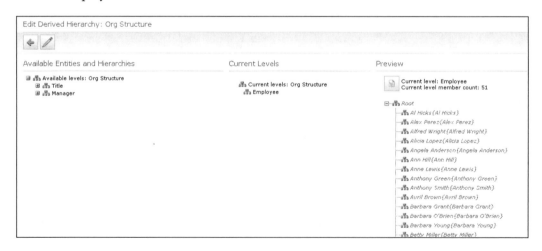

8. In the leftmost pane, click Manager and drag it to the Employee label on the Current Levels pane. When you release the mouse button, in the Preview pane, the CEO (or other employees without a manager assigned) is displayed at the highest level of the hierarchy, and the system recognizes that this hierarchy is recursive.

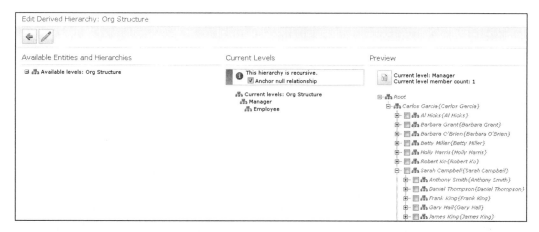

As you expand and collapse the hierarchy, you can see that each employee is listed only once. If you were to clear the "Anchor null relationship" check box, each employee would be listed individually, with any of his or her direct reports listed underneath. Anchor null relationship means that Carlos Garcia, who has a NULL value for his Manager attribute value, is considered the "anchor" for all other relationships. If there were multiple null relationships, these would all be displayed at the top of the hierarchy.

If you clear this check box, all employees are displayed
with the employees who report to them underneath.

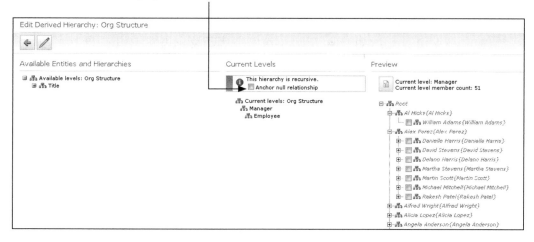

Derived Hierarchies with Explicit Caps

The last type of derived hierarchy within MDS is the derived hierarchy with explicit cap. This is a standard derived hierarchy that has an explicit hierarchy on top. The topmost entity of the derived hierarchy must be the bottom level of the explicit hierarchy.

Explicit cap hierarchies allow you to provide the best of both worlds. At the lower levels are derived levels that correspond to specific entities. At the top levels, you have the freedom to adapt the complex ragged structures allowed by explicit hierarchies. Explicit cap hierarchies allow you to define many lower bases to the same explicit hierarchy. These hierarchies are primarily used in finance domains such as Chart of Accounts and Organization Structure.

A global chart of accounts allows you to map disparate financial systems into your standard chart of accounts. This mapping allows corporate employees at large organizations to have common nomenclature when discussing financials with divisions across the globe. When working within multinational corporations, the complexities of accounting are further complicated by regional accounting laws that must be enforced. Corporate controllers cannot be expected to understand the intricacies of all these accounting practices worldwide, yet they must be able to hold individual business units accountable for their financial budgets and numbers. By creating a global chart of accounts and having each individual business unit map their country's unique chart of accounts into the global master account structure, individual countries can manage finances according to their regional requirements and corporate managers can still discuss their financials in a common manner.

As you can see in Figure 6-5, a company can use an explicit hierarchy for its global chart of accounts. This allows a ragged structure that's flexible and easy to update.

Each business unit can have its own standard chart of accounts that it maintains in a level-based derived hierarchy, as shown in Figure 6-6.

When you combine the derived hierarchy with the explicit hierarchy, the top levels are dictated by the explicit hierarchy and the bottom levels are populated by the derived hierarchy, as shown in Figure 6-7.

Procedure: How to Create a Derived Hierarchy with an Explicit Cap

To create a derived hierarchy with explicit cap, you must have your explicit hierarchy already created. You should also have an entity with domain-based attributes that you plan to use to create the derived hierarchy.

In this explicit hierarchy, leaf members from the Account entity
are grouped by consolidated members from the Account entity.

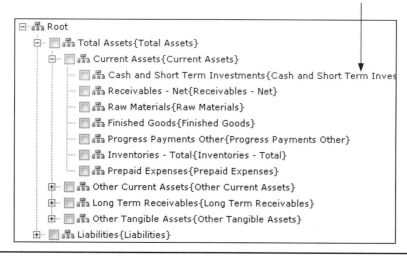

Figure 6-5   *An explicit hierarchy showing a multinational corporation's chart of accounts*

In this derived hierarchy, leaf members from the Account
entity are used to group leaf members from another entity.

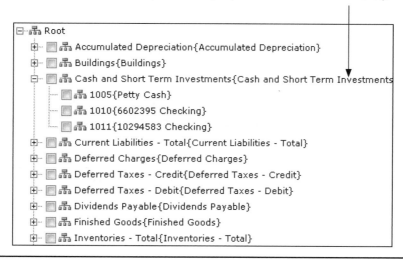

Figure 6-6   *A derived hierarchy for one division of the multinational corporation*

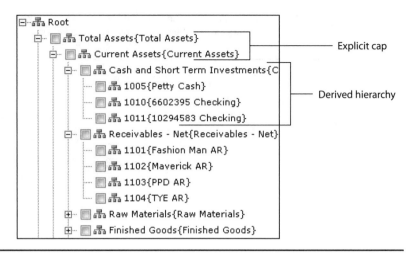

Figure 6-7 *A derived hierarchy with explicit cap*

Then follow the directions for creating a derived hierarchy (in System Administration, choose Manage | Derived Hierarchies). Drag the entities for the derived hierarchy over to the Current Levels pane. When your derived hierarchy is complete and the top level of the hierarchy is the bottom level of the explicit hierarchy, drag the explicit hierarchy to the Current Levels pane and drop it above the other levels.

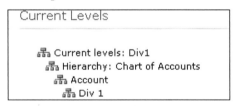

The structure of the hierarchy looks similar to that of a derived hierarchy; the results, however, are ragged at the top and level-based at the bottom.

NOTE

You can use the same explicit hierarchy as a cap for multiple derived hierarchies.

Collections

While hierarchies provide structures to manage consolidations of entire entities, you or your users might need to group a small number of members for your personal use. Master Data Services provides the ability to manage these personal consolidations through collections. Collections are containers for members from a single entity. Collections can hold either leaf, consolidated, or other collections within them. Collections do not follow the same rules as hierarchies. Collections can contain a member twice, as long as that member is contained in separate objects within the collection.

There are many different scenarios where collections can be a valuable tool. Collections can be used to manage personal charts of account consolidations or employee shifts. The Main Street Clothing Company will use collections a few times each year to manage sets of clothing (for example, a seasonal shirt, pants, belt, and hat). Collections allow Main Street to group members without using a hierarchy where all members need to be accounted for. It is simply a combination of random members that Main Street uses for analysis.

Limitations of Collections

Because Master Data Services is a version 1 product, collections have been implemented with a number of limitations. For example, the ability to use weighting on collections does not surface in the released product. Weighting on collections, if implemented, would provide users with the ability to apportion values across all members in a collection. This process can be invaluable in managing partnerships. This functionality still exists within the database tables, and weight continues to be exposed in the collections subscription view type. Because weighting is hidden from the UI, using it is slightly complicated, but it is possible. See www.mdsuser.com for more information.

Procedure: How to Create a Collection

In this example, you'll create a collection that represents a set of clothes for boys. Main Street Clothing Company sells two sets every season: one set for boys and one set for girls.

Before you can create a collection, you must enable the entity to have collections. Some organizations never use collections, but Main Street uses a few. To create a collection, you are going to complete the following tasks:

1. Enable the Product entity for hierarchies and collections.
2. Create a collection.
3. Add members to the collection.

Enable the Entity for Hierarchies and Collections

As with explicit hierarchies, you cannot create a collection for an entity until you enable the entity for hierarchies. To do so, complete the following steps:

1. On the Master Data Manager home page, click System Administration.
2. On the menu bar, choose Manage | Entities.

3. Select the Product model.

4. In the list, click Product and then the "Edit selected entity" button.

5. From the "Enable explicit hierarchies and collections" list, select Yes.

6. You are prompted to enter a name for an explicit hierarchy. Even though you don't need an explicit hierarchy, you must create one. Type **Product** for the name and leave the "Include all leaf members" check box selected.

7. Click the Save entity button.

Create the Collection

To create a collection, complete the following steps:

1. Go back to the Master Data Manager home page by clicking the SQL Server image in the top left.

2. Ensure the Product model and VERSION_1 are selected and click Explorer.

3. If you point to Hierarchies on the menu bar, you can see that a hierarchy is now displayed. This is the one you just created. Again, you don't need this hierarchy, but it is required to create collections.

   To create your collection, on the menu bar, choose Collections | Product. The Collections item on the menu bar shows the name of all entities that are enabled for explicit hierarchies and collections. None of the other entities in the model has enough members to merit collections, though, and right now you've enabled collections for Product only.

4. To create a collection, click the Add collection button above the grid.

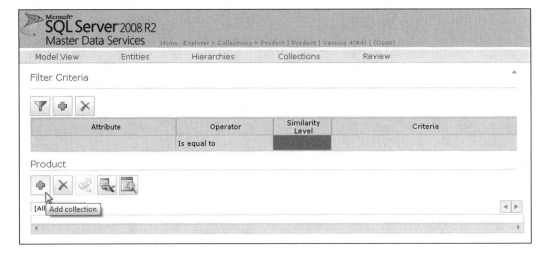

5. Enter the name and code, just as you would when you create a member. Enter **Boys Winter Set** for the name and **BWS** for the code.

6. Click the "Save and go back" button.

   The collection is displayed in the grid. Every collection has a Name, Code, Description, and Owner attribute. (You can see the owner if you scroll to the right in the grid.) By default, the user who created the collection is listed as the owner.

   If you want to type a brief description for your collection, you can double-click the cell in the Description column, type a description, and press ENTER.

Add Members to the Collection

Now that the collection exists, you can add members to it:

1. In the list of collections, click the arrow at the left of the row and, from the submenu, click Edit members.

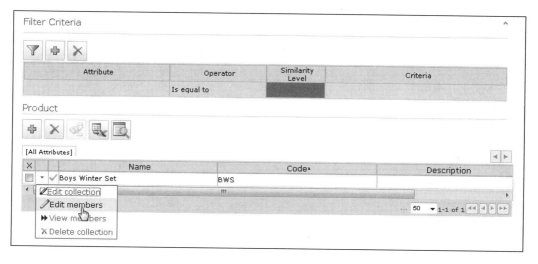

The page that is displayed has two panes. On the left is the explicit hierarchy that you created. All of the product members are displayed at the root.

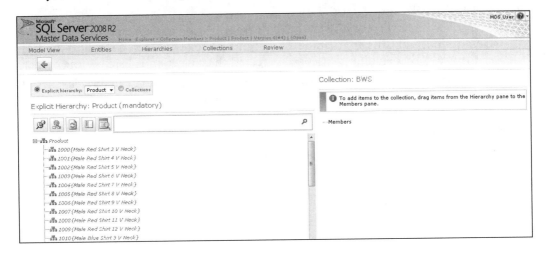

2. From the left pane, click and drag the following members to the Members label on the right: 1000, 1363, 1471, and 1477. These represent a boy's shirt, pants, belt, and hat, which are sold together as a set.

Drag members here to add them to the collection.

If you have trouble finding any of these members, you can type the code in the Search box above the hierarchy and click the magnifying glass icon to start the search. Click the Refresh hierarchy button to clear the search.

NOTE

When searching, you must enter the full, exact name or code to get results.

Notice that no matter where you drag and drop members, they are always added to the root of the collection. Members are added to the collection based on the structure of where they come from. If you were to add consolidated members from an explicit hierarchy, and that hierarchy already had a ragged structure, when you bring the members to the collection, that ragged structure is maintained.

Also note that on the bottom left of the page is a Clipboard you can use to copy and paste members into the collection if you decide not to drag and drop. To copy a member to the Clipboard, click the member in the left pane and then click the "Copy to clipboard" button. Then click the location in the right pane and click either the "Paste as child" or "Paste as sibling" button. Similar clipboards exist in other areas of the application; see Chapter 7 for instructions for moving data in hierarchies—these same instructions apply to collections.

Creating Hierarchies by Using Web Services

While there are two types of hierarchies discussed within this chapter, we have only provided a derived hierarchy example here. Explicit hierarchies can be created as part of the MetadataCreate operation.

Creating a Derived Hierarchy with the MetadataCreate Operation

Derived hierarchies are created as a series of connected attribute levels. Each of these levels must be related properly within the system or the hierarchy will not be created. While creating derived hierarchies within the UI will limit the entities or hierarchies available at the current level, creating derived relationships within the web service does not provide this information until the error response is returned.

The following operation creates a three-level derived hierarchy that groups Products by Line by Manufacturer.

```
public OperationResult CreateDerivedHierarchy(string ModelName, string
DHName)
    {
        // Create the request objects
        MetadataCreateRequest request = new MetadataCreateRequest();
        request.Metadata = new Metadata();
```

```
request.Metadata.DerivedHierarchies =
newCollection<DerivedHierarchy>();

//Create the initial derived hierarchy container
DerivedHierarchy dHier1 = new DerivedHierarchy();
dHier1.Identifier = new ModelContextIdentifier
        {
            Name = DHName,
            ModelId = new Identifier { Name = ModelName }
        };
dHier1.Levels = new Collection<DerivedHierarchyLevel>();

//Level 1 - Product
DerivedHierarchyLevel DHLevel1 = new DerivedHierarchyLevel();
DHLevel1.LevelNumber = 1;

//Levels will default to invisible without explicitly setting
//visible to true
DHLevel1.IsVisible = true;
DHLevel1.Identifier = new DerivedHierarchyContextIdentifier
{ Name ="Product" };
DHLevel1.DisplayName = "Product";
DHLevel1.ForeignType = HierarchyItemType.Entity;
DHLevel1.ForeignId = new Identifier { Name = "Product" };
dHier1.Levels.Add(DHLevel1);

//Level 2 - Line
DerivedHierarchyLevel DHLevel2 = new DerivedHierarchyLevel();
DHLevel2.LevelNumber = 2;
DHLevel2.IsVisible = true;
DHLevel2.Identifier = new DerivedHierarchyContextIdentifier
{Name = "Line" };
DHLevel2.DisplayName = "Line";

//For standard MDS derived hierarchies all additional levels
//will have the foreign type of DBA
DHLevel2.ForeignType = HierarchyItemType.DBA;
DHLevel2.ForeignId = new Identifier { Name = "Line" };

//Provide the ForeignEntityID Connector for this DBA entity
DHLevel2.ForeignEntityId = new Identifier { Name = "Product"};
dHier1.Levels.Add(DHLevel2);
```

```
//Level 3 - Manufacturer
DerivedHierarchyLevel DHLevel3 = new DerivedHierarchyLevel();
DHLevel3.LevelNumber = 3;
DHLevel3.IsVisible = true;
DHLevel3.Identifier = new DerivedHierarchyContextIdentifier
{ Name = "Manufacturer" };
DHLevel3.DisplayName = "Manufacturer";
DHLevel3.ForeignType = HierarchyItemType.DBA;
DHLevel3.ForeignId = new Identifier { Name = "Manufacturer" };
DHLevel3.ForeignEntityId = new Identifier { Name = "Line" };
dHier1.Levels.Add(DHLevel3);
request.Metadata.DerivedHierarchies.Add(dHier1);

//Send the request object to the MetadataCreate Operation
MetadataCreateResponse response =
mds_Proxy.MetadataCreate(request);
return response.OperationResult;
}
```

Summary

In this chapter we discussed a number of methods for managing relationships in Master Data Services. We showed derived hierarchies, which enforce a level-based structure based on domain-based attribute relationships. We showed explicit hierarchies, which allow ragged structures but still prevent duplicates or loss of data. We talked about the system settings that affect hierarchies and showed real-world examples meant to help you build your own hierarchies. Finally, we showed collections and special hierarchies that can be used to manage more complex relationships within MDS.

Chapter 7

Working with Master Data

In This Chapter

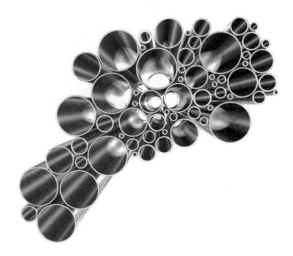

I n previous chapters we focused on creating the environment and architecture for managing master data in your organization. In this chapter, we begin to talk about how to work with your master data on a daily basis. We discuss the grid and filter that allow you to work with data within your master data entities. We also review how to manage data within entities while leveraging the organization of hierarchies. Finally, we discuss the transaction management logic in Master Data Services and how to reverse transactions within the system.

The majority of MDS users will be entering the system to update data. Data stewardship activities in the Master Data Manager web application are managed within the Explorer functional area. A vast majority of users will only have access to the Explorer functional area. In this functional area, there are two major areas where users will work with data:

▶ In the Explorer grid, where they can update consolidated or leaf members within a grid control.

▶ On the hierarchy page, where they can navigate through a hierarchy to manage data changes in an integrated grid control.

Viewing the Base Entity

The entity that is set as the "base" entity is displayed when you first open Explorer. The attributes for the base entity are displayed on the left and any hierarchies and collections for the entity are displayed on the right. For more information on base entities, see Chapter 4.

In this book, we show you how to take actions in Explorer by using the menu bar. However, you can open attributes, hierarchies, and collections for the base entity without using the menu bar by clicking the links and buttons displayed on this page.

Product is the base entity in this model.

Click to edit an entity.

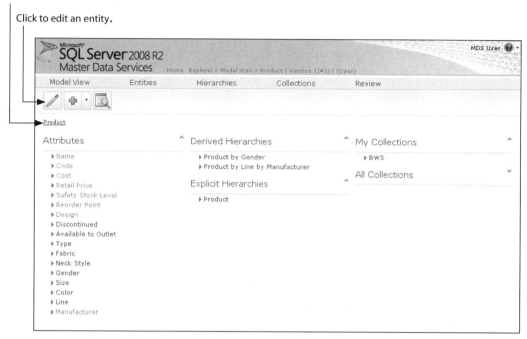

Finding Data by Filtering

To begin working with data, you open an entity and if necessary, filter the list of members to show those that you want to work with. To open an entity, point to Entities on the menu bar and then click the entity you want. All of the entity's members are displayed in a grid.

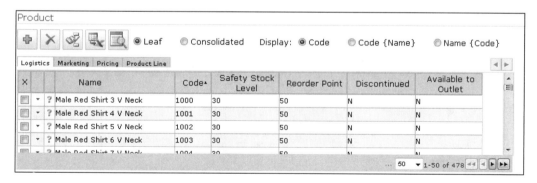

Above the grid, a Filter Criteria section is displayed. To activate a cell in this section, double-click it. Select an attribute, operator, and criteria. The cells here act like the cells in the grid. Each time you make a selection, you have to press ENTER or TAB. Similarity Level is used only for the "Matches" or "Does not match" operator.

When you're ready to apply the filters to the members in the grid, click the Apply filter button.

NOTE

You can filter by multiple attributes by clicking the "Add filter row" button and adding multiple rows of criteria before applying.

To clear a filter, click anywhere in the row. The row's background changes color and a "Delete selected filter row" button is displayed. You must delete one filter row at a time.

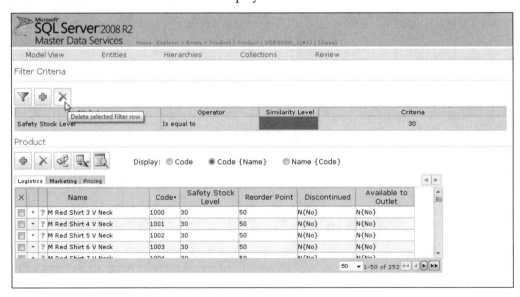

Operators

The operator determines how you're going to filter the list.

Operator	Use
Is equal to	Finds values that match your filter criteria exactly.
Is not equal to	Finds values other than those that match your filter criteria exactly.
Is like	Allows you to use the T-SQL "LIKE" expression.
Is not like	Allows you to use the T-SQL "NOT LIKE" expression
Is greater than	Finds values greater than your filter criteria. This works with both letters and numbers.
Is less than	Finds values less than your filter criteria. This works with both letters and numbers.
Is greater than or equal to	Finds values greater than or equal to your filter criteria. This works with both letters and numbers.
Is less than or equal to	Finds values less than or equal to your filter criteria. This works with both letters and numbers.
Matches	Finds values based on fuzzy match logic. This operator uses the Similarity Level displayed in the grid. For more information, see the "Using Similarity Level" section that follows this table.
Does not match	Finds values based on fuzzy match logic. This operator uses the Similarity Level displayed in the grid. For more information, see the "Using Similarity Level" section that follows this table.
Contains pattern	Matches pattern expressed in Microsoft .NET Framework regular expressions format.
Does not contain pattern	Does not match pattern expressed in Microsoft .NET Framework regular expressions format.
Is NULL	Finds NULL values.
Is not NULL	Finds all values that are not NULL.

Using Similarity Level

When you select the "Matches" or "Does not match" operator, you must choose a Similarity Level in the Filter Criteria grid. The default value is 0.3 but you can double-click to change it. The closer the number is to 1, the more specific the results. To return a wider variety of results, specify a number closer to 0 (for example, 0.2, 0.1, or 0).

The following example shows the Matches operator and the default Similarity Level of 0.3.

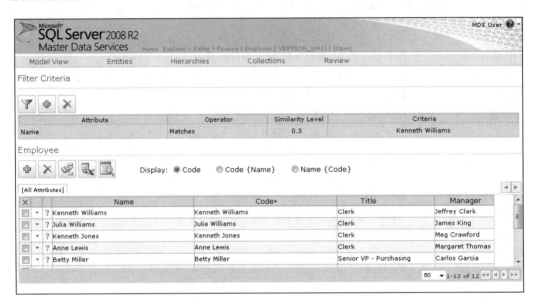

You can see that 12 results were found by looking at the number of records displayed in the lower right.

If you change the Similarity Level to 1, you retrieve only exact results.

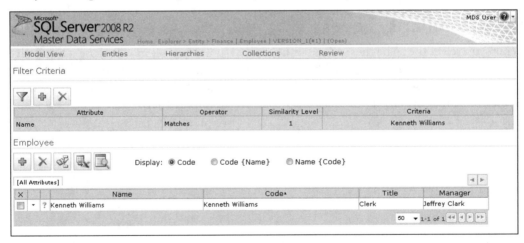

In general, 0.3 is a good level to use to retrieve a list of results. If you want the default to be something other than 0.3, you can change it in the Master Data Services database, in the tblSystemSetting table. GridFilterDefaultFuzzySimilarityLevel determines the default Similarity Level.

NOTE

Some MDS system settings have not been exposed in Master Data Services Configuration Manager, and this is an example of one. All of the settings in Configuration Manager are in tblSystemSetting, and you can change the settings directly in the table or in Configuration Manager. Use care and ensure you're comfortable working in the database if you decide to make the change directly in the table.

Sorting and Pagination

When working in the grid, it is useful to understand sorting and pagination.

Sorting

By default, the members in the grid are sorted in ascending order by code. You can click any column heading to sort the members by that column. Click once to sort in ascending order, and again to sort in descending order. You can sort by the values in only one column at a time. Each time you leave the page and return to the grid, the default sort is displayed.

Pagination

Pagination is important to understand because it affects how you update members. Some actions update the members on the displayed page only, while other actions update all members, whether they're displayed or not.

The drop-down list on the left controls how many members are displayed on the current page. Change this as needed. The number of records is then displayed, followed by arrows that you use to page through the members.

When you apply business rules, or when you use the left column of check boxes to select all members (for updating attribute values or for deleting), only the members displayed on the current page of the grid are affected. You must go to each page individually if you want to update or select members other than those on the current page. Applying business rules in Explorer is covered in detail in Chapter 8.

If you export to Excel, all members are included, not just those on the current page. For example, if you've filtered the list to show 250 members, but your pagination is set to 50 members, when you export, your spreadsheet still contains all 250 members.

Editing Attributes

There are a few different ways to edit attributes. As long as you are viewing the entity that contains attributes you want to update, you can use any of the following procedures.

Edit One Attribute for One Member

To edit an attribute directly in the grid, double-click the cell for the attribute. When you've updated it with the value you want, press ENTER or TAB to save the value. Domain-based attribute values are displayed in a drop-down list.

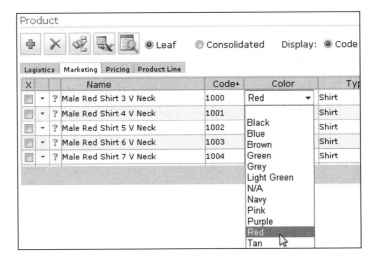

Change the Number of Domain-Based Attributes Displayed in List

In MDS Configuration Manager, you can change whether a list of attribute values or a searchable dialog box is displayed when you double-click the cell of a domain-based attribute value. The setting is called "Number of domain-based attributes in list" and you set the maximum number of members that will be displayed. If you have more than that number, a dialog box is displayed instead of a list.

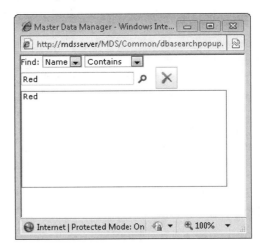

Edit One Attribute for Multiple Members

To edit multiple members at the same time, use the check boxes in the leftmost row of the grid. You can select the check box for individual members or click the X at the top of the column to select all members.

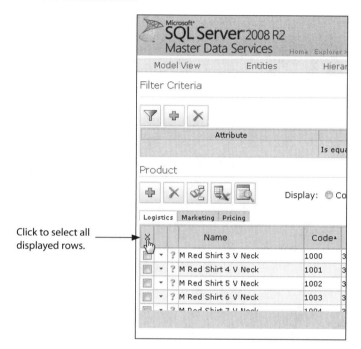

Click to select all displayed rows.

After the rows you want are selected, double-click a cell and update the attribute value. When you press TAB or ENTER, the attribute values for all selected members are updated. (If you have 50 members displayed on the page of the grid, the attributes of those 50 members will be updated. The attribute values for members on the other pages are not updated.)

TIP

You can click the X one time to select all displayed members, and click the X a second time to clear all the check boxes.

Edit Multiple Attributes for One Member

You can open a member and update multiple attributes by clicking the arrow in the second column from the left. When you do, a submenu is displayed.

1. Click Edit member.

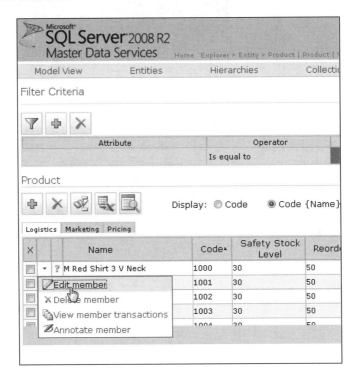

2. On the Member Information page, you can edit the Name and Code attributes by clicking the top Edit button. To edit any of the other attributes, click the bottom Edit button.

NOTE

Before you click Edit, ensure you've selected the tab for the attribute group you need, and ensure you've selected how you want the attributes to be displayed (by Code, Code {Name}, or Name {Code}).

Update the Name and/or
Code attribute.

Update any of the other attributes
for this member.

3.   Edit the attributes you want and then click Save.

Exporting Members

Above the grid, you can click the "Export to Excel" button to export the displayed members to Excel. You don't need Excel installed to take advantage of this functionality. The file is saved with the .xls extension to the location you specify.

If the list is filtered, only the members displayed in the filtered list are included in the spreadsheet. If the list is not filtered, all members are exported; pagination doesn't affect exporting to Excel.

In the Master Data Services database, you can set the maximum number of members that are exported to Excel. In tblSystemSetting, change the value for DataExportRowCountLimit to the number you want. Again, use caution when working directly in the database.

Working with Data in Hierarchies

In the Explorer functional area of the user interface, you can move members in a hierarchy. There are a few different methods for moving members; the one you choose will be based on how many members you want to move and the type of hierarchy you are working with. Moving members in a derived hierarchy is slightly different from moving members in an explicit hierarchy.

Moving Members by Dragging and Dropping

This procedure is the same for both hierarchy types. The only difference is the location you can paste members to. If you are working in an explicit hierarchy, you can:

▶ Paste a leaf member beneath a consolidated member or at the root.

▶ Paste a consolidated member beneath a consolidated member or at the root.

If you are working in a derived hierarchy, you can:

▶ Paste a leaf member anywhere beneath a domain-based attribute value that applies to the member. For example, you can paste products beneath colors, because Color is a domain-based attribute of Product.

To move a member in a hierarchy, click the label of the member you want to move. (The mouse pointer will be a hand icon.)

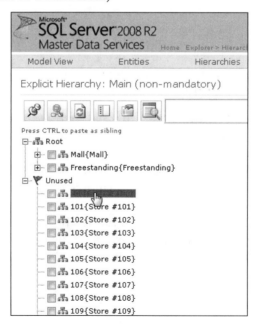

Holding the mouse button down, drag the member to the new location and, when the cursor becomes a plus sign (+), release the button.

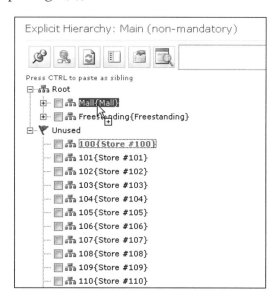

The member is moved to the new location.

Moving Members by Using the Clipboard

This procedure is also the same for both hierarchy types. To move members in any type of hierarchy by using the Clipboard, complete the following steps:

1. In the hierarchy tree, select the check box for each member you want to move.
2. Click the "Copy to clipboard" button.

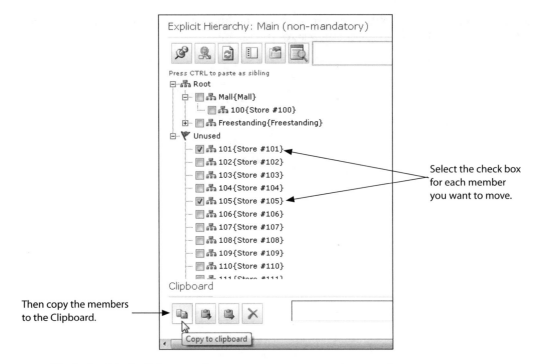

Select the check box for each member you want to move.

Then copy the members to the Clipboard.

3.   Click the label of the member you want to move the members to.

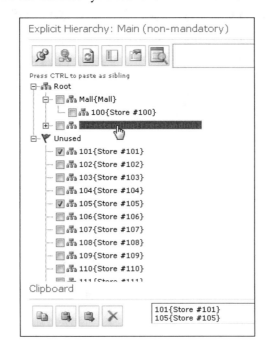

4. Click the "Paste as child" button or the "Paste as sibling" button, depending on what you want to do.

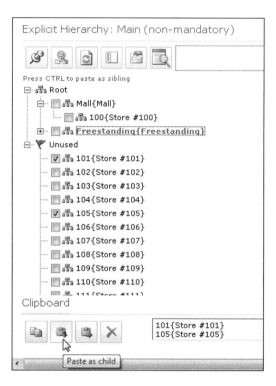

5. In the confirmation dialog box, click OK.
    The members are displayed in the location you specified.

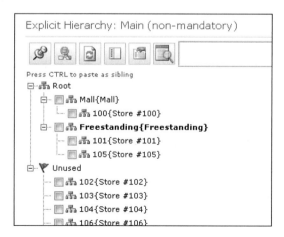

Searching for Members in a Hierarchy

You can use the search field above the hierarchy to find members. Unfortunately, the search functionality has a number of limitations:

▶ The text you enter must be an exact match of either the full name or code. To search for partial matches, use the % wildcard.

▶ The search does not find members in the Unused node of explicit hierarchies.

▶ If you have so many members in your hierarchy that the …more… label is displayed, members that aren't displayed aren't included in the search results.

To use the search field, type your search text and click the magnifying glass icon. Your search is applied and the hierarchy is updated. To remove the search, click Refresh hierarchy.

Set the Number of Members That Are Displayed

In MDS Configuration Manager, you can change the number of members displayed in each hierarchy node before you have to click …more….

The setting is called "Number of members in the hierarchy by default," and you set the maximum number of members that will be displayed. If you have more than that number, the …more… label is displayed.

Show Names in a Hierarchy by Default

In MDS Configuration Manager, you can also change whether or not the member name is displayed when you view hierarchies. By default, both the name and code of each member are displayed. Change "Show names in hierarchy by default" to No to display the code only.

NOTE

You can always change this setting while viewing the hierarchy in Explorer, by clicking the "Show/hide names" button above the hierarchy tree structure.

Moving Members in a Derived Hierarchy by Updating Attribute Values

In addition to using the Clipboard or dragging and dropping, you can move members in a derived hierarchy by updating the member's attribute value that determines its location in the hierarchy.

When you first open a derived hierarchy, the top levels are displayed in the hierarchy structure on the left.

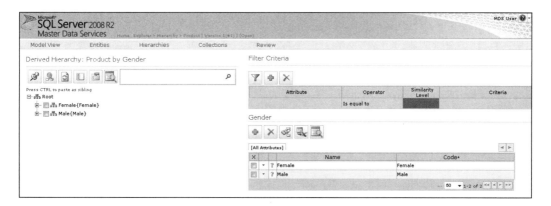

In the grid on the right, the top-level members are displayed. To display the members contained in any level, click a node in the hierarchy tree. The grid on the right refreshes. For example, when you click Female in the hierarchy tree on the left, all of the female products are listed in the grid on the right.

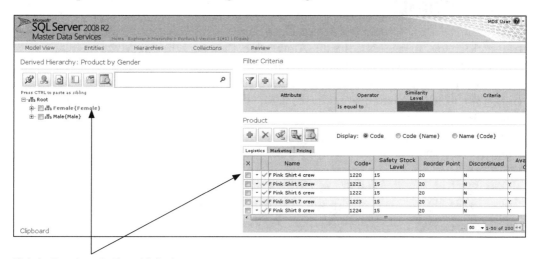

Click the Female node. The grid displays all the members underneath.

Now in the grid, find the attribute that determines where the member is displayed in the hierarchy. In this example, we'll click the Marketing tab and scroll to the right until the Gender column is visible. Then, find the member you want to move and, just as you would do to update any other attribute value, double-click the cell, as shown next.

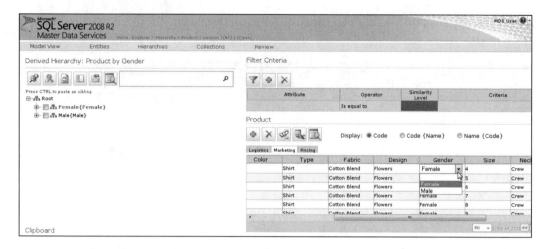

Now change the value. When you press TAB or ENTER, the grid and hierarchy are updated, and the member is moved to the node based on your selection. In this case, the product moved from the Female to the Male hierarchy node.

Transactions

Every change made to data in Master Data Services is logged as a transaction. All transactions log the type, prior value, new value, the user who made the change, and the time the change was made. In the Explorer functional area, all users have access to their own transactions and can reverse any transaction they have access to. In the Version Management functional area, administrators can review and reverse transactions for all users.

The following types of transactions are logged and displayed in the Master Data Manager web application:

Transaction Type	Description
Member created	A new leaf or consolidated member has been added to the entity.
Member status changed	The member has been deleted from the system. Because this is a soft delete, the member can be reactivated by reversing the transaction. The reversal will display as a status change as well.
Attribute value specified	An attribute value has changed.
Member moved to parent	A member was moved to a new location, based on its parent's location.
Member moved to sibling	A member was moved to a new location, based on its sibling's location.
Member annotated	An annotation was added to the member or an annotation was modified. You cannot reverse these types of transactions.

NOTE

By default, transactions are not logged for data that's staged into the system. Transaction logging for staging can be turned on in the MDS Configuration Manager system settings.

Reviewing Transactions

In either the Explorer or Version Management functional area, on the menu bar, choose Review | Transactions. Transactions are displayed in a grid. You can filter the grid by using the Filter Criteria section, and you can export the contents of the grid to Excel by clicking the "Export to Excel" button above the grid.

Export transactions to Excel.   Filter the list of transactions.

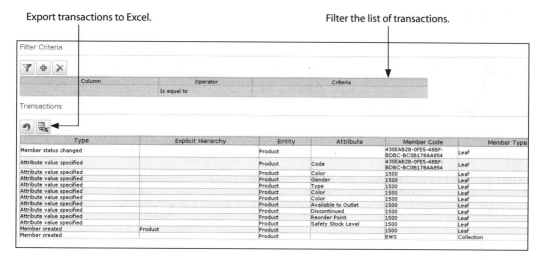

Reversing Transactions

To reverse a transaction, in the grid, click the row of the transaction you want to reverse and click the "Reverse selected transaction" button.

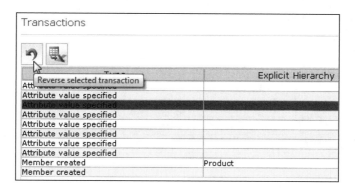

If you want to reactivate a member, you have to reverse two transactions:

▶ The transaction that shows the member changing from Active to De-Activated

▶ The transaction that shows the member code changing to a 36-character GUID

If you reverse these transactions in this order, the member and its original code will be reactivated. The member will be part of all hierarchies and collections it was a member of before it was deleted; it will be as though the member was never deleted in the first place.

Annotations

You can annotate transactions to explain why you took an action, but these actions can be hard to find after you've entered them. Instead, you can annotate individual members; this adds a transaction to the list of transactions, where it is more visible.

Annotating Members

To annotate a member, open Explorer and then open the entity. In the grid, click the down arrow to the left of the member and then click Annotate member.

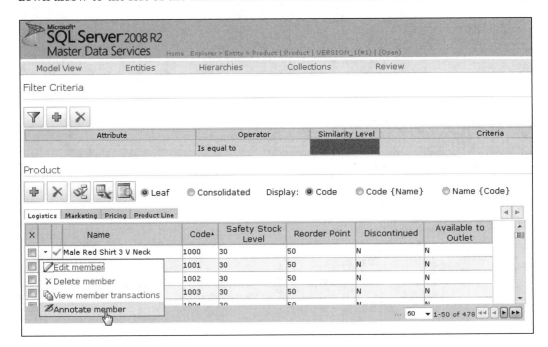

In the dialog box that opens, type your annotation and click the Save annotation button. In the confirmation dialog box, click OK.

Now review your transactions and you will see that the member was annotated—a row in the grid will have the "Member annotated" type. To view the text of the annotation, click the row and scroll down.

Click the row.

The annotation is displayed.

Annotating Transactions

Annotating a member might not always suit your needs. If you are reviewing transactions and you want to add more detailed information, you can.

While reviewing transactions, click the row of the transaction you want to annotate. Scroll down until the Transaction Annotations pane is displayed. Type your text in the box and click the Save annotation button.

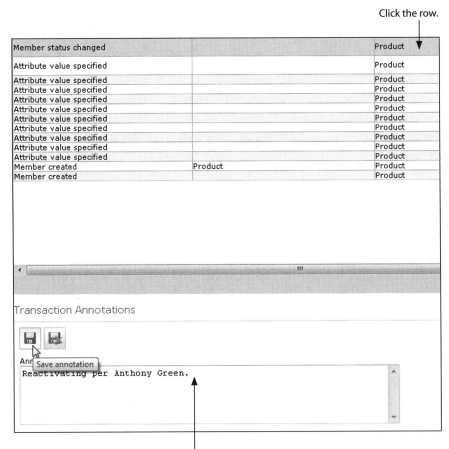

Click the row.

Enter an annotation for the transaction.

You must scroll to the bottom of the screen to view the saved annotation. No new "Member annotated" entries are added to the transaction list; the annotation is visible only when you click the related transaction in the grid.

Metadata

You may have noticed that there are several places in Explorer where a View metadata button is displayed. Metadata is another way to track data about your data. It will be covered in detail in Chapter 10.

Using Web Services to Work with Members

The calls associated with getting and changing master data within Master Data Services are the most used web service calls by organizations looking to customize their MDS implementation. These calls allow users to enter new member records, update existing member records, or bring back existing entity member record sets.

Retrieving Members

The EntityMembersGet operation will bring back member records from any entity that exists within MDS. This operation supports paging to allow users to show a subset of the entity within a customized UI. This operation also supports subselecting a set of attributes to be retrieved. If you are going to you use the paging criteria to bring back a subset of records, be sure to lock down the sort criteria before you page; otherwise, inconsistent records will be returned.

There are three types of member return options. An EntityMembersGet operation can return either data, counts, or both data and counts. Some systems may require the total number of records to be returned before they return any member detail, and the "record counts only" return option provides this functionality. For organizations interested in using the paging mechanism to return records, the "data and counts" return option can help ensure that all records are collected over the course of all pages returned.

In the following code sample, we provide an example that returns a standard EntityMembersGet request with a standard page size of 50 members. This request has no complex filter.

```
public EntityMembers GetMembersFromEntity(string ModelName,
string VersionName, string EntityName, MemberType memType)
{
    //Create the Request and Criteria Objects
    EntityMembersGetRequest Request = new EntityMembersGetRequest();
    EntityMembersGetCriteria Criteria = new EntityMembersGetCriteria();
    //Build Context Criteria for Member Request
    Criteria.ModelId = new Identifier { Name = ModelName };
    Criteria.VersionId = new Identifier { Name = VersionName };
```

```
    Criteria.EntityId = new Identifier { Name = EntityName };
    Criteria.MemberType = memType;

    //Add Return Options to Criteria
    Criteria.MemberReturnOption = MemberReturnOption.DataAndCounts;
    Criteria.PageNumber = 1;
    Criteria.PageSize = 50;
    Criteria.SortColumnId = new Identifier { Name = "Name" };
    Criteria.SortDirection = SortDirection.Asc;

    //Assign Criteria to the Get Request
    Request.MembersGetCriteria = Criteria;
    EntityMembersGetResponse Response =
     mds_Proxy.EntityMembersGet(Request);
    return Response.EntityMembers;
}
```

When retrieving large amounts of data from the web service, it is quite likely that you will run into the following error:

System.ServiceModel.CommunicationException was unhandled
    Message=The maximum message size quota for incoming messages (65536) has been exceeded. To increase the quota, use the MaxReceivedMessageSize property on the appropriate binding element.

This is to protect users from themselves. Each organization must determine how large the maximum message size can be, but this can be set in the client's app.config file by changing the following parameter:

    maxReceivedMessageSize="2147483647"

Creating and Updating Members

Master Data Services provides the following three operations for managing entity members within the system. They support three different types of data loads.

- ▶ **EntityMembersCreate** Only new member records with unique codes can be created with this operation. If a member code already exists, an error will be thrown in the returned error collection and the member will not be created or updated.

- ▶ **EntityMembersUpdate** Only existing members can be updated using this operation. If a member code or ID is provided that does not exist within the system, an error will be returned in the error collection passed in the operation result and the member will not be created.

▶ **EntityMembersMerge**   Many users have been confused by this operation and believe it has something to do with record survivorship or match merge functionality. This operation does nothing to look for possible matches or provide any survivorship functionality; it only allows users to create and update records simultaneously within MDS.

The following example shows only the EntityMembersMerge operation because this operation provides the most flexibility for users programming against MDS. For simplicity in programming and to show all of the capabilities of setting attributes, we have hard-coded some defaults from the Main Street Clothing Company product example. If you are using this call within your organization, you need to replace the defaults with attribute parameters that are passed into the operation.

```
public OperationResult SimpleEntityMembersMerge(string ModelName,
string EntityName, string VersionName, MemberType memType,
string memCode, string memName)
{
    EntityMembersMergeRequest request = new EntityMembersMergeRequest();
    request.Members = new EntityMembers();

    //Set Context Identifiers for EntityMembers Object
    request.Members.ModelId = new Identifier { Name = ModelName };
    request.Members.EntityId = new Identifier { Name= EntityName };
    request.Members.VersionId = new Identifier { Name = VersionName };
    request.Members.MemberType = memType;

    //Create Members Collection object
    request.Members.Members = new Collection<Member>();

    //Add member to member collection
    Member newMem = new Member();
    newMem.MemberId = new MemberIdentifier { Code = memCode,
    Name = memName, MemberType = memType };
    newMem.Attributes = new Collection<MDS_WS.Attribute>();

    //Add default attribute values (In this example we are
    //adding attribute values for product)
    newMem.Attributes.Add(new MDS_WS.Attribute { Identifier =
     new Identifier { Name = "Safety Stock Level" },
     Type = AttributeValueType.Number, Value = 50 });
    newMem.Attributes.Add(new MDS_WS.Attribute { Identifier =
     new Identifier { Name = "Discontinued" },
```

```
      Type = AttributeValueType.Domain,
      Value = new MemberIdentifier { Code = "N" } });

    //Add the new member to the members collection
    request.Members.Members.Add(newMem);

    EntityMembersMergeResponse Response =
      mds_Proxy.EntityMembersMerge(request);
    return Response.OperationResult;
}
```

Summary

In this chapter we looked at how users will manage data within Master Data Services on a daily basis. We discussed using the Explorer grid to update members quickly as well as using the Member Information screen to update members in a form-based approach. Every change made in MDS is logged as a separate transaction. All users can manage their own transactions, reviewing and filtering prior changes. Transactions can be reversed, changing the current value back to the prior value.

Chapter 8

Using Business Rules

In This Chapter

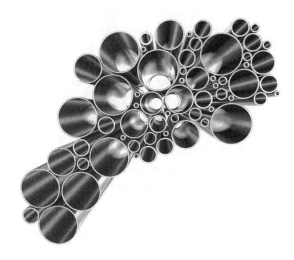

anaging data is not just about storing the data in a customized entity; it is also about ensuring that the data is both accurate and complete. Master Data Services provides business rules to achieve this aim. In this chapter, we review business rules and discuss how to create both simple and complex rules. We discuss how to create simple workflows in MDS and how to integrate with external workflows such as those provided by SharePoint.

Business Rules Overview

In many organizations, no matter what the size, the business owners responsible for managing the master data don't have the technical knowledge needed to implement the related processes. If the business owners don't know how to use SQL Server or how to code business rule engines, they can be left at the mercy of their IT departments. At the same time, because the IT department has the technical know-how, the burden often falls on them to learn business domains they don't necessarily need to know. MDS strives to simplify the creation of business rules to empower business users to manage their own data quality.

In MDS, business rules are declarative expressions that govern the conduct of business processes. These expressions are compiled into stored procedures that perform the task of validating the data. The area of the Master Data Manager web application used for business rules was created to empower business users to write relatively complex business rules without knowledge of Transact-SQL.

Business Rule Structure

Business rules are IF…THEN statements. IF certain conditions evaluate to true, THEN perform specific actions. Conditions can be combined using either AND or OR logical operators. These operators can be used to create extremely complex business rules. You can use as many as seven levels for complex conditioning.

Although you have the ability to create complex rules, there are some real benefits in creating multiple, more granular rules. You should consider breaking any rule that uses the logical OR operator into multiple rules. This makes rules easier for other users to read and understand. Multiple rules also allow you to exclude specific rules and to provide more granular notifications. Rules built with the AND operator must be kept together to function as a unit.

Business rules are always applied to attribute values. For example, if an attribute value is blank, you might want to send an e-mail to notify someone or set the value to Pending.

Or you might want to update the value of one attribute based on the value of another attribute. Because business rules are applied to attribute values, you should determine which attributes you're going to work with before you start creating rules. Each time you create a rule, you must select the model, entity, and type of member that contains the attribute you're looking for.

Business Rule Workflow

Business rules must be created, configured, and published before you can validate data against them. The workflow includes the following steps:

1. Create a business rule, which adds it to the list of available rules.
2. Edit the rule and configure its expression.
3. Publish the rule so it's active and can be used to validate data.
4. Apply the rule to members.

When you apply the rule to members, the attribute values for each member are validated and they either pass or fail validation. If they pass, no action is required. If they fail, you must update the attribute values and re-validate your data successfully against the rules. If you don't take action, your hierarchies may not be complete or your data might otherwise be invalid.

Creating a Business Rule

The first step in the workflow is to create a business rule. Creating a rule means adding it to the list of existing rules. This procedure doesn't configure the rule to do anything, nor does it publish the rule. It's simply the first step necessary in using business rules to validate data.

1. On the Master Data Manager home page, click System Administration.
2. On the menu bar, choose Manage | Business Rules.
3. On the Business Rule Maintenance page, choose a model, entity, and member type for your rule to apply to. In this example, select Product, Product, and Leaf, respectively. For the attribute, leave it as the default, All. The Attribute list works as a filter for the list of business rules. In general, you should leave this as All to ensure that all rules are displayed.

4. Click the "Add business rule" button.

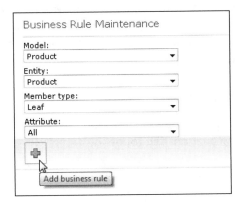

A new row with a light blue background is displayed in the table. The blue highlight indicates that the row is selected.

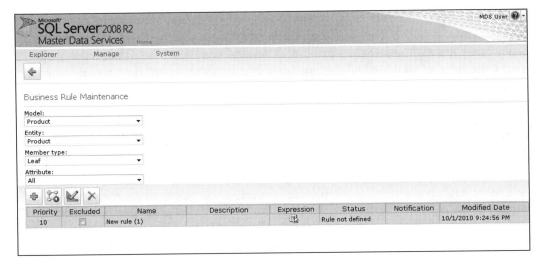

You are now ready to edit the business rule and configure an expression.

Configuring a Rule's Expression

A business rule frequently consists of a condition and an action. The condition is evaluated, and if it evaluates to true, one or more actions are initiated. If a rule contains no conditions, the rules engine will always initiate the actions.

Rules on the Edit Business Rule page are defined by using the following format:

IF *<condition>* THEN *<action>*

You can configure business rules to evaluate a wide variety of expressions. In this chapter we will strive to show you some common business rules and give you the knowledge needed to create some of your own.

Procedure: How to Require Attribute Values

In this first example, a business rule ensures that the Cost, Retail Price, and Gender attributes of all products are populated with values. The expression for this rule will be

IF <nothing, because it applies to all cases>
THEN require an attribute value for Cost, Retail Price, and Gender

To create the structure of a rule to perform this type of validation, complete the following steps:

1. Follow the procedure to create a new business rule. In this example, on the Business Rule Maintenance page, select the Product model, Product entity, Leaf member type, and All attributes and click the "Add business rule" button.
2. Click the row for the rule you want to edit and then click the "Edit selected business rule" button.

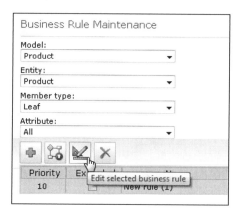

3. The Edit Business Rule page is displayed. In the Components pane on the top left, expand the Actions node.

4. Scroll down. Under the Validation node, click "is required" and drag it to the THEN pane in the middle right. Drop it on the Actions label.

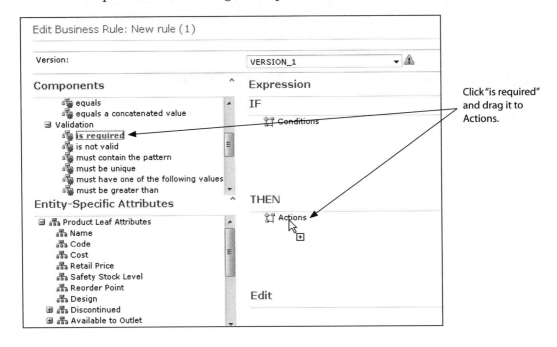

5. The Edit pane in the lower right becomes the Edit Action pane. In the Entity-Specific Attributes pane on the lower left, click Cost and drag it to the Edit Action pane. Drop it on the Select attribute label.

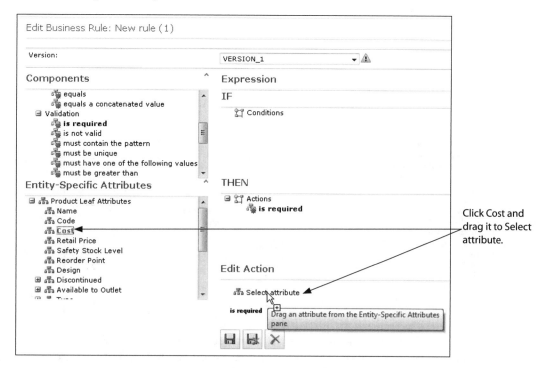

6. At the bottom of the Edit Action pane, click the Save item button. This saves the action you just added.

7. Repeat steps 4, 5, and 6 for the Retail Price and Gender attributes. When you're done, you should have three actions displayed in the THEN pane.

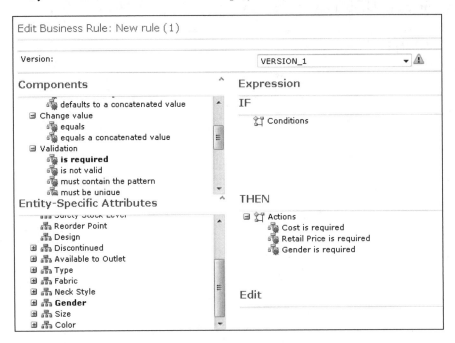

8. In the top-left corner, click the green arrow to return to the Business Rule Maintenance page. Because the rule was saved as you created it, there is no need to save again when you leave the page.

Now that the rule exists, you must publish it if you want to apply it to your data.

Deleting a Condition or Action

While you're working on the Edit Business Rule page, you may realize you've selected the wrong action or condition. In either the IF or the THEN pane, you can right-click any condition or action and click Delete to remove it.

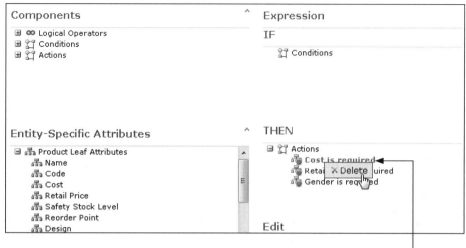

Right-click any action or
condition to delete it.

More Expression Examples

Now we'll continue with other examples of business rules you might want to create.
Later in this chapter, we'll explain how to validate your data against active business rules.

Procedure: How to Populate One Value Based on Another Value

You can populate an attribute value based on other attribute values. This is probably the
most common use for business rules.

In this example, we want to indicate that discontinued products that have fewer than
50 items in stock are now available to outlet stores. The expression will be

> If Discontinued = Y and Safety Stock Level < 50
> THEN Available to Outlet = Y

To create this rule, complete the following steps:

1. Follow the procedure to create a new business rule. In this example, on the Business
    Rule Maintenance page, select the Product model, Product entity, Leaf member
    type, and All attributes and click the "Add business rule" button.
2. Click the row for the rule you want to edit and then click the "Edit selected
    business rule" button. The Edit Business Rule page is displayed.
3. In the Components pane, expand the Conditions node.

4. Under the Value comparison node, click "is equal to" and drag it to the IF pane on the top right. Drop it on the Conditions label.

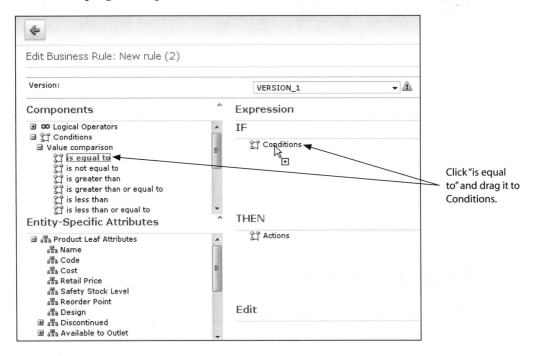

5. The Edit pane in the lower right becomes the Edit Condition pane. In the Entity-Specific Attributes pane, click Discontinued and drag it to the Edit Condition pane. Drop it on the Select attribute label.

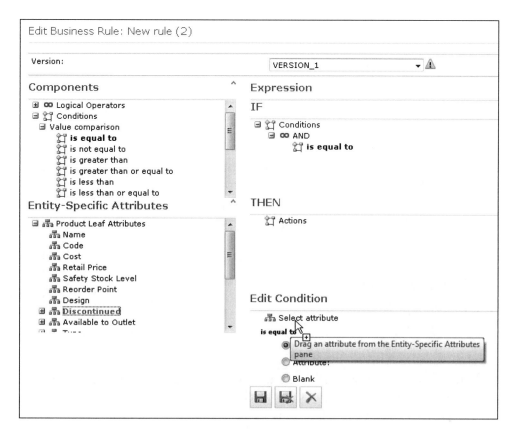

6. The Attribute value radio button is selected. Next to it, select Y from the list.

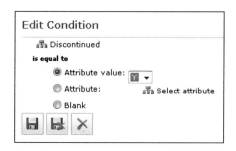

7. At the bottom of the Edit Condition pane, click the Save item button. The IF pane is populated with the condition: Discontinued is equal to Y.

8. In the Components pane, click "is less than" and drag it to the IF pane. Drop it on the And label.

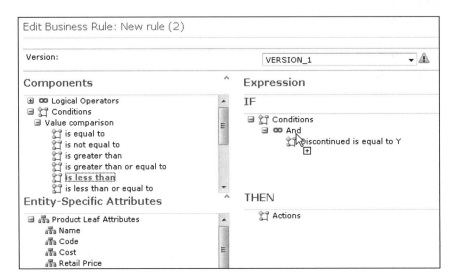

9. In the Entity-Specific Attributes pane, click Safety Stock Level and drag it to the Edit Condition pane. Drop it on the Select attribute label.

10. The Attribute value radio button is selected. Next to it, type **50**.

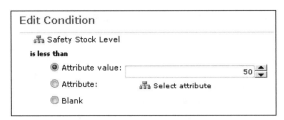

11. At the bottom of the Edit Condition pane, click the Save item button. The IF pane is populated with the condition: Safety Stock Level is less than 50.

12. In the Components pane, expand the Actions node.

13. Scroll down. Under the Change value node, click "equals" and drag it to the THEN pane. Drop it on the Actions label.

14. In the Entity-Specific Attributes pane, click Available to Outlet and drag it to the Edit Action pane. Drop it on the Select attribute label.

15. The Attribute value radio button is selected. Next to it, select Y from the list.

16. At the bottom of the Edit Action pane, click the Save item button.

The business rule is complete.

Procedure: How to Concatenate Values

In this example, a business rule creates a member name that is a concatenation of several attribute values. For example, one of our product names is

> M Red Shirt 3 V Neck

This is a concatenation of these attribute values:

> Gender Code + Color Name + Type Name + Size Name + Neck Style Name

Before we imported our products, we did this concatenation in Excel. Now we want to do this concatenation in MDS for all products, new and existing. We've also decided to use the full Gender name (Male) as part of the product name, rather than just the code (M). To create this rule, complete the following steps:

1. Follow the procedure to create a new business rule. In this example, on the Business Rule Maintenance page, select the Product model, Product entity, Leaf member type, and All attributes and click the "Add business rule" button.

2. Click the row for the rule you want to edit and then click the "Edit selected business rule" button. The Edit Business Rule page is displayed.

3. In the Components pane, expand the Actions node.

4. Under the Change value node, click "equals a concatenated value" and drag it to the THEN pane. Drop it on the Actions label.

5. In the Entity-Specific Attributes pane, click Name and drag it to the Edit Action pane. Drop it on the Select attribute label. (You drag the attribute whose value you want to concatenate; in this case, you want to concatenate the Product's Name value.)

6. Also in the Entity-Specific Attributes pane, expand the Gender node and click Name. Drag it to the Edit Action pane and drop it on the Value label.

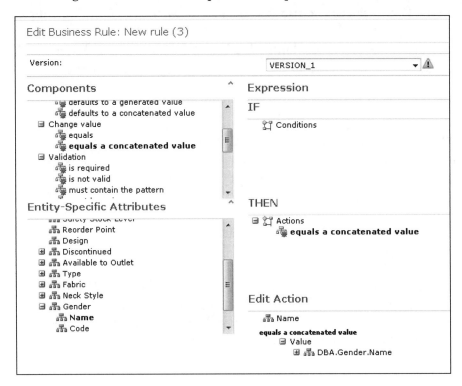

7. Right-click DBA.Gender.Name and choose Add text.

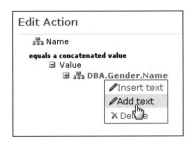

8. Double-click the label. A text box is displayed. Type a single space to indicate the space between values. Then click away from the field to make the text box back into a label.

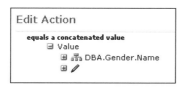

9. In the Entity-Specific Attributes pane, expand the Color node and click Name. Drag it to the Edit Action pane and drop it on the Value label.

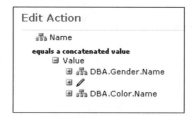

10. Right-click DBA.Color.Name and choose Add text.
11. Double-click the label. A text box is displayed. Type a single space to indicate the space between values.
12. Repeat steps 9–11 for Type Name, Size Name, and Neck Style Name.
13. At the bottom of the Edit Action pane, click the Save item button. The THEN pane is updated with all of the actions you specified.

> THEN
> ⊟ ⚙ Actions
>   Name equals a concatenated value DBA.Gender.Name + + DBA.Color.Name + + DBA.Type.Name + + DBA.Size.Name + + DBA.Neck Style.Name

The business rule is complete. Now, when you validate your data, all product names will be updated based on this rule.

TIP

You can use concatenation to create link attributes, like those used for Bing maps (for example, http://bing.com/ maps/default.aspx?where1=15%20Cherry%20Street%20Springfield%20WA%2098000). In this case, you would concatenate the Name attribute values for the Location entity's Street Address, City, State, and Zip Code attributes to create a link.

Procedure: How to Populate an Attribute Value from a Different Entity

In Chapter 6, we created a three-level hierarchy:

> Product > Line > Manufacturer

In this example, the Product entity had a Line attribute, and the Line entity had a Manufacturer attribute. But the Product entity did not have a Manufacturer attribute.

This structure is required in order to create the hierarchy. But you probably want to see the manufacturers at the same time as you look at the products; that is, you want the Product entity to have a Manufacturer attribute.

You can set up the structure required for the hierarchy but then use business rules to populate the Manufacturer value, in this case. The following procedure describes how to show the manufacturers along with the products without losing the hierarchy structure. This is going to require some work before we proceed to creating the business rule.

1. For the Product entity, create a free-form attribute called **Manufacturer**. See Chapter 4 for information on how to create free-form attributes.

2. For the Product entity, create an attribute group called **Product Line** and add the Manufacturer and Line attributes to it. You can also see Chapter 4 for how to create attribute groups.

3. Create a business rule to populate products with the appropriate manufacturer. This means that the rule will populate the Product entity's Manufacturer attribute with the Line entity's Manufacturer attribute values.

    a. Follow the procedure to create a new business rule. In this example, on the Business Rule Maintenance page, select the Product model, Product entity, Leaf member type, and All attributes and click the "Add business rule" button.

    b. Click the row for the rule you want to edit and then click the "Edit selected business rule" button. The Edit Business Rule page is displayed.

    c. In the Components pane, expand the Actions node.

    d. Under the Change value node, click "equals" and drag it to the THEN pane. Drop it on the Actions label.

e. In the Entity-Specific Attributes pane, click Manufacturer and drag it to the Edit Action pane. Drop it on the Select attribute label. (You drag the attribute whose value you want to populate; in this case, you want to populate the Manufacturer value.)

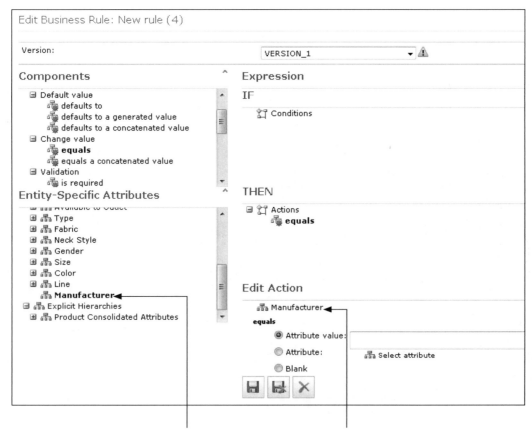

Ensure you select Manufacturer at the top level.   Drag it here.
This is the free-form attribute of the Product entity.

f. In the Entity-Specific Attributes pane, expand the Line node and click Manufacturer. Drag it to the Edit Action pane and drop it on the Select attribute label.

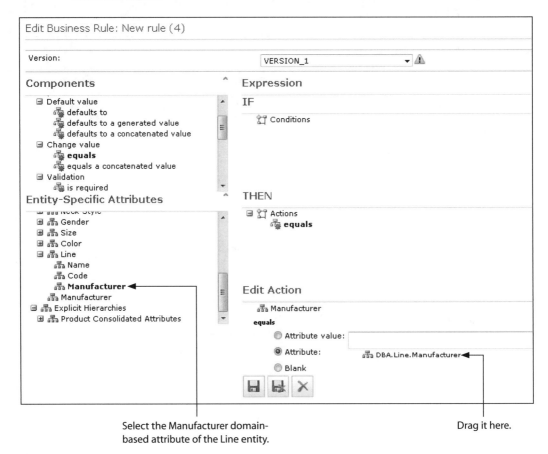

Select the Manufacturer domain-based attribute of the Line entity.

Drag it here.

g. At the bottom of the Edit Action pane, click the Save item button.

The business rule is complete.

Procedure: How to Use Incremental Values for Codes

You might want to populate an attribute value with an incremental number. For example, maybe you want each new product to have a unique number as its Code value and you want to increment each new product number by five. You can use business rules to do this.

In the current Finance model, the Code attribute values for the Location entity start with 100 and additional Code values are incremented by one. As new locations are added, the Code value should be one number higher than the highest number that's already used. The following example shows how to create a business rule to do this incremental numbering.

NOTE

Because you're going to populate the Code attribute, you will notice in Explorer that the Code attribute is not editable, because the code is being generated by a business rule.

To create this business rule, complete the following steps:

1. In this example, on the Business Rule Maintenance page, select the Finance model, Location entity, Leaf member type, and All attributes and click the "Add business rule" button.
2. Click the row for the rule you want to edit and then click the "Edit selected business rule" button. The Edit Business Rule page is displayed.
3. In the Components pane, expand the Actions node.
4. Under the Default value node, click "defaults to a generated value" and drag it to the THEN pane. Drop it on the Actions label.

5. In the Entity-Specific Attributes pane, click Code and drag it to the Edit Action pane. Drop it on the Select attribute label. (You drag the attribute whose value you want to populate; in this case, you want to populate the Code value.)

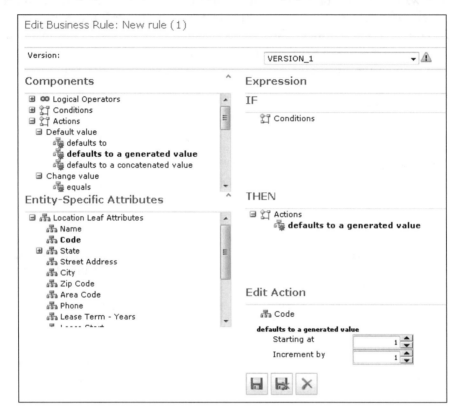

6. If you are not sure which number to start with, you can leave 1 for the Starting at value. MDS will populate the Code value with the next possible value. We want to increment each value by 1, so we will leave the Increment by value at the default.

7. At the bottom of the Edit Action pane, click the Save item button.

The business rule is complete.

Creating Your Own Expressions

The following reference tables explain the possible conditions and actions you can use to create business rule expressions.

Conditions

If a condition evaluates to true, an action is taken. For example, if an attribute value is greater than another attribute value (the condition), then the attribute value is changed (the action).

Condition	Description	Column Types Supported
Is equal to	The value must match exactly.	Text, Number, DateTime, Link
Is not equal to	The value must not be equal.	Text, Number, DateTime, Link
Is greater than	The value must be greater.	Number, DateTime
Is greater than or equal to	The value must be greater or equal to.	Number, DateTime
Is less than	The value must be less than.	Number, DateTime
Is less than or equal to	The value must be less than or equal to.	Number, DateTime
Starts with	The value must start with the value.	Text, Link
Ends with	The value must end with the value.	Text, Link
Contains	The value must contain the value.	Text, Link
Contains pattern	The value must contain a .NET regular expressions pattern.	Text, Link
Contains subset	The value must contain a subset of a string value from either a provided value or another attribute. The match must occur at the provided starting position.	Text, Link
Has changed	The value has changed since the last time business rules were applied.	Change Tracking Group 1 - 31
Is between	The value is between two other attribute values.	Number, DateTime

Actions

There are four categories of actions you can take by using business rules.

Default Value Actions   Default value actions set a blank value to a value specified by the rule. If a value is already populated, default actions do not have an effect.

Action	Description	Supported Attribute Types
Defaults to	Change the value.	Text, Number, DateTime, Link
Defaults to generated value	Increment the value. You can specify a starting value and a number to increment by.	Number
Defaults to concatenated value	Concatenate the value. You can type text and use attributes to create the value.	Text, Number, DateTime, Link

Change Value Actions   Change value actions update values to new values each time business rules are applied.

Action	Description	Supported Attribute Types
Equals	Change the value.	Text, Number, DateTime, Link
Equals a concatenated value	Concatenate the value. You can type text and use attributes to create the value.	Text, Number, DateTime, Link

Validation Actions   Validation actions are used to send e-mail notifications when data fails business rule validation.

Action	Description	Supported Attribute Types
Is required	Require the value (it cannot be null or blank).	Text, Number, DateTime, Link
Is not valid	The value is not valid. Use this action in conjunction with conditions, otherwise all values will be considered not valid.	Text, Number, DateTime, Link
Must contain the pattern	Require the value to contain a .NET regular expressions pattern.	Text
Must be unique	Require each value for members in the entity to be distinct. You can also specify unique combinations. For example, you might want the Name and Color attributes to be unique when combined, but Color by itself does not need to be unique.	Text, Number, DateTime, Link
Must have one of the following values	Require the value to be one of those you specify.	Text, Number, DateTime, Link
Must be greater	Require the value to be greater than the specified value.	Number, DateTime
Must be equal to	Require the value to be equal to the specified value.	Number, DateTime
Must be greater than or equal to	Require the value to be greater than or equal to the specified value.	Number, DateTime
Must be between	Require the value to be between the specified values.	Number, DateTime
Must have a minimum length of	Require the value to be longer than the specified value.	Text, Link
Must have a maximum length of	Require the value to be shorter than the specified value.	Text, Link

External Actions   External actions start applications outside of Master Data Services.

Action	Description	Supported Attribute Types
Start Site Workflow	Initiates a SharePoint workflow or triggers an external process. For more information, see "Triggering an External Workflow" later in this chapter.	Not applicable. You can select any attribute; it's not used as part of the rule.

Publishing Business Rules

After you have created a rule, you must publish it. Publishing a business rule means making it available to validate data against it. You can create as many rules as you want, but if you don't publish them, they aren't applied to your data when you start validation.

After you publish a business rule, you can always exclude it if you decide you don't want to apply it to data. Any time you edit a rule, you must republish it or it won't be applied to data as part of the validation process.

Procedure: How to Publish a Business Rule

To publish a business rule, click the "Publish business rules" button.

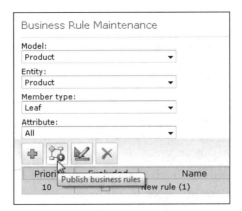

For all business rules that have expressions defined, the value in the Status column changes to Active. Data can now be validated against the rules. You can exclude rules you do not want to publish. For more information, see "Procedure: How to Exclude Business Rules," later in this chapter.

Business Rule Statuses

The following table describes all possible statuses for rules on the Business Rule Maintenance page.

Status	Description	Can Data Be Validated Against?
Rule not defined	A complete expression for the rule has not yet been defined.	No
Active	The rule expression is complete and the rule has been published to the validation process. Subsequent validations will include this rule.	Yes
Excluded	The rule is saved but has been excluded from the validation process.	No
Activation pending	The rule is complete, but until the rule is published, the rule will not be enforced when validation is triggered.	No
Changes pending	Changes have been made to the rule; the rule must still be published.	Previous business rule is still considered active.
Exclusion pending	The business rule is still active and needs to be removed from the validation procedure by publishing business rules.	Yes
Deletion pending	The business rule is still active and needs to be removed from the validation procedure by publishing business rules.	Yes

Applying Business Rules

Business rules are not valuable until you validate data against them. Data can be validated against business rules in the following ways:

▶ You can validate the members for a single entity at a time in the Explorer functional area of the Master Data Manager web application. Business users with Explorer permissions can do this.

▶ You can validate all entities in a model in the Version Management functional area of the Master Data Manager user interface.

▶ You can use web services to validate all or some members as they are passed in.

▶ You can run a stored procedure to validate at different model object levels. While using the stored procedures directly is not encouraged, you may find it necessary to implement the data management process for your organization.

▶ Validations can be triggered through the staging process stored procedure. For more information about this stored procedure, see Chapter 5.

Procedure: How to Apply Business Rules in Explorer

Users with permission can apply business rules in Explorer. To do so, complete the following steps:

1. On the Master Data Manager home page, select the Product model and VERSION_1 from the drop-down lists.
2. Click Explorer.
3. On the menu bar, choose Entities | Product (or whichever entity you want to validate against business rules).
4. Above the grid, click the "Apply business rules" button.

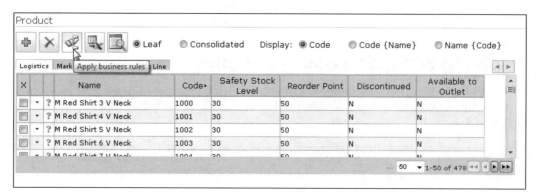

5. In the confirmation dialog box, click OK.

A green check mark indicates success. A red exclamation point indicates failure.

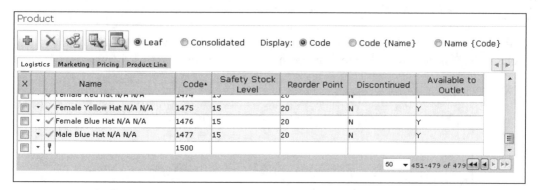

NOTE

Only the members on the current page in the grid are validated. So if you are showing 50 members, only those 50 members are validated against business rules.

Number of Members to Apply Business Rules To

In Explorer, when you apply business rules to members in the grid, you can set the maximum number of members in the grid to apply business rules to at one time. You do this by using the "Number of members to apply business rules to" setting in Master Data Services Configuration Manager.

You cannot show more than 100 members at a time in the grid, so it doesn't make sense to set this value higher than 100. However, the default value is 500.

Resolving Validation Issues in Explorer

In Explorer, you can view the validation issues you are an e-mail recipient for. To do so, in Explorer, choose Review | Validation Issues. The My Validation Issues page is displayed.

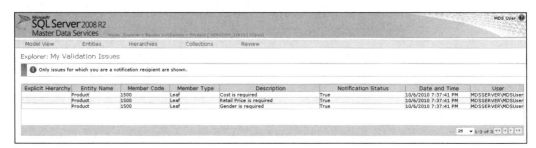

You can go directly to the member that failed validation by clicking the row and then clicking the "Go to selected item" button that's displayed above the grid.

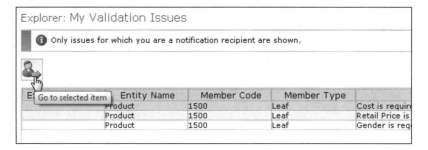

The Member Information page opens and you can correct the issue. After you resolve all of the issues and reapply business rules, the errors are removed from the My Validation Issues page.

Procedure: How to Validate a Version

In the Version Management functional area of Master Data Manager, you can validate an entire model version at once. For more information and full instructions, see Chapter 9.

Other Business Rule Tasks

Now that you have created rules, you might want to update the name and description of each to ensure you can tell them apart. You can also change the order in which the rules run, or exclude rules from running.

Procedure: How to Change the Rule Name and Description

You should give each business rule a name and description so you can keep track of what the rule is used for. To change the name or description of a business rule, complete the following steps:

1. On the Business Rule Maintenance page, in the row for the rule you want to rename, double-click the Name column. The cell becomes editable.

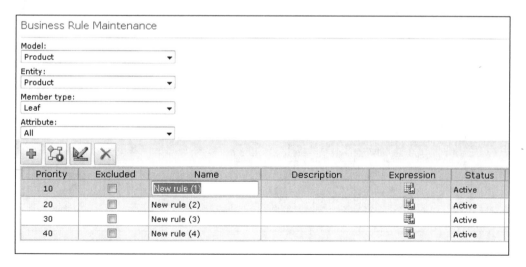

2. Type the text you want and press ENTER. The Status column changes to Changes pending.
3. Click the "Publish business rules" button.
4. In the confirmation dialog box, click OK. The status changes to Active.

The text is updated. Follow this same procedure to update values in the Description column.

> **NOTE**
>
> *The name cannot be more than 50 characters and the description cannot be more than 255 characters.*

Procedure: How to Set the Rule's Priority Order

Business rules execute based on the priority order provided in the Priority column. If you change the priority, you're changing the order in which the rules are applied to data. It is possible to have two rules with the same priority. In this case, MDS will determine the order for these two rules, usually the order of creation.

To change a business rule's priority, complete the following steps:

1. On the Business Rule Maintenance page, in the row for the rule with the priority you want to change, double-click the Priority column. The cell becomes editable.

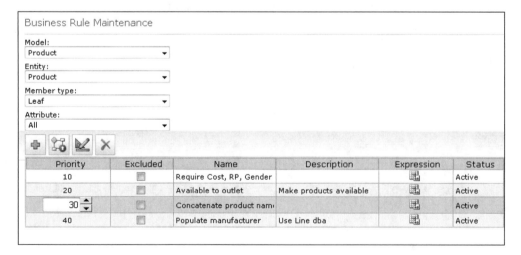

2. Type the text you want and press ENTER. The status changes to Changes pending.
3. Click the "Publish business rules" button.
4. In the confirmation dialog box, click OK. The status changes to Active.

TIP

You can click the column heading to sort by the Priority column.

In Master Data Services Configuration Manager, you can change the number that the Priority column is increased by when you create a new rule. The default is 10 but you can change it by updating the "Number to increment new business rules by" setting.

Procedure: How to Exclude Business Rules

You can exclude rules if you're not ready to publish or if you're troubleshooting. If you wish to save the business logic but temporarily exclude the rule from validation processes, you can check the Excluded check box and republish the rules.

To exclude a business rule, complete the following steps:

1. On the Business Rule Maintenance page, in the row for the rule you want to exclude, select the Excluded check box. The status changes to Exclusion pending.

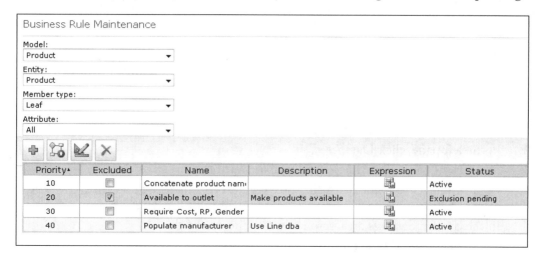

2. Click the "Publish business rules" button.
3. In the confirmation dialog box, click OK. The status changes to Excluded.

Configuring E-Mail Notifications

You can configure MDS to send e-mail notifications when an attribute value fails validation against certain types of business rules. First, you must configure e-mail settings to ensure e-mail can successfully be sent. Then, you must edit the business rule to indicate who to send e-mail notification to if validation fails. If you don't need e-mail notifications, you can skip this section.

A few notes before you get started:

▶ If you trigger e-mails to a group, only the users who have accessed the Master Data Manager web application will receive the mails.

▶ To confirm that the e-mail is sent to the user's correct address, on the Master Data Manager home page, click User and Group Permissions. To the left of the user, click the down arrow, then choose Edit | General. If the e-mail address listed is not correct, click the Edit button and update it.

Procedure: How to Configure E-Mail Notifications

Before you can configure e-mail notifications, you must know the IP address of the SMTP server that will send the mail. You should also have an e-mail address and display name for the account that will send the mail.

After you get this information, you can configure e-mail notifications by completing the following steps:

NOTE

This is a one-time process in Configuration Manager. If you need to update the Database Mail profile after you've set it up initially, you must do so in SQL Server Management Studio.

1. Open Master Data Services Configuration Manager.
2. In the left pane, click Databases.
3. In the right pane, click the Select Database button.
4. In the Connect to Database dialog box, connect to a database and click OK. The System Settings section is populated with settings for the database.
5. In the System Settings area, scroll down to the end of the list.
6. Click the Create Profile button.

7.   Populate the Create Database Mail Profile and Account dialog box as follows:

Setting	Description
Profile name	A unique name for the mail profile. It must be different from the name of any other mail profile in the database. An example might be MDS Email Profile.
Account name	A unique name for the account that's associated with the profile. Again, it must be different from the name of any other account in the database. This account name is used to create the account in SQL only; it is not a domain or local computer account. An example for this might be MDS Email Account.
E-mail address	The e-mail address that will be the From address on e-mails sent from MDS.
Display name	Optional. The display name for the e-mail address.
Reply e-mail address	Optional. If a user replies to an e-mail from MDS, this is the address replies are sent to.
SMTP server	The SMTP server used to send e-mail. You can use a server name or IP address.
Port number	The port number for the SMTP server, if needed.
This server requires a secure connection (SSL)	Select if you use SSL encryption.
SMTP Authentication	**Windows Authentication**—Database Mail uses the credentials of the service account used for SQL Server Database Engine. **Basic Authentication**—Specify a user account that can authenticate on the SMTP server. **Anonymous Authentication**—No credentials will be used when accessing the SMTP server.

8.   Click OK to save and close. The Database page is updated with the name of your Database Mail profile.

Other E-Mail Settings in Configuration Manager

There are a few other settings you can use to customize e-mails for your implementation:

▶   **Master Data Manager URL for notifications**   The URL that's used in the link in the e-mail notification. You should enter the name of your web site so users who get the e-mail can go directly to the validation issue by clicking the link.

▶   **Notification e-mail interval (in seconds)**   How often e-mails are sent. The default is every two minutes.

▶ **Number of notifications in a single e-mail** How many validation issues are included in a single e-mail.

▶ **Default e-mail format** Format for e-mails.

▶ **Regular expression for e-mail address** Used to validate e-mail addresses in the User and Group Permissions functional area of Master Data Manager. It determines the format that is allowed when entering e-mail addresses. Unless you have reason to change it, leave the default setting.

▶ **Database Mail account** You cannot change this setting. It is intended to show you the name of the Database Mail account in SQL Server in case you need to update it.

Procedure: How to Configure a Business Rule to Send E-Mail

After you configure Database Mail in Configuration Manager, you must specify who will be notified when data fails validation against business rules.

NOTE

To send e-mail notifications, the rule must have a validation action. (Validation actions are listed on the Edit Business Rule page, in the Components pane, under Actions | Validation.) Other types of actions do not send e-mail.

To configure a business rule to send e-mail, complete the following steps:

1. On the Master Data Manager home page, click System Administration.
2. On the menu bar, choose Manage | Business Rules.
3. On the Business Rule Maintenance page, choose a model, entity, and member type for your rule to apply to. In this example, select Product, Product, and Leaf. For the attribute, leave All.
4. For the business rule for which you want to send e-mail, double-click the Notification column. Expand the Users or Groups node to find the user or group you want to send mail to.

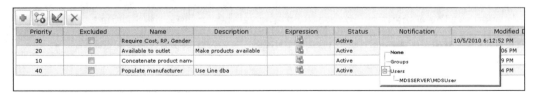

Priority	Excluded	Name	Description	Expression	Status	Notification	Modified D
30	☐	Require Cost, RP, Gender			Active		10/5/2010 6:12:52 PM
20	☐	Available to outlet	Make products available		Active	None	06 PM
10	☐	Concatenate product nam			Active	Groups	9 PM
40	☐	Populate manufacturer	Use Line dba		Active	Users	4 PM
						MDSSERVER\MDSUser	

5. Click the name of the user or group. The Notification column is updated with the value you selected. The Status column is updated to Changes pending.

Priority	Excluded	Name	Description	Expression	Status	Notification	Modified Date
30	☐	Require Cost, RP, Gender			Changes pending	MDSSERVER\MDSUser	10/6/2010 12:21:06 PM
20	☐	Available to outlet	Make products available		Active		10/6/2010 12:14:06 PM
10	☐	Concatenate product name			Active		10/5/2010 6:14:59 PM
40	☐	Populate manufacturer	Use Line dba		Active		10/5/2010 6:10:04 PM

6. Click the "Publish business rules" button.
7. In the confirmation dialog box, click OK.

Creating and Triggering Workflows

By using business rules and customizing your data model, you can create relatively simple workflows for managing the flow of data through Master Data Services. If you want to manage a one- or two-step approval process or notify users when more data is required, you can simply use the MDS interfaces provided to create these workflows.

Some organizations will require more complex event processing. If your organization requires multitiered approvals or complex decision trees, then integration with a SharePoint workflow may better suit your needs. Integration with SharePoint workflow will require some coding expertise and basic understanding of Windows workflow foundation.

Creating a Workflow in MDS

A simple MDS workflow might include getting approval when an attribute changes. For example, if someone in Purchasing needs to change the cost of a product, the head of Purchasing might want to be notified so that he can approve or deny that change.

You can create workflows in MDS based on any condition, but we're going to show you an example where an attribute value changes. In this case, you don't know what the attribute has changed to; you just know that it has changed.

To address this scenario, MDS uses change tracking groups attached to attributes. Each entity within Master Data Services has up to 31 change tracking groups that can have any number of attributes allocated to them. An attribute can be managed by only one change tracking group at a time.

NOTE

Change tracking is not triggered through the staging process in the SQL Server 2008 R2 release of MDS. If you require automatic updates to trigger change tracking, you must use the web service to update data.

To create a workflow within MDS, you will complete the following steps:

1. Add attributes to a change tracking group (so you can be notified when their values change).
2. Add a domain-based attribute named Approved and populate it with Yes, No, and Pending members.
3. Create a business rule to send notification when the attribute values change.

These steps create a simple workflow. Any time the cost of a product changes, the Approved attribute changes to Pending and the purchasing manager is notified. It is the purchasing manager's job to open MDS, review the change, and approve or deny it.

Procedure: How to Add an Attribute to a Change Tracking Group

You must add an attribute to a change tracking group before you can use rules to determine if the attribute value has changed. To add an attribute to a tracking group, complete the following steps:

1. On the Master Data Manager home page, click System Administration.
2. On the menu bar, choose Manage | Entities.
3. Select a model from the Model list. In this case, select Product.
4. Click the row of the entity that contains the attribute and click the "Edit selected entity" button. In this example, edit Product.
5. In the Leaf attributes section (or whichever section contains your attribute), click the attribute and click the "Edit selected attribute" button. In this example, edit Cost.
6. At the bottom of the page, select the "Enable change tracking" check box.
7. The "Change tracking group" field is displayed. You can set this number to any number you want. It is just used as a grouping for multiple attributes. If you want to include more than one attribute in this group, use the same group number for each attribute.

8. Click the Save attribute button.

Now if you want, you can edit other attributes and add them to the group with the same number. To do this, follow the same steps and make sure to use the same number for the group.

Procedure: How to Create an Approved Attribute

Now you're going to create an attribute that will change whenever the Cost attribute changes. This attribute acts as a flag to make others aware that the cost has changed.

By now, you should be able to create an entity and attribute in System Administration and create members in Explorer. If you need a refresher, see the procedures in Chapter 4.

To continue with this example:

1. In System Administration, for the Product model, create an entity named **Approved**. This entity does not need to be enabled for hierarchies.

2. Then in System Administration, create a leaf-level domain-based attribute for the Product entity. This domain-based attribute should be based on the Approved entity and be named **Approved**.

3. Add the Approved attribute to the Pricing attribute group so you can view the attribute in Explorer.

4. In Explorer, open the Approved entity and create three members: **Yes, No,** and **Pending**. If you have created multiple versions of the Product model, make sure you do this in the latest version.

Procedure: How to Create a Business Rule That's Triggered by Change Tracking

Now you're going to create the business rule to update the Approved attribute when the Cost attribute changes. You can create your own rules for any attributes that change by using similar steps.

1. On the home page, click System Administration.

2. On the menu bar, click Manage | Business Rules.

3. Select a model, entity, member type, and attribute. In this case, choose Product, Product, Leaf, and All.

4. Click the "Add business rule" button.

5. The row is highlighted. Select the "Edit selected business rule" button. The Edit Business Rule page is displayed.

6. In the Components pane, expand the Conditions node.

7. Under the Value comparison node, click "has changed" and drag it to the IF pane. Drop it on the Conditions label.

8. In the Entity-Specific Attributes pane, click Cost and drag it to the Edit Condition pane. Drop it on the Select attribute label. (Important: The attribute you drag here does not have any effect on MDS. It's required to create the rule, but the group, not the attribute, is what the rule is based on.)

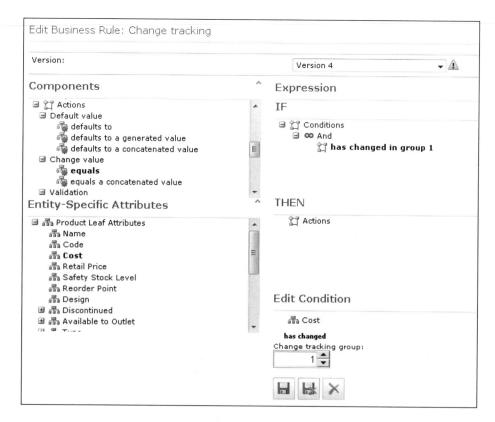

9. Click Save item.

10. In the Components pane, expand the Actions node. In the Change value node, click "equals" and drag it to the THEN pane. Drop it on the Actions label.

11. In the Entity-Specific Attributes pane, click Approved and drag it to the Edit Action pane. Drop it on the Select attribute label.

12. Select Pending from the list.

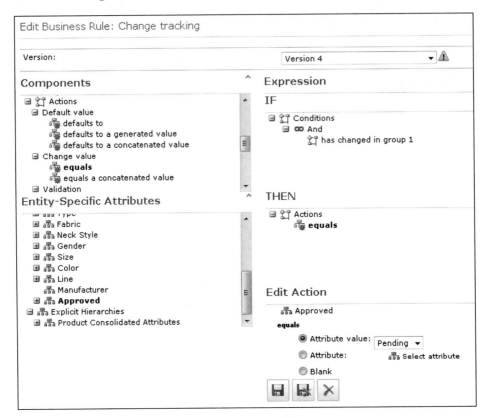

13. Click Save item.
14. Click the Back button in the top-left corner.
15. Click the "Publish Business Rules" button.

Now any time a cost changes and business rules are applied, the Approved column changes to Pending.

To have e-mail sent to the manager, create another business rule that sends e-mail when the Approved column is Pending. To do this, use the "is equal to" condition and the "is not valid" action.

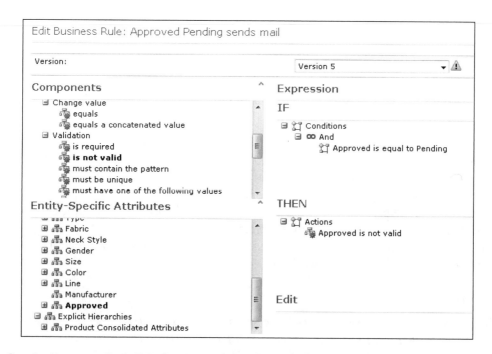

On the Business Rule Maintenance page, in the Notification column, choose the user or group you want to notify. This user or group is responsible for changing the Approved attribute from Pending to Yes or No.

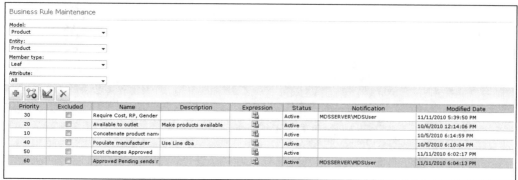

NOTE

You might want to create an additional business rule that notifies a different user or group if the Approved attribute value changes to No.

Triggering an External Workflow

Workflows external to MDS are triggered by using the external action business rule. When business rules are applied, all entity members that evaluate to true by the conditions provided are sent to the external action Service Broker queue.

To enable external actions, the workflow integration service must be installed separately. Otherwise, the data gathered by external action business rules just sits in the external action Service Broker queue without triggering any effect. Because this workflow listener pulls requests from a Service Broker queue, only a single workflow listener should be connected to an MDS database at a time and no other custom components should be pointed at the external action Service Broker queue.

A diagram of the process is shown in Figure 8-1. The workflow integration service queries the database periodically, and if the external action business rule has put data in the Service Broker queue, the data is passed by the service to either a SharePoint workflow or some other, custom workflow.

NOTE

If the SharePoint or other workflow is not configured properly, the service still clears the data from the queue and attempts to pass it to the workflow. At this point, even if you re-validate against business rules, the change tracking has already occurred and the data won't be re-added to the queue.

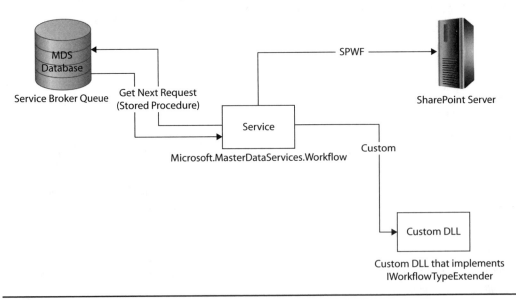

Figure 8-1   *The workflow integration service interacting with workflows external to MDS*

The following procedures should help you get started with installing the workflow integration service and configuring MDS to trigger external workflows. We've also written a white paper specific to triggering SharePoint workflows, which you can view here: http://msdn.microsoft.com/en-us/library/ff459274(SQL.100).aspx.

Installing the Workflow Integration Service

The first step in triggering an external workflow is to install the workflow integration service. It is called Microsoft.MasterDataServices.Workflow.exe and it can be found in Program Files\Microsoft SQL Server\Master Data Services\WebApplication\bin. You can use InstallUtil.exe to install the service. When you are ready to begin pulling data from the Service Broker queue, you will start this service.

Updating the Web Configuration File

Depending on the type of external action you want to trigger, different settings must be made in the Workflow configuration file. This file is called Microsoft.MasterDataServices .Workflow.exe.config and can also be found in Program Files\Microsoft SQL Server\ Master Data Services\WebApplication\bin.

If the only external actions that will be triggered are SharePoint workflows, then only the link to the MDS database is necessary. An example of the database connection string needed for a SharePoint workflow is shown here:

```xml
<?xml version="1.0" encoding="utf-8" ?>
<configuration>
    <configSections>
        <sectionGroup name="applicationSettings" type="System.Configuration.ApplicationSettingsGroup, System,
Version=2.0.0.0, Culture=neutral, PublicKeyToken=b77a5c561934e089" >
            <section name="Microsoft.MasterDataServices.Workflow.Properties.Settings"
type="System.Configuration.ClientSettingsSection, System, Version=2.0.0.0, Culture=neutral,
PublicKeyToken=b77a5c561934e089" requirePermission="false" />
        </sectionGroup>
    </configSections>
    <applicationSettings>
        <Microsoft.MasterDataServices.Workflow.Properties.Settings>
            <setting name="ConnectionString" serializeAs="String">
                <value>Server=MDSServer;Database=MDS;Integrated Security=SSPI</value>
            </setting>
        </Microsoft.MasterDataServices.Workflow.Properties.Settings>
    </applicationSettings>
</configuration>
```

Update this value with your server and database names.

In this example, MDSServer is the name of the server and MDS is the name of the database.

For each external DLL that you want to install into MDS, you must add a reference in the configuration file. Multiple external references must be added to the same XML node and separated by a semicolon. An example of two external actions is shown here:

```
<?xml version="1.0" encoding="utf-8" ?>
<configuration>
    <configSections>
        <sectionGroup name="applicationSettings" type="System.Configuration.ApplicationSettingsGroup, System,
Version=2.0.0.0, Culture=neutral, PublicKeyToken=b77a5c561934e089" >
            <section name="Microsoft.MasterDataServices.Workflow.Properties.Settings"
type="System.Configuration.ClientSettingsSection, System, Version=2.0.0.0, Culture=neutral,
PublicKeyToken=b77a5c561934e089" requirePermission="false" />
        </sectionGroup>
    </configSections>
    <applicationSettings>
        <Microsoft.MasterDataServices.Workflow.Properties.Settings>
            <setting name="ConnectionString" serializeAs="String">
                <value>Server=MDSServer;Database=MDS;Integrated Security=SSPI</value>
            </setting>
        </Microsoft.MasterDataServices.Workflow.Properties.Settings>
        <setting name="WorkflowTypeExtenders" serializeAs="String">
            <value>TAS=IntegrationWorkflow.AddressStandardizationIntegrationWorkflow, IntegrationWorkflow,
                Version=1.0.0.0, Culture=neutral, PublicKeyToken=null;
            TEST=Microsoft.MasterDataServices.Workflow.WorkflowTypeTest,Microsoft.MasterDataServices.Workflow,
                Version=10.0.0.0, Culture=neutral, PublicKeyToken=89845DCD8080CC91
            </value>
        </setting>
    </applicationSettings>
</configuration>
```

Multiple workflows are both between the <value> tag and are separated by a semicolon.

Creating a SharePoint Workflow in Visual Studio

If you decide you want to use SharePoint for your workflow, use these steps to get started designing a workflow in Visual Studio:

NOTE

You must use Microsoft Visual Studio 2010 and Microsoft SharePoint Foundation 2010 or Microsoft SharePoint Server 2010 to create your SharePoint workflow.

1. Open Visual Studio 2010.
2. Using the SharePoint 2010 templates, create a Sequential workflow project.
3. Drag the OnWorkflowActivated control from the toolbox to the designer area.
4. Right-click the control and choose Generate Handlers.

The data passed from the business rule process into the Service Broker queue will be contained in the string MDSData = workflowProperties.InitiationData. You must now parse the MDS data string into separate data fields and use the MDS web service to interact with Master Data Services.

Creating a Business Rule That Starts a Workflow

To trigger an external workflow from within MDS, you must create a business rule that starts the workflow. To do so, create a business rule as you normally would.

NOTE

Workflow business rules should always contain a condition. Otherwise, the workflow would be continually triggered.

The action needed to start the workflow is the last item in the Conditions node of the Components pane. Under the External action node, choose "start Workflow," as shown in the illustration on the following page. Then populate the Edit Action pane as follows:

Field	Description
Select attribute	Choose any attribute; this field is not used by MDS in this case.
Workflow type	SPWF for SharePoint; name of DLL file if other custom workflow.
Include member data in the message	Select this check box to include attribute names and values in the information passed to the workflow.
Workflow site	SharePoint only—the name of the site, e.g., http://site.
Workflow name	The name of the workflow. In Visual Studio Solution Explorer, this value is in the Display Name field.

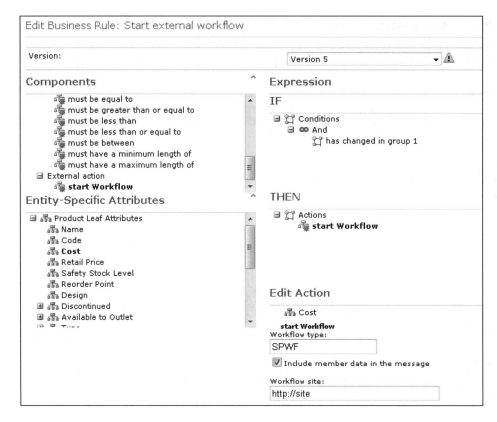

Then save the item and publish the business rule as you normally would. When the business rule is applied, it populates the queue. When you start the service, the queue is cleared and an attempt is made to pass the data to the workflow.

Using Web Services to Manage Business Rules

Business rule management is the most complicated process exposed by the Master Data Services web service. Although we provide a couple of simple examples in this section, writing more complex business rules is significantly more intricate and would require a significant amount of this book to explain. Automation of MDS business rules should only be attempted by experienced developers working on a specific project that requires business rule automation.

Getting a List of Rules

There may be instances where you want to programmatically consume Master Data Services' business rules in external systems. While we have seen significant interest in this, we believe the internal ruleset limits the capability for MDS to be used as a rule warehouse. Users interested in this type of solution should look at using standard MDS entities to store this data. For users interested in getting rules out of MDS, the following procedure shows a common request to get a list of business rules:

```
public BusinessRules GetBusinessRules(string ModelName,
string EntityName, BREntityMemberType memType)
{
    //Instantiate the request and criteria
    BusinessRulesGetRequest Request = new BusinessRulesGetRequest();
    Request.GetCriteria = new BRGetCriteria();

    //Set Model, Entity, and MemberType
    //to filter the business rule request
    Request.GetCriteria.ModelId = new Identifier { Name = ModelName };
    Request.GetCriteria.EntityId = new Identifier { Name = EntityName };
    Request.GetCriteria.MemberType = memType;
    Request.ResultOptions = new BRResultOptions();
    Request.ResultOptions.BusinessRules = ResultType.Identifiers;
    BusinessRulesGetResponse Response =
      mds_Proxy.BusinessRulesGet(Request);
    //This operation will primarily return a BusinessRuleSet
    return Response.BusinessRuleSet;
}
```

Creating a Business Rule

The most complex operations in MDS are the creation and update of business rules in MDS. If you are interested in automating the business rule process, we suggest that you keep the processes simple, by not adding complex conditions or actions in the beginning. At the conclusion of this procedure, a new business rule will be created but will not be published. You will need to publish the rule in another operation or through the UI.

```
public OperationResult MandatoryAttributeBusinessRuleCreate
(string BRName, string ModelName, string EntityName, string AttributeName,
 MemberType memType, int Priority)
    {
```

```
BusinessRulesCreateResponse Response = new
  BusinessRulesCreateResponse();
BusinessRulesCreateRequest Request = new
  BusinessRulesCreateRequest();
Request.ReturnCreatedIdentifiers = true;
Request.BusinessRuleSet = new BusinessRules();
Request.BusinessRuleSet.BusinessRulesMember =
  new Collection<BusinessRule>();

//Create New Business Rule Object and assign the properties
BusinessRule newBR = new BusinessRule();
newBR.Identifier = new  MemberTypeContextIdentifier
{ Name = BRName };
newBR.Identifier.ModelId = new Identifier
{ Name = ModelName };
newBR.Identifier.EntityId = new Identifier
{ Name = EntityName };

//Each Business Rule must be given a priority order to run
newBR.Priority = 1;
newBR.Identifier.MemberType = memType;

//Add Action to Action Collection
newBR.BRActions = new Collection<BRAction>();
BRAction BRActionItem = new BRAction();

//Add Attribute and Action type to the collection
BRActionItem.PrefixArgument = new BRAttributeArgument();
BRActionItem.PrefixArgument.PropertyName = BRPropertyName.Anchor;
BRActionItem.PrefixArgument.AttributeId = new Identifier();
BRActionItem.PrefixArgument.AttributeId.Name = AttributeName;
BRActionItem.Operator = BRItemType.Mandatory;

//All Action and Condition Items must have a sequence
//greater than zero
BRActionItem.Sequence = 1;
newBR.BRActions.Add(BRActionItem);

//Add the New Business Rule to the Business RuleSet
Request.BusinessRuleSet.BusinessRulesMember.Add(newBR);
Response = mds_Proxy.BusinessRulesCreate(Request);

return Response.OperationResult;
}
```

Summary

In this chapter we discussed the ability to manage master data by using business rules. These business rules were created to allow business users to quickly and efficiently create logical constructs to manage the data within their entities. Business rules are entity and type centric. Using notifications and business rules, simple workflow processes can be managed using only Master Data Services functionality. If more complex workflows need to be managed, you can trigger SharePoint workflows using the external action business rule. In the next chapter we will discuss using validation as part of a version management process.

Chapter 9

Creating Versions of Data

In This Chapter

A fter you understand the workflow for adding and modifying the data stored in MDS, you must learn how to manage that data over time. For each model within MDS, a historical record of the data can be stored. These data snapshots are called *versions*.

Each time you create a version of a model, the data for all the entities within the individual model are versioned at the same time. Only the data is stored; any changes to the structure of the model affect all versions and can create unintended consequences.

Version flags are another important component of versioning in MDS. By assigning flags to versions, integration with other systems can be better managed.

Versions Overview

In order to manage data within your organization effectively, you may be required to create versions of the data stored within a model. In MDS, the data in all entities within each model is versioned simultaneously. A benefit of this design is that you can manage relationships between entities without worrying about time and version. A side effect of this design is that entities in different models cannot interact with one another.

There is often a natural cadence to many data domains. This cadence can help define which entities should be managed in the same model. For example, in many organizations, the accounting department manages structural changes on a monthly basis. As each month ends, everyone in the accounting department goes through standard routines to ensure that the month's books can be closed properly. Any entities related to this process—accounts, divisions, departments, or other internal business entities that are central to this process—should be managed together, versioned in concert with the month-end process.

In another example, an organization may release products on a quarterly basis. All entities central to the product development process would follow this quarterly versioning scheme. Other entities may not require a versioning scheme at all.

Versions provide a number of benefits to the data management process:

▶ **Complete model history for a specific point in time**   MDS model versions can be committed to ensure that an exact record of a model's data can be stored for later review. These committed versions can provide a portion of the required audit trail for new, more rigorous compliance requirements.

▶ **Limited access during sensitive processes**   When performing certain processes, like validating the entire model or loading large numbers of records, it may be prudent to restrict access to the model by locking it.

▶ **Additional version copies for analysis**   Additional versions can be created outside of the standard cadence for a variety of purposes. These versions can be used to examine new hierarchy configurations or potential acquisitions without affecting the current regular processes.

Changing the Structure of Your Model

MDS does not version metadata changes. Any changes to the model structure affect all open and committed versions. If an attribute or entity is deleted, for example, all history for that attribute or entity is lost from all versions *forever*. When you need to maintain historic data, we suggest that you use security permissions to hide attributes or entities instead of deleting them. You can also hide attributes by setting the display width to zero or by not adding them to attribute groups.

When you add an attribute or entity, the model structure is updated in all versions as well. You can add the corresponding data to any version of the model; if you add data to a later version, the structure exists in the earlier versions but the data does not.

Committing Versions

Sometimes users and downstream systems need to be certain that all data has been validated and reviewed. Because MDS allows incomplete members to be added to the system and encourages users to manage the data creation and correction workflow from within MDS entities, it may not be reliable for external production systems to use open or locked versions. Only committed versions ensure that all members in every entity within the model have passed all business rules successfully. Once a version is committed, no additional changes can be made to the data, and the status of the version cannot be changed.

Figure 9-1 shows the most common version control workflow. A few notes about Figure 9-1:

- ► Each time the status changes, if notifications are configured, an e-mail is sent to model administrators. For more information about notifications, see Chapter 8.

- ► You can change a setting in MDS Configuration Manager so that you can copy versions with a status other than Committed, but Figure 9-1 shows the default behavior.

- ► You can validate a version at any time. Locking the version ensures that users don't make changes after you've validated, but it's only necessary if you plan to commit the version or otherwise prevent users from making changes.

Versioning for Main Street Clothing Company

Main Street Clothing Company has separated its entities into two separate domains: Account and Product. A major reason for this split was the version cadence of each domain.

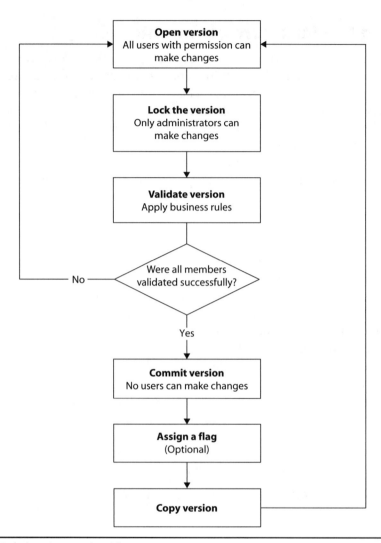

Figure 9-1 *Default version control workflow*

As a clothing company, Main Street finds that its product lines change significantly based on the season. This creates a natural cadence for managing major changes to its product list on a quarterly basis. The account model is managed on a monthly basis as part of the accounting team's regular month-end close process.

Updating Your Version Name and Description

Before you lock, validate, commit, or copy a version of your model, you might want to customize the version name and description. You can do this at any time. The new version name is displayed in many places in the Master Data Manager web UI, but you will probably notice it most on the home page, when you select the model name and version from the drop-down lists.

Procedure: How to Change the Version Name and Description

To change the version name and description, complete the following steps:

1. On the Master Data Manager home page, click Version Management.
2. From the Model list, select the model with the version name or description you want to change.
3. Double-click the cell that contains the version name or description that you want to change. The cell becomes editable.

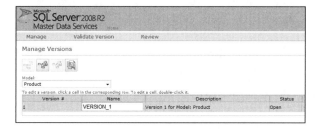

4. Change the text.
5. Press ENTER.
6. Double-click the cell with the version description.
7. Change the description to the text you want.
8. Press ENTER.

The name and description are updated.

NOTE

The date/time shown in the Last Changed Date column is based on the last change to any of the version information on this page, including the status.

Version Statuses

As you work with versions of your model and its data, you change the status of the version and then make copies of it. The version status indicates whether or not the model structure and its data can be updated. The following table lists the possible statuses for a version.

Status	Meaning
Open	Users can change the data; model administrators can change the data and the model structure. (See Chapter 11 for more information about model administrators.)
Locked	Users cannot change the data; model administrators can change the data and the model structure.
Committed	Neither users nor administrators can change the data or the structure. At this point, you can copy the model. *Note:* MDS Configuration Manager has a setting you can use to change which statuses you can copy. By default, you can copy Committed only.

Procedure: How to Lock a Version

When you're ready to save a version of the model, you first lock it. Then you can validate the model data and work on resolving issues that occur when data fails validation against business rules. To lock a version, complete the following steps:

1. On the Master Data Manager home page, click Version Management.
2. From the Model list, select the model you want to lock.
3. Select the row for the version you want to lock. The background is shaded when the row is selected.
4. Click the "Lock selected version" button.

5. In the confirmation dialog box, click OK.

The Status column changes to Locked.

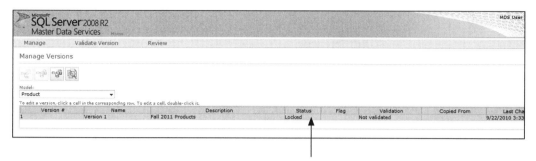

The status changes to Locked.

Now you can proceed with validating the version against business rules so that you can commit the version and create a copy of it.

Validating a Version

When you validate a version against business rules, all the members in the model are validated against business rules. You can validate subsets of members in the Explorer functional area, but you use the following procedure to validate all members at the same time.

Procedure: How to Validate a Version

To validate the members from a version against business rules, complete the following steps:

1. On the Master Data Manager home page, click Version Management.
2. On the menu bar, click Validate Version.
3. Select the model and the version you want to validate.

4. Click the Validate version button.

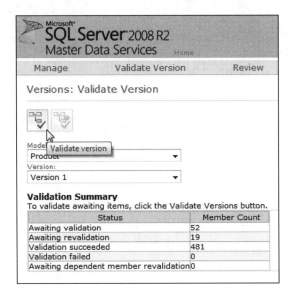

5. In the confirmation dialog box, click OK.

(You may have to do steps 4 and 5 twice. You will know that the process is complete when the Commit version button is enabled.)

Validation Statuses

The statuses that are displayed on this page help you determine which members have passed business rule validation and which members have failed. The following table lists the possible validation statuses.

Status	Meaning
Awaiting validation	These new members have never been validated.
Awaiting revalidation	These existing members are waiting to be validated.
Validation succeeded	These members passed business rule validation and there are no issues to fix.
Validation failed	These members failed validation and you must resolve the issues before you can commit.
Awaiting dependent member validation	These consolidated members are validated after leaf members are validated.

Procedure: How to Resolve Validation Issues

Before you can commit the version, you must resolve all business rule validation issues by completing the following steps:

> **NOTE**
>
> *In Explorer, users can view their own individual business rule issues, if they are recipients of notifications that are sent when validation fails. As an administrator, you can view all issues for all users by following this procedure.*

1. On the Master Data Manager home page, click Version Management.
2. On the menu bar, choose Review | Validation Issues.
3. Select the model and the version.

    A list of all validation issues is displayed. Unlike the Explorer functional area, this page shows validation issues for all users.

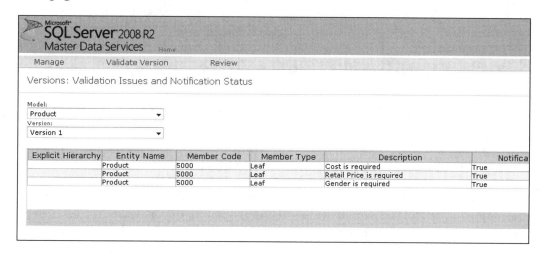

4. If you need to unlock the version at this point so that users can update data, return to the Manage Versions page, select the model, and click the "Unlock selected version" button.

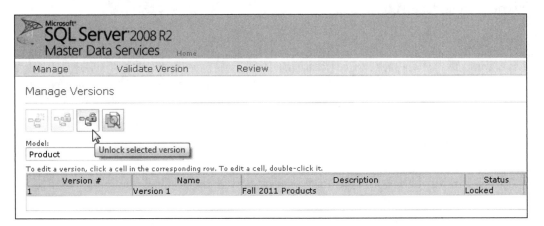

Reviewing and Reversing Transactions

To help resolve business rule validation issues, you can review transactions for all users in the Version Management functional area. To do so, choose Review | Transactions. For the steps required to reverse a transaction or annotate it, see Chapter 7.

Committing and Copying a Version

You should not commit a version until you are sure it's complete and accurate. Once you commit a version, you cannot undo it without opening the database. You also have the ability to delete a version, but you must also go into the database. In either case, you should only do these procedures if you're not concerned with compliance issues and if you're comfortable working in the database.

In general, you should commit the version and then copy it, giving users the ability to continue updating the data.

Procedure: How to Commit a Version

When all members pass validation against business rules and the version is locked, you can commit the version by completing the steps that follow.

CAUTION

After you commit a version, you cannot reopen it from the UI. Before committing, you should be sure that you no longer want to work with the data.

1. On the Master Data Manager home page, click Version Management.
2. On the menu bar, click Validate Version.
3. If all rows in the table show 0 except the Validation succeeded row, then the version can successfully be committed. Click Commit version.

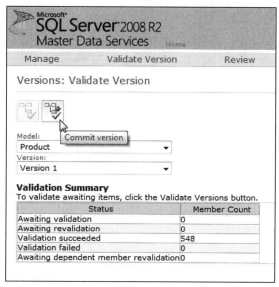

4. In the confirmation dialog box, click OK.

When the version is successfully committed, a success message is displayed. Back on the Manage Versions page, the Status column is updated to Committed.

Now you can copy the version.

Procedure: How to Reopen a Committed Version

You can change a committed version back to an open version by completing the steps that follow.

CAUTION

This action should be performed by a DBA only in those rare situations in which the version was committed by mistake. If production systems have pulled this data and used the results for reporting that is subject to compliance, the more appropriate action is to copy the version and commit a new, revised version for compliance purposes.

1. Open SQL Server Management Studio and connect to the MDS database.
2. In the table mdm.tblModel, in the ID column, note the ID of the model.
3. In the table mdm.tblModelVersion, in the Model_ID column, find the ID from step 2.
4. In the row for the version of the model you want to open, change the value in the Status column from 3 (Committed) to 1 (Open) or 2 (Locked).

The version is now displayed as open or locked in the web UI.

Procedure: How to Copy a Version

When you copy a version, a new version with the next version number is created. Newly created versions have the status of Open and are available for editing by users and administrators. To copy a version, complete the following steps:

> **NOTE**
>
> *By default, you can copy Committed versions only.*

1. On the Master Data Manager home page, click Version Management.
2. On the menu bar, choose Manage | Versions.
3. From the Model list, select a model.
4. Click the row for the version you want to copy.
5. Click the "Copy selected version" button.
6. In the confirmation dialog box, click OK.

A new row is displayed in the grid. You can update the name and description to indicate which version you want this to be.

Copy Versions Other Than Committed

In MDS Configuration Manager, you can change whether you can copy models with any status or just those with a status of Committed. The setting is called "Copy only committed versions" and the default is Yes. Set it to No if you want to copy versions of any status.

If your organization acquires another organization, or you want to work with a hypothetical version of the data, it can be useful to copy other versions of the data. If you have more than one open version, however, remember that users can modify it. You can set security to prevent access, but it is not a straightforward process. See "Hierarchy Member Permissions" in Chapter 11 for more information.

Version Flags

While versions can provide a myriad of benefits, managing the integration with other systems can be a nightmare as the current version changes over time. MDS addresses this issue with the implementation of version flags. Each version in MDS can be flagged with a custom flag specific to the selected model. These flags allow data stewards to tag a version as current, prior, draft, or some unique identifier for downstream systems. Each version can have only one version flag associated with it at a time.

Because downstream systems rely on the type of data being presented in a version, MDS can require versions to be committed before the flag can be applied. For most production systems, it is important to ensure that committed versions require flags. This check will be the only way to ensure that a specific version has passed validation before being used by downstream systems.

Procedure: How to Create a Version Flag and Assign It to a Version

To create a version flag and assign it to a version of a model, complete the following steps:

1. On the Master Data Manager home page, click Version Management.
2. On the menu bar, choose Manage | Flags.
3. From the Model list, select a model.
4. Click the Add flag button.

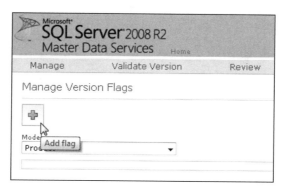

5. A grid is displayed. Type a name and description and select whether the flag is available to apply to Committed versions only (True) or to versions of any status (False).

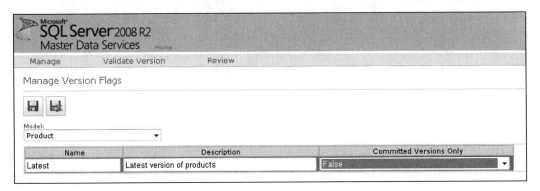

6. Click the Save flag button.
7. On the menu bar, choose Manage | Versions.
8. In the row of the version you want to assign the flag to, double-click the Flag column. A list is displayed.
9. Select the flag from the list.

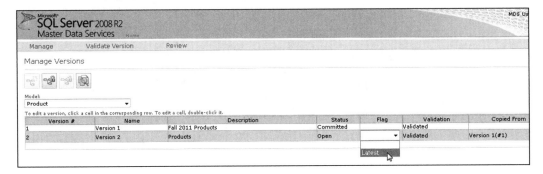

10. Press TAB or ENTER.

The Flag column is updated.

NOTE

You can assign a flag to one version at a time only.

Viewing a Version's Ancestry

You can copy any previous versions to create new versions; for example, you can copy versions in this order:

- ▶ Version 1 to Version 2
- ▶ Version 2 to Version 3
- ▶ Version 1 to Version 4

If you create several versions of a model and you are trying to determine where each version came from, you can view the Copied From column on the Manage Versions page.

This column shows where the version came from.

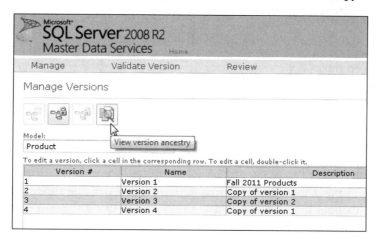

This column shows only the most recent version in the version's history. You can view a more in-depth historical record by viewing the version ancestry. On the Manage Versions page, click the row you want to see a history for and click the "View version ancestry" button. In this example, we'll view Version 3, which was a copy of Version 2.

The Version Ancestry dialog box that is displayed shows the history. You read this dialog box from bottom to top; 0 is the first time the version was generated, 1 is the second time, 2 is the third, and so on. In this case, the first version of this model was Version 1, then it was copied to Version 2, and then to Version 3.

Version Ancestry

Generation #	Version #	Name	Status
2	3	Version 3	Open
1	2	Version 2	Committed
0	1	Version 1	Committed

Procedure: How to Delete a Version

Normally, you should not need to delete a version of your model. This procedure is intended to help you with testing or if some circumstance forces you to take this action. Use with caution.

CAUTION

If you delete the only version for the model, the model becomes unusable.

To delete a model version, complete the following steps:

1. Open SQL Server Management Studio and connect to the MDS database.
2. In the view mdm.viw_SYSTEM_SCHEMA_VERSION, determine which version of the model you want to delete, and copy the value in the ID field.
3. Create a new query similar to the following:

```
EXEC [mdm].[udpVersionDelete] @Version_ID='value from step 2'
```

Replace *value from step 2* with the ID from step 2.

When you run the query, the version is deleted. The Master Data Manager web application reflects this change shortly after. You should close and reopen your Internet browser to confirm the change.

Using Web Services to Work with Versions

Web services can be used to update information related to versions within a model. In this example, we use the MetadataUpdate method for the first time. Unlike the MetadataCreate operation, identifiers cannot be created using the name field only to allow people to update the name.

Returning a List of Versions

When managing versions through the MDS web services, the GetVersion helper class will be very useful because version updates cannot be managed based on the name directly, as we have discussed. In this helper class, we will return the version based on the model and version name. Similar helper classes would be required to update any metadata objects.

```
public Collection<MDS_WS.Version>
GetVersion(string modelName, string verName)
        {
            MetadataGetRequest Request = new MetadataGetRequest();

            //Create all required Search Criteria Objects
            Request.SearchCriteria = new MetadataSearchCriteria();
            Request.SearchCriteria.Models = new Collection<Identifier>();
            Request.SearchCriteria.Versions = new Collection<Identifier>();
            Request.SearchCriteria.SearchOption =
               SearchOption.UserDefinedObjectsOnly;

            //Create model and version Search Identifiers
            Identifier modelIdentifier = new Identifier { Name = modelName };
            Identifier versionIdentifier = new Identifier { Name = verName };

            //Add these identifiers to search criteria
            Request.SearchCriteria.Models.Add(modelIdentifier);
            Request.SearchCriteria.Versions.Add(versionIdentifier);

            //Add Result Options to request
            Request.ResultOptions = new MetadataResultOptions();
            Request.ResultOptions.Versions = ResultType.Details;

            MetadataGetResponse Response = mds_Proxy.MetadataGet(Request);

            return Response.Metadata.Versions;
        }
```

Changing the Version Status

Version information is updated using the MetadataUpdate operation. The following code leverages the helper class outlined in the prior section to retrieve the identifier for the version you want to update. In this code, we lock the version. A similar method could be used to commit the version, but committing a version requires that the version has been successfully validated first.

```
public OperationResult UpdateVersion(string modelName,
string verName, string verDesc, bool locked)
    {
        MetadataUpdateRequest Request = new MetadataUpdateRequest();

        Request.Metadata = new Metadata();
        Request.Metadata.Versions = new
          Collection<MDS_Wrapper.MDS_WS.Version>();

        //Run the helper class to get reference to version
        MDS_WS.Version targetversion = GetVersion(modelName, verName)[0];

        //Create local instance of version and apply retrieved identifier
        MDS_WS.Version ver1 = new MDS_Wrapper.MDS_WS.Version();
        ver1.Identifier = targetversion.Identifier;

        //Description or Name properties can be updated
        ver1.Description = verDesc;

        //VersionStatus can be freely changed between locked and open
        //but committed requires a successfully validated model
        if (locked == true)
        {
            ver1.VersionStatus = VersionStatus.Locked;
        }
        else
        {
            ver1.VersionStatus = VersionStatus.NotSpecified;
        };

        //Add the version to the versions collection
        Request.Metadata.Versions.Add(ver1);

        //Make the MDS Web Service request
        MetadataUpdateResponse Response =
          mds_Proxy.MetadataUpdate(Request);

        return Response.OperationResult;
    }
```

Summary

Versioning provides you with the flexibility to manage models over time. Versions can be in one of three states: open, locked, or committed. Committed versions can provide users and downstream systems with the assurance that all members have been validated and the committed version will not be changed in the future. Integration with downstream systems can be facilitated by using version flags. Version flags can be used on draft versions, or you can require that versions be committed before they can be flagged. In the next chapter, we will discuss how to provide descriptions for MDS model objects.

Chapter 10

Using Metadata

In This Chapter

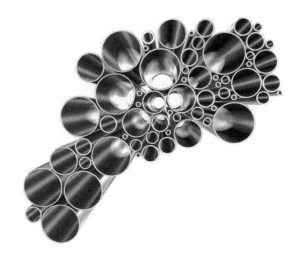

I n general, "metadata" is an overloaded term. In Master Data Services, this term is overloaded as well. Structural changes in MDS are manifest in the web service through "metadata" calls. By using the simplest definition of metadata—data about data—these calls provide internal information about the models, entities, and hierarchies created in MDS. Other companies consider the actual attribute data for master data members as "metadata."

Microsoft recognized that users want to add descriptions to their models, entities, and attributes. Thus, this is the definition of *metadata* that we will be using: the data used to describe your MDS objects. In this chapter, we review the methods for adding and updating metadata attribute values for the MDS object types.

The Metadata Model

The MDS metadata feature leverages a system model to allow model administrators to add attributes to MDS objects. This system model is called Metadata, and when you first create an MDS database, this is the only model that exists in the system. There are five entities within the Metadata model, one for each object type. For example, the Model Metadata Definition entity is used to store metadata about models, the Entity Metadata Definition entity is used to store metadata about entities, and so on for attributes, attribute groups, and hierarchies. The entities in the Metadata model cannot be deleted by any user, no matter what the user's level of access is.

What Happens When Model Objects Are Added or Deleted

As objects in the model are added and deleted, the Metadata model is updated. For example, if you create a new attribute, it will be displayed in the Attribute Metadata Definition entity. If you delete an attribute, it will be deleted, along with its corresponding metadata.

Each model object has a unique code in the Metadata model. For example, the Product entity has a unique code, and the Size attribute has a unique code. The code for each object in the Metadata model is based on the internal Object ID for the related object. As objects become more granular, the code in the Metadata model becomes a combination of the IDs of all objects that are a part of the context, in order of importance.

You have the ability to change the Name and Code attributes of any member in the Metadata model; it doesn't affect the metadata that's displayed in Explorer for the object.

Viewing Metadata

There are two primary actions related to metadata. You, as the administrator, will add the metadata. Your users will view metadata to get more information about the data they're working with. Let's start with how users will view metadata; this will help you determine where and how to add it.

In the following examples, we'll use the Product model to show you where metadata is displayed for each object type. You can use the same procedures for any model (other than the Metadata model).

Metadata for Entities

To view metadata for an entity, complete the following steps:

1. On the Master Data Manager home page, select an active model and version and click Explorer. In this example, select the latest version of the Product model.
2. From the menu bar, choose Entities | Product. The products are displayed in the grid.
3. Above the grid, click the View metadata button.

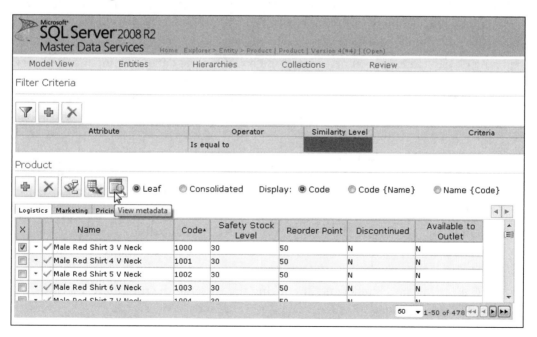

The Metadata Explorer dialog box is displayed. This dialog box can be confusing at first sight.

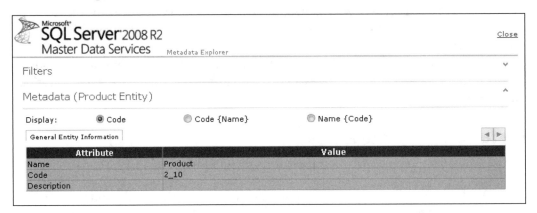

There are several things to note about this dialog box:

▶ The grid displays information from the Metadata model. For example, the Name and Code are for the Product entity, based on how the Product entity is referred to in the Metadata model. No text is displayed in the Description field yet, because no one has added metadata about the Product entity to the Metadata model.

▶ The Code field helps you determine which table in the database contains the entity. In this example, the Code is 2_10. If you open SQL Server Management Studio and view the tables in your MDS database, a table named mdm.tbl_2_10_EN is displayed. This table contains a list of all members in the Product entity.

▶ The Code field also indicates the code for the member that represents the Product entity in the Metadata model. This is the code for the member you must update if you want to display metadata in this dialog box. The Code value is a concatenation of two codes from the MDS database: the ID in tblModel and the ID in tblEntity.

▶ A tab is displayed above the grid. If you were to create attribute groups for the Entity Metadata Definition entity in the Metadata model, the tabs that indicate attribute groups would be displayed here.

▶ If you expand the Filters pane by clicking the arrow in the top right, you can change the filters and view metadata for other model objects.

Click to expand the Filters pane.

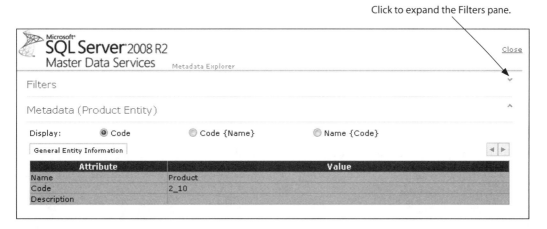

When the Filters pane is expanded, you can confirm which object you're viewing metadata for. In this case, when you view the filters, it is clear that you're viewing metadata for the Product entity.

You use these filters to view metadata for attributes and attribute groups. You can also use the filters to view metadata for models and hierarchies, though you can view metadata for those objects on their specific screens as well.

NOTE

If a filter is disabled (as Attribute is in this example), you cannot select it. Change the Metadata type to view other metadata.

Metadata for Attributes

To view metadata for attributes, follow the same procedure as you did for entities, but in the Filters pane, select a Metadata type of Attribute.

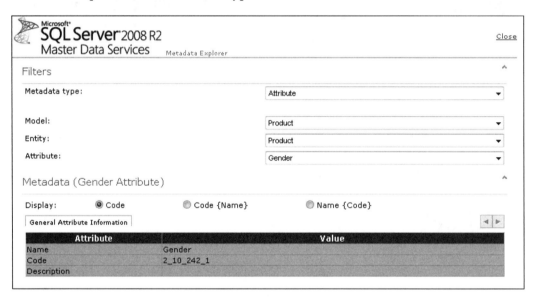

The Code value is a concatenation of three codes from the MDS database: the model ID from tblModel, the entity ID from tblEntity, and the attribute ID from tblAttribute. For example, 2_10_242_1 is model ID 2, entity ID 10, and attribute ID 242.

Metadata for Attribute Groups

To view metadata for attribute groups, follow the same procedure as you did for entities, but in the Filters pane, select Attribute group for the Metadata type.

The Code value is a concatenation of two codes from the MDS database: the entity ID from tblEntity and the attribute group ID from tblAttributeGroup. For example, 6_5 is entity ID 6 and attribute group ID 5.

Metadata for Hierarchies

To view metadata for hierarchies, in Explorer, choose Hierarchies | *<the name of the hierarchy>*. Above the hierarchy structure, click the View metadata button to view metadata.

The Code value (for example, 2_D_1) is a concatenation of the model ID, the hierarchy type ("D" for Derived, "E" for Explicit), and the hierarchy ID from tblHierarchy.

Metadata for Models

To view metadata for a model, click Explorer. On the first page that's displayed, click the View metadata button in the top left.

The Code value is a single digit that indicates the internal ID for the model. This ID represents the integer order in which the model was created. Since the Metadata model was created at the time of initial implementation of the database, the ID for the Metadata model is always 1. The table mdm.tbl_1_1_EN contains one row for every model in the database.

Adding Metadata

Now it's time to populate the Description field that we've been referring to. This will be the metadata that users are looking for in Explorer. In this example, we add metadata to the Product model.

CAUTION

You cannot create a package of the Metadata model to deploy to a production environment from a test environment; if you want to keep the changes you make to this model, use the production instance of your MDS installation.

1. On the Master Data Manager home page, select the Metadata model and Version 1. Then click Explorer.
2. On the menu bar, choose Entities | Model Metadata Definition. The models are displayed in a grid. Each model has a code, based on the order in which it was created.

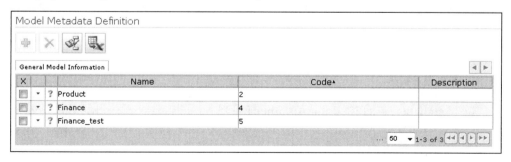

In this example, you can see that the first and third models that were created were deleted, because none of the models has a code of 1 or 3.

3. For the model you want to update, double-click the cell in the Description column and type a description.

4. Press ENTER to save the description.

Now when you open the Product model in Explorer and open the Metadata Explorer dialog box, the description is displayed.

The description is displayed.

Now that you understand how to add metadata for a model, you can use the same procedure to add metadata for any other object. For example, you can choose the Hierarchy Metadata Definition entity and update the Description attribute for a hierarchy.

Extending the Metadata Model

Description might be a useful attribute for you, but you may want to track other types of metadata. For example, you might want to list the owner of a specific attribute so that other users know who to contact if there is disagreement over how the attribute is managed. To do this, you would create an attribute for the Attribute Metadata Definition entity and name it "Owner" or something similar.

As another example, you might want to ensure that a free-form attribute is periodically evaluated to make sure users aren't entering text that veers too far from corporate standards. You can create a "Reviewed Date" attribute and then create a business rule that sends e-mail if this date is more than three months in the past.

The Metadata model is similar to other MDS models, so you can use the procedures outlined in other chapters to create additional attributes or business rules. You can create entities and use them as domain-based attribute values, just as you would in any other model.

Limitations of the Metadata Model

You cannot add or delete members in the Metadata model, add metadata to the model, or create versions or version flags for the model. As stated previously, you cannot create a package of the Metadata model to deploy from test to production. You cannot change the model name or delete the model.

You also cannot add metadata to the Name and Code attributes of any entity.

Using Web Services with Metadata

There are no special calls to get or create metadata in MDS. Despite their names, all calls in the web service labeled Metadata will create, update, or delete the structural elements of MDS. None of these calls should be used to interact with the descriptive metadata feature, as these objects are created programmatically when the underlying structures are created.

Determining the Metadata Member Code

The toughest part about managing metadata is determining the code for the member in the Metadata model that you want to view or update. The following operation combines the internal IDs needed to give you the Code for the metadata type you request.

Before reviewing the code sample, note the following:

▶ Because the future of some metadata entities, like hierarchy and attribute group, are in doubt, we have chosen not to add their complexity here.

▶ The code brings in strMemType as a string parameter, rather than an integer, to eliminate recasting from integer to string within the code.

```
public string CreateMetadataCode(string MetadataType, string modelName,
string entityName, string AttributeName, string strMemType)
{
    MetadataGetRequest Request = new MetadataGetRequest();
    MetadataGetResponse Response = new MetadataGetResponse();

    //Limit the returned metadata to a single model, entity,
    //and/or attribute when provided
    Request.SearchCriteria = new MetadataSearchCriteria();
    Request.SearchCriteria.Models = new Collection<Identifier>();
    Request.SearchCriteria.Models.Add(new Identifier {
    Name = modelName });
    if (entityName != null)
    {
        Request.SearchCriteria.Entities = new Collection<Identifier>();
        Request.SearchCriteria.Entities.Add(new Identifier {
        Name = entityName });
    }
```

```
        if (AttributeName != null)
        {
            Request.SearchCriteria.Attributes =
            new Collection<Identifier>();
            Request.SearchCriteria.Attributes.Add(new Identifier {
            Name = AttributeName });
        }

        //Set Result options to load all data for the required type
        Request.ResultOptions = new MetadataResultOptions();

        //Only identifiers are required for this operation
        Request.ResultOptions.Models = ResultType.Identifiers;
        Request.ResultOptions.Entities = ResultType.Identifiers;
        Request.ResultOptions.Attributes = ResultType.Identifiers;

        Response = mds_Proxy.MetadataGet(Request);

        switch (MetadataType)
        {
        case "Model":
        //Models are just the internal id for the model
        return Response.Metadata.Models[0].Identifier.InternalId.ToString();

        case "Entity":
        //Entities are a combination of internal ids for the model and
entity
        return Response.Metadata.Models[0].Identifier.InternalId.ToString()
+ "_" + Response.Metadata.Entities[0].Identifier.InternalId.ToString();

        case "Attribute":
        //The standard part of the base attribute code is
        //model and entity internal ids

        string BaseCode =
        Response.Metadata.Models[0].Identifier.InternalId.ToString()
+ "_" + Response.Metadata.Entities[0].Identifier.InternalId.ToString();

        //The attributes, Name and Code, are in the metadata
        //attribute code
        if (AttributeName == "Name" | AttributeName == "Code")
            {
            string AttrCode = BaseCode + "_" + AttributeName
            + "_" + strMemType;
            return AttrCode;
            }
                else
            {

            //otherwise they use the attribute internal id and
            //the integer for the membertype
            string AttrCode = BaseCode + "_" +
            Response.Metadata.Attributes[0].Identifier.InternalId.ToString()
              + "_" + strMemType;
```

```
                    return AttrCode;
            }
        };
        return "MetadataType Not Found";
    }
```

Getting Metadata for a Model, Entity, or Attribute

Pulling descriptive metadata from MDS requires using the EntityMembersGet
operation. Since all descriptive metadata is stored in the Metadata model in one of five
system entities, these are the entities to pull data from, using a valid search term to
limit the results to the specific metadata you are interested in:

```
public MDS_WS.EntityMembers GetMetaData(string modelName, string
entityName, string attributeName, string MetadataType)
{
    EntityMembersGetRequest Request = new EntityMembersGetRequest();
    EntityMembersGetResponse Response = new EntityMembersGetResponse();

    //Create all required Search Criteria Objects
    Request.MembersGetCriteria = new EntityMembersGetCriteria();

    //data must be returned from the Metadata model and the entity
    //for the specific metadata type
    Request.MembersGetCriteria.ModelId = new Identifier
    { Name = "MetaData" };
    switch (MetadataType)
    {
        case "Model":
            Request.MembersGetCriteria.EntityId = new Identifier {
            Name = "Model MetaData Definition" };
            break;
        case "Entity":
            Request.MembersGetCriteria.EntityId = new Identifier {
            Name = "Entity MetaData Definition" };
            break;
        case "Attribute":
            Request.MembersGetCriteria.EntityId = new Identifier {
Name = "Attribute MetaData Definition" };
            break;
    };
    //Each of these criteria are for the Metadata model objects
```

```
//(this model cannot be versioned)
Request.MembersGetCriteria.VersionId = new Identifier {
Name = "Version 1" };
Request.MembersGetCriteria.MemberType = MemberType.Leaf;
Request.MembersGetCriteria.MemberReturnOption =
MemberReturnOption.Data;

//Use the helper class to build the MetadataCode
string strmcode = CreateMetadataCode(MetadataType, modelName,
entityName, attributeName, "1");

//The search term can hold multiple filters but for now let's
//pass the code
Request.MembersGetCriteria.SearchTerm = "Code = '" + strmcode + "'";
//Pass the request to the proxy
Response = mds_Proxy.EntityMembersGet(Request);

return Response.EntityMembers;
}
```

Summary

Many times you may want to add additional descriptions to your master data objects. These descriptions can help provide users with context for an entity or attribute. Metadata entities can be appended to any type of attribute, but all structural objects of that type will have access to those attributes. The five main entities in the Metadata model cannot be deleted because they are system objects and their members will be created automatically as new models, entities, attributes, attribute groups, or hierarchies are created in the system. In the next chapter we will discuss the different ways that you can secure your models.

Chapter 11

Implementing Security

In This Chapter

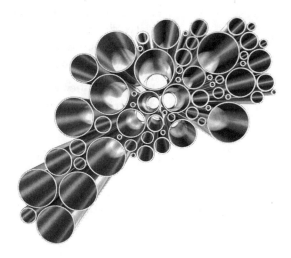

B y the time you are ready to implement security, most of the functionality in MDS has been enabled. Models have been built and refined, rules have been written, and the application has been integrated into your organization. In order to deploy MDS, everyone needs access to the application. While transaction management can provide some accountability, limiting access based on needs and roles ensures that users are unable to change data without authorization. Limiting the number of models and functions available to users can also help them focus more quickly on the data they need. The ability to provide specific data access within the MDS system is the single most important feature of the application. The focused security access provided by MDS empowers business users and frees the IT organization to manage the overall process, not maintain the individual data points.

In this chapter we provide an overview of the security framework in Master Data Services. We discuss the process of managing user and group permissions and explain the highly customized access that can be granted. The rest of the chapter drills into each level of security by showing how permissions can be applied to your data.

Security Overview

MDS security is broken into three distinct areas:

- ▶ **Functional security** Corresponds to each of the five functional areas displayed on the home page of the Master Data Manager web application. Most users need access only to the Explorer functional area of the web UI. All other functional areas are available only to administrators.

- ▶ **Model object security** Provides access control to attributes, based on the model objects within the MDS architecture. For example, you can set permissions on an entity, which determines permissions for all attributes for the entity. Or you can set permissions on a single attribute, which affects that attribute only. Model object security is required; without it, a user cannot perform any tasks in MDS.

- ▶ **Hierarchy member security** Provides the most granular level of security, and is optional. It is used to grant access to specific members, based on their location in a hierarchy.

Model object permissions (which apply to attributes) and hierarchy member permissions (which apply to members) are combined to determine the exact level of security for every attribute value. Figure 11-1 shows how attribute and member permissions intersect so that security can be determined for an individual attribute value.

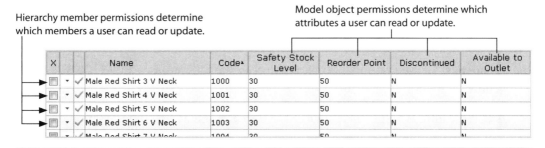

Hierarchy member permissions determine which members a user can read or update.

Model object permissions determine which attributes a user can read or update.

X			Name	Code▲	Safety Stock Level	Reorder Point	Discontinued	Available to Outlet
☐	▼	✓	Male Red Shirt 3 V Neck	1000	30	50	N	N
☐	▼	✓	Male Red Shirt 4 V Neck	1001	30	50	N	N
☐	▼	✓	Male Red Shirt 5 V Neck	1002	30	50	N	N
☐	▼	✓	Male Red Shirt 6 V Neck	1003	30	50	N	N
☐	▼	✓	Male Red Shirt 7 V Neck	1004	30	50	N	N

Figure 11-1   *Model object and hierarchy member permissions are combined to determine permissions for every attribute value.*

Users and Groups

MDS relies on Active Directory for user and group authentication. While all security permissions are stored in the MDS database, no passwords or group memberships are managed in MDS.

To keep security as simple as possible, you should do the following:

▶ Create either Active Directory or local groups and add either Active Directory or local users to those groups.

▶ Assign security in MDS to these groups, rather than to individual users.

▶ If you decide to assign security to a user, don't also assign security to groups that the user is a member of. While MDS has rules for determining which permissions take effect, security becomes more complicated when you do this.

Before you begin working with security, you should take some time to determine which groups your users might be part of, and which attributes or members those groups might need access to. The following list should give you a general idea of the groups that Main Street Clothing Company might use. Some of the examples in this chapter show how you would assign permissions like these.

▶ **Product Administrators**   This group will have permission to all functional areas and to take any action available for the Product model. This includes changing the model structure and modifying all members, among many other things.

▶ **Finance Administrators**   This group will have the same type of permission as the Product Administrators, but for the Finance model.

- ▶ **Purchasing** This group will be able to update the Cost attribute for all products.
- ▶ **Warehouse** This group will be able to update the attributes on the Logistics tab only.
- ▶ **Logistics** This group will be able to update the Safety Stock Level, Reorder Point, and Discontinued attributes. All other attributes will be read-only.

All of these groups will be able to access MDS after being assigned functional area and model object permissions. Main Street might also assign hierarchy member permissions to a few select members of the Purchasing group. These users should be able to view products for only the manufacturers they are responsible for.

Even though we recommend that you assign permissions to groups, for the rest of this chapter we'll refer to permissions that users receive, because at the end of the day, groups wouldn't mean anything if users weren't in them. Users are ultimately the ones who will access the data.

Procedure: How to Add a Group

After you've created your groups either locally or on the domain, you can add the group to the web UI by completing the following steps:

NOTE

Adding a group to the web UI does not give the users in the group permission to access models or data. It simply adds the group to a list, so that you can start to assign permissions.

1. On the Master Data Manager home page, click User and Group Permissions. The administrator account you specified in Configuration Manager when you set up MDS is shown in the Users list; for more information about administrators, see the following section.
2. On the menu bar, click Manage Groups.
3. Click the Add groups button.

4. In the Groups field, type the name of the group in the format Domain\
   GroupName or Computer\GroupName.

5. Click OK.

Now that the group is displayed in the list, you can continue with assigning
functional and model object permissions, which are described in upcoming sections.
If you need to add a user instead of a group, click Manage Users on the menu bar and
then click Add users.

NOTE

When you use groups, the users in the group aren't displayed in the list of users until after they have logged in.

Administrators

In MDS there are two types of administrators:

► The system administrator you specified in the Administrator Account field when
  creating the MDS database. This user has full control over all models and data.
  When new models are created, this user automatically has access. This user also
  has permission to access all functional areas of the web UI. To change this user,
  you must run a stored procedure in the database. See "Procedure: How to Change
  the Administrator Account" for more information.

► A model administrator who is manually assigned Update permission to a model,
  and no other model object or hierarchy member permissions. This user has full
  control over the model he or she has Update permission to. Model administrators
  do not necessarily have permission to access all functional areas of the application.
  For example, a model administrator might be responsible for integration only.
  However, they can perform all tasks in whichever functional area they have
  permission to access.

All model administrators with access to the User and Group Permissions functional area can assign permissions for other users. Keep this in mind when you're assigning someone permission to update a model.

In the following sections we explain how to manually assign the permissions that turn any MDS user into an administrator.

Procedure: How to Change the Administrator Account

When you created your database, you specified an administrator account. This user has access to everything, including any sensitive data you may be storing. If you want to change this user, complete the following steps:

CAUTION

This procedure deletes the former administrator's account from MDS.

1. On the Master Data Manager home page, click User and Group Permissions.
2. Add the new administrator to the list of users by clicking the Add user button.
3. Open SQL Server Management Studio and connect to your MDS database.
4. In the table mdm.tblUser, find the user you just added and copy the value listed in the SID column.
5. Create the following query:

```
EXEC [MDS_database].[mdm].[udpSecuritySetAdministrator]
@UserName='DOMAIN\user',
     @SID = 'SID', @PromoteNonAdmin = 1
```

6. Replace *MDS_database* with the MDS database name, *DOMAIN\user* with the new administrator's username, and *SID* with the value you copied.
7. Run the query.

This user now has permission to take all actions on all models and members. The former administrator is deleted from the list of MDS users. Note that if the former administrator was a member of a group that has security permissions, the user retains the permissions assigned to the group. You must remove the administrator from the local or domain group to fully remove his or her privileges.

Testing Permissions

As you begin assigning permissions to groups, you'll quickly realize that it would be great to log in as the user and confirm that they have the access you intended them to have. You can do this by creating a test user or group and assigning permissions to it. Then you can access the Master Data Manager web application by using the credentials of the test user and view the data that the user views.

To have Internet Explorer prompt you for credentials when you open an intranet site like Master Data Manager, you can change IE's security settings. Open IE and choose Tools | Internet Options. On the Security tab, ensure that Local intranet is selected and click the Custom level button. Scroll to the bottom, and in the User Authentication section, click the "Prompt for user name and password" option.

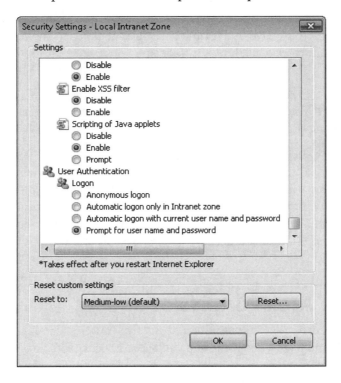

Now when you open a new browser, you are prompted for credentials.

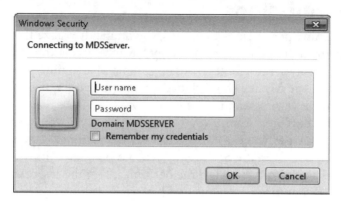

After you enter the credentials of your test user, you can confirm that they have the access you expect them to have. Each time you make changes to the test user's security, you should close and reopen the browser to ensure you're viewing the latest changes.

NOTE

You will learn later in this chapter that hierarchy member permissions are not applied immediately. Keep this in mind when testing security.

If you are using IE 8, another setting to change before you start working with permissions is Compatibility View, which you should turn off. To do so, click Tools | Compatibility View. This makes the User and Group Permissions functional area work better. However, when you open the browser by using the test user's credentials and want to view data in the Explorer functional area, you should turn Compatibility View back on.

Functional Area Permissions

Functional area security determines which of the five functional areas on the Master Data Manager home page a user or group can access. Security at this level is either permitted or denied. If permission to access a specific functional area is denied, the area is not displayed in the web UI and related web service operations are denied.

The Explorer functional area is where users manage data. When you assign access to Explorer, you must assign access to specific model objects, so the user gets access to a specific set of data. When you assign access to any of the other functional areas, the user must have access to the entire model (on the Models tab) in order to use those areas. Without this access, the user can open the functional areas but no models are displayed. This is how MDS handles permission for administrators.

Procedure: How to Assign Functional Area Permissions

To assign functional area permissions, complete the following steps:

1. On the Master Data Manager home page, click User and Group Permissions.
2. On the menu bar, click Manage Groups.
3. To the left of the group you want to edit, click the down arrow.
4. On the submenu, click Edit | Functions.

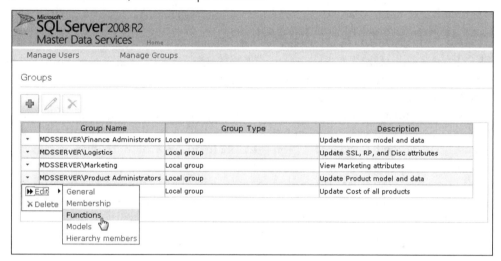

5. At the top of the page, click the Edit button.

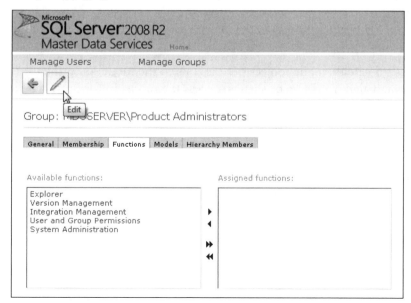

6. From the Available functions list, select the functional areas you want the user to have access to.

7. Click the arrows to add functional areas to the Assigned functions list.

8. Click the "Save and continue" button to go to the Models tab, where you will set model object permissions.

At this point, the users in the group cannot do anything in MDS. If they open the web UI, they will see the functional areas but will not see models displayed either on the home page or in any of the functional areas.

Model Object Permissions

Model object permissions, assigned on the Models tab, are required. Users cannot view any models or data if they do not have model object permissions.

When you give users permission to model objects, you are giving them the ability to edit attributes for members, based on the object you select. For example, if you set Update permission on the Product entity, all attributes for all Product members (leaf and consolidated) can be updated. If you set Update on the Color attribute of the Product entity, only the Color attribute can be updated.

In addition to giving a user the ability to update attribute values, if you assign Update model object permissions to a model, entity, or to the word "Leaf" or "Consolidated," the user can also create and delete members. If permissions are assigned at a lower level, the user cannot create and delete members.

NOTE

Permissions automatically cascade to all child objects within the current model unless permissions are assigned at a lower level. You do not need to explicitly set permission on every object.

If you assign Update model object permissions to the model only, the user is an administrator, which means he or she can access the model in functional areas other than just Explorer.

Quick Facts About Model Object Permissions

Things to remember about model object permissions include the following:

▶ They are required.

▶ They determine which attributes a user can view or update (as opposed to which members).

▶ They apply to all lower-level objects unless another permission is explicitly assigned.

▶ Update permission to Leaf or Consolidated model objects and above gives users the ability to create and delete members.

▶ Update permission at the model level only makes the user an administrator.

Best Practice for Model Object Permissions

There are many different model objects you can assign permission to. Giving access to specific models, entities, or attributes should fulfill most of your security needs. Before you assign model object permissions to objects other than these (derived or explicit hierarchies, attribute groups), take a moment to determine if entity or attribute permissions would meet your needs. When you assign model object permissions to other object types, security begins to overlap and permissions become more complicated.

Procedure: How to Assign Model Object Permissions

To assign model object permissions, complete the following steps:

1. On the Master Data Manager home page, click User and Group Permissions.
2. On the menu bar, click Manage Groups. In this example, we're going to update the Finance Administrators group.
3. To the left of the group you want to edit, click the down arrow.

4. On the submenu, click Edit | Models.

5. At the top of the page, click the Edit button.

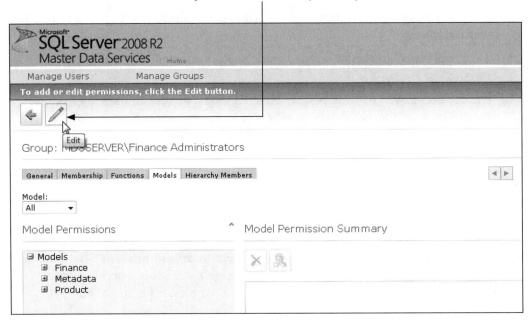

Ensure you click Edit before you do anything else.
Otherwise you won't be able to save your changes.

6. Optional. In the Model list, select the model you want to view. In this case we'll select Finance.

7. Expand and collapse nodes in the tree until you see the object you want to give permission to.

8. Right-click the object you want to give permission to, and from the menu that's displayed, click Update, Read-only, or Deny. In this example, we're going to right-click the Finance model and choose Update.

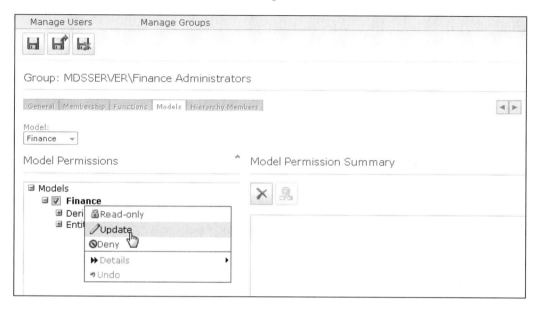

9. Click Save. If you intend to assign hierarchy member permissions, you can click the "Save and continue" button.

The Model Permission Summary grid is populated with the permissions you've assigned.

NOTE

You do not have to explicitly deny access to model objects you don't want users to see. Permissions cascade, so the user is implicitly denied access to any object that doesn't inherit permissions.

This was the simplest example, where you assign Update to the model and no other permissions. In this case, all of the users in the group can access all Finance members, as well as access the Finance model in any functional areas they have permission to access.

Procedure: How to Delete Model Object Permissions

Before you can test other permissions, you may want to delete those you already assigned. To do so, complete the following steps:

1. On the Models tab, in the Model Permission Summary grid, click the down arrow for the row that shows permissions you want to delete.

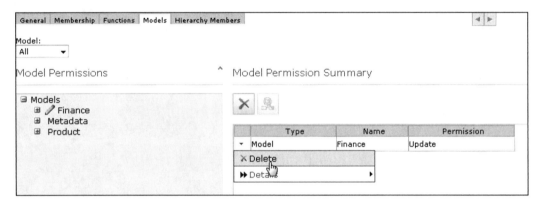

2. From the submenu that's displayed, click Delete.
3. In the confirmation dialog box, click OK.

The page refreshes and the permissions are deleted.

Now let's go through all of the possible model object permissions you can assign.

Access to Entities

When you assign Update permission to an entity, the user can create and delete members as well as update all attributes for the entity (assuming no other permissions are assigned). When you assign Read permission, the user can view all attributes for the entity.

Here is what Update permission to a single entity (in this case, the Line entity) looks like after you save:

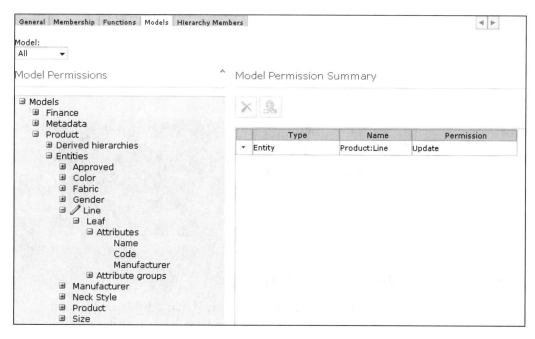

And here is what Update access to the Line entity looks like in Explorer:

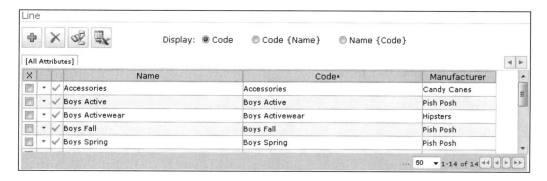

As you can see, the user can update all attributes for all members in the Line entity. The user can also create and delete members when you assign permissions at this level. If the Line entity had hierarchies or collections, they would also be editable. When you have permission to read or update an entity, you can read or update any explicit hierarchies and collections for the entity.

On the menu bar, if you choose Entities | Manufacturer, you'll notice that you have Read-only permission to any domain-based attributes for the entity. You can't do anything with these members—you can't create or delete this entity's members—but you can view them.

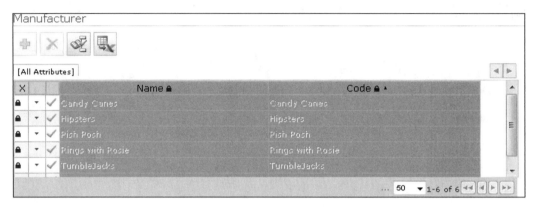

Access to Leaf Member Attributes

In the tree, you can assign permission to the word "Leaf" that's displayed beneath an entity. This is a shortcut for giving permission to all attributes for all leaf-level members. If you assign Update permission, the user can create and delete members, just as if you assigned permissions to the entity itself.

NOTE

If an entity does not have explicit hierarchies enabled, there is no difference between assigning permission to an entity and assigning permission to Leaf.

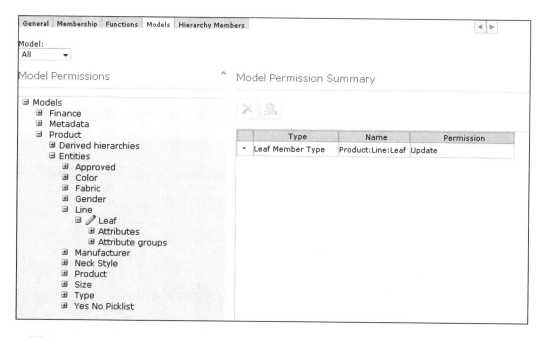

If the entity is enabled for explicit hierarchies, use this permission to give a user access to update attributes for all leaf members or for all consolidated members. Otherwise, this permission does not need to be used, because you can assign permission directly to the entity.

Access to Individual Attributes

When you assign Update or Read permission to a specific attribute, the user can update or read that attribute. It doesn't matter if the attribute is domain-based; the user is able to update the attribute value for the entity that the attribute applies to only.

In this example, the user has Update permission to the Product entity's Cost attribute:

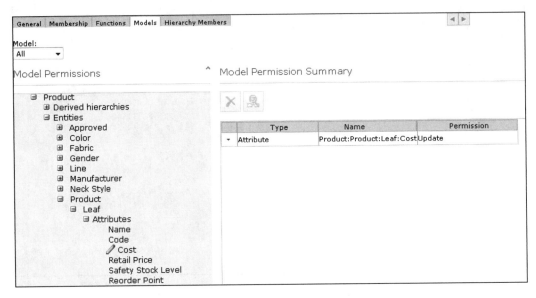

When the user accesses the Product entity in Explorer, the Name and Code attributes are read-only but the Cost attribute can be updated.

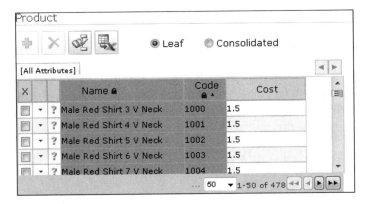

Note that when you assign permission to an attribute, the user can't create or delete members. Also note that if the attribute is domain-based, the user can't make changes to the entity the attribute is based on. For example, if a user has permission to update the Color attribute for the Product entity, the user can change a product's color, but the user cannot open the Color entity itself and change the color name from Blue to Light Blue.

If you wanted the user to be able to do both these things, you would choose these permissions:

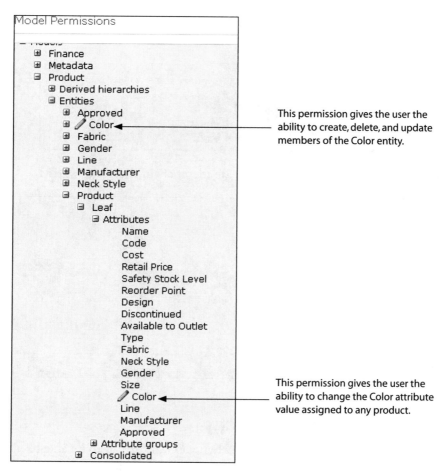

This permission gives the user the ability to create, delete, and update members of the Color entity.

This permission gives the user the ability to change the Color attribute value assigned to any product.

In Explorer, you can view the results. The user can update the Color attribute for all products.

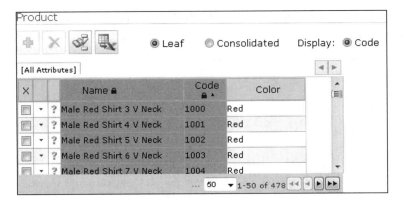

The user can also create, delete, and update members of the Color entity.

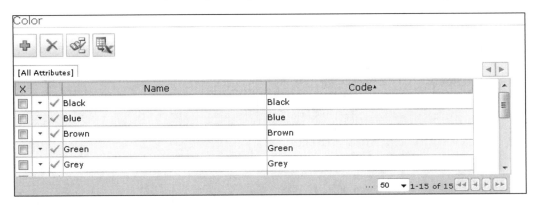

Access to an Explicit Hierarchy

Assign permission to an explicit hierarchy when you want a user to be able to move members in an explicit hierarchy but not create and delete members.

If you assign Update permission to an explicit hierarchy, the user can move members in the hierarchy. If you assign Read-only permission, the user can view the hierarchy but not make any changes.

In this example, the user is assigned Update permission to the Chart of Accounts explicit hierarchy:

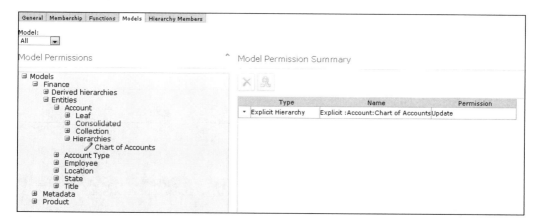

When you open Explorer to view the results of these permissions, you can open the hierarchy and move members in it. You can also view the members in the entity the hierarchy is for (in this case the Account entity), but you can't update attributes for these members.

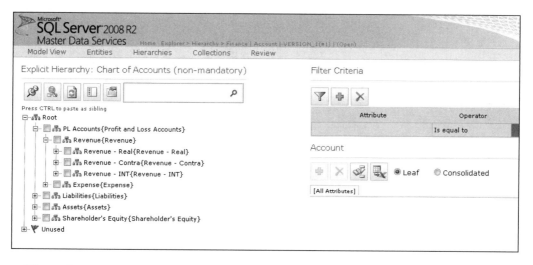

The only way to give a user permission to move members in an explicit hierarchy without giving the user the ability to create and delete members is by assigning permission to the explicit hierarchy. If the user has Update permission to an entity, the user can also view and update all explicit hierarchies for the entity.

Access to Collections

When you assign Update or Read permission to the Collection object, you are assigning access to all collections. You can't give permission to an individual collection—it is an "all or nothing" scenario.

If a user has Update permission, he or she can create, delete, and update collections. In this example, the user has permission to update collections for the Product entity:

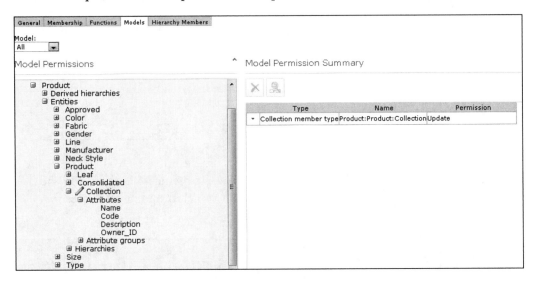

In Explorer, all collections for the Product entity are displayed, and the user can create and delete collections, as well as update collection attributes like Name, Code, Description, or Owner_ID.

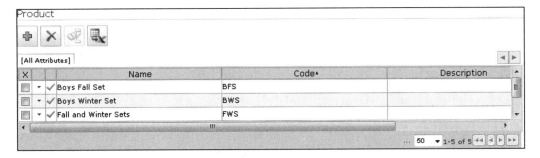

At this point, the user can delete members from the collection but can't add any members because the user doesn't have permission to other model objects. If the user had a minimum of Read-only permission to the Product entity, he or she could add members to the collection.

In User and Group Permissions, on the Models tab, you can give permission to attributes of collections, so you can lock down the description or names of all of your collections, for example. You can also set permission on attribute groups, just as you would with attribute groups that apply to entities. For more information, see the "Access to an Attribute Group" section a bit later in this chapter.

Access to Other Model Objects

The model objects described in this section can make your security story more complex. Assigning permission to these model objects can be useful in certain circumstances; just read the explanations thoroughly and test your permissions before you implement them in production.

If you have permissions already assigned to entities or attributes, assigning permissions to these objects can cause overlapping permissions that must be resolved to determine which permission takes effect. After we describe each type of access, we'll provide details about how these overlaps are resolved.

Access to a Derived Hierarchy

When you assign Update permission to a derived hierarchy, you are assigning permission to update the domain-based attributes that the hierarchy is based on. It's similar to assigning permission to the specific attributes, except that you can also update the hierarchy tree in Explorer.

In this example, the user is assigned permission to the hierarchy that groups products by Line and then groups lines by Manufacturer:

When you open Explorer with this user's credentials, you can update the Line attribute of the Product entity.

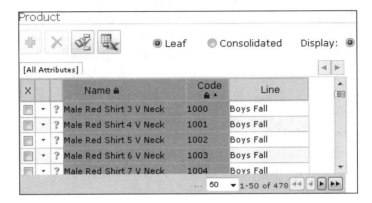

You can also update the Manufacturer attribute of the Line entity.

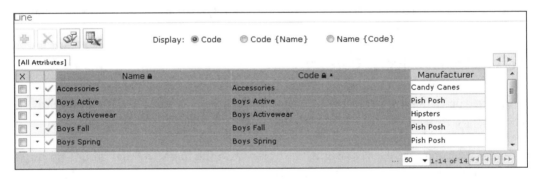

By updating either of those attributes, you change the location of a member in the hierarchy. For example, if you change the Line attribute value for member 1000, the member would be displayed under the new line in the hierarchy. You don't need to view the hierarchy to know that this change has taken place.

However, assigning permission to a derived hierarchy does allow the user to view the hierarchy structure and move members in the tree, rather than just updating attribute values.

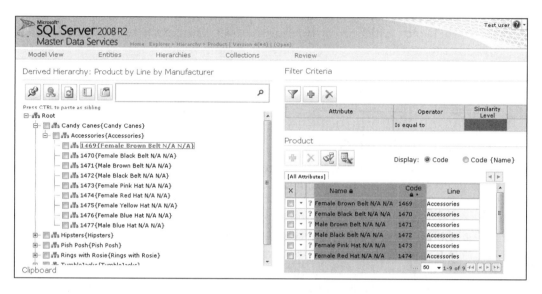

Although you can assign permissions to individual attributes, the user cannot work with the hierarchy structure unless you give him or her permission to the entity, model, or derived hierarchy model object.

Overlapping Objects   If you assign a user permission to an entity or attribute and it is different from the permission you assigned to the derived hierarchy object, you have overlapping permissions that must be resolved:

▶ If one entity or domain-based attribute from the hierarchy is assigned Deny permission, then the hierarchy is not displayed, no matter which permission is assigned to the derived hierarchy object.

▶ If one entity or domain-based attribute from the hierarchy is assigned Read-only permission, the entity or domain-based attribute is read-only when displayed in the hierarchy. If the entity or domain-based attribute is assigned Update permission, the entity or domain-based attribute can be updated in the hierarchy.

If multiple domain-based hierarchies contain the same attributes and you've assigned different permissions to each, overlapping permissions must also be resolved:

► If one of the hierarchies is assigned Deny permission, then that hierarchy is not displayed. If the entities or domain-based attributes from the hierarchy exist in any other hierarchies, those hierarchies are not displayed.

► If one of the hierarchies is assigned Read-only permission and another is assigned Update permission, then any attributes from the hierarchy assigned Update can be updated when they are displayed in the Read-only hierarchy.

Access to an Attribute Group

Permissions assigned to attribute groups can make security simple and effective. However, because multiple attribute groups can contain the same attributes, permissions can quickly become complicated.

When you assign permission to attribute groups, the Name and Code attributes are always Read-only and the user cannot create and delete members. It doesn't matter if you assign Update permission; Name and Code are always Read-only.

In this example, the user has Update permission to the Logistics attribute group and Read-only permission to Product Line. There are no attributes that are included in both groups.

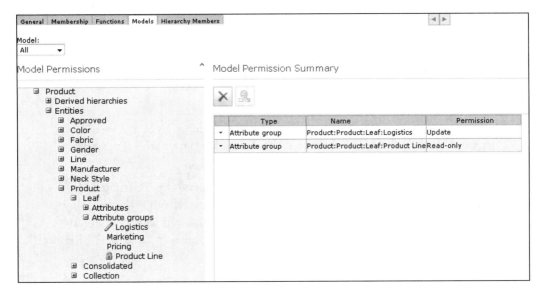

When you open Explorer with the user's credentials, you see that you can update all attributes on the Logistics tab.

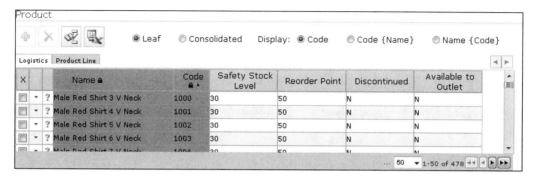

All attributes on the Product Line tab are Read-only.

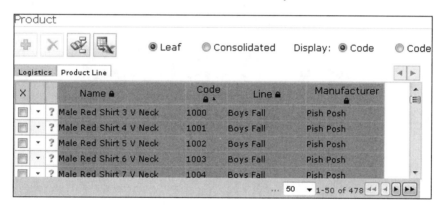

No other attribute groups are displayed.

Overlapping Objects   If the same attribute exists in multiple groups, you have overlapping permissions that must be resolved:

▶   If one group is assigned Update permission and another is assigned Read-only, the attribute can be updated in both groups (on both tabs).

▶   If one group is assigned Update or Read-only permission and another is assigned Deny, the attribute is not displayed on the tab that's assigned Update.

If the permission assigned to an attribute is different from the permission assigned to the attribute group the attribute belongs to, you must also resolve overlapping permissions:

► If an attribute from the attribute group is assigned Deny permission, then the attribute is not displayed in the attribute group.

► If an attribute from the attribute group is assigned Read-only permission, the attribute is read-only when displayed in the attribute group. If the attribute is assigned Update, the attribute can be updated when displayed in the attribute group.

Attribute Groups in System Administration   You may have noticed when you were creating attribute groups that users and groups were displayed on the Attribute Group Maintenance page. The Users and Groups nodes on this page are for viewing users and groups who have Update permission (users with Read-only permission are not displayed).

CAUTION

Do not attempt to edit users and groups on this page.

You should *not* use this page to try to administer security for attribute groups. It is not guaranteed to show what's been set in the User and Group Permissions functional area, and updates you make on this page may not be reflected in the user's security.

Deny Permissions

You'll notice that when you right-click a model object, Deny is listed on the submenu. In most cases you won't need to explicitly deny access to an object. Permissions cascade so that all lower-level objects inherit the assigned permissions. Objects that are at the same level or higher, and that don't have permissions explicitly assigned, are inherently denied.

For example, if you set Update permissions on the Product model but not on the Finance model, the user is denied permission to access the Finance model. You don't have to explicitly deny access. Or for example, if you set Update permissions on the Color entity but not on any other entities, permission to access all other entities is denied.

These same rules apply to hierarchies on the Hierarchy Members tab. Hierarchy nodes at the same level and higher are inherently denied as soon as any Read-only or Update permissions are set. All other permissions cascade down the hierarchy.

Navigational Access

Every user needs a certain degree of access to the system in order to open the members and attributes he or she has permission to. For example, if a user has permission to access three specific attributes, but not the model itself, the user can still view the list of models in the drop-down list on the home page. Users also have to be able to see the Name and Code attributes for the members so that they know what they are updating. This bare minimum required access is sometimes referred to as *navigational access*. We're not going to delve into the specifics of each model object, but you should know that when you give permissions to a user, you are also giving the user the navigational access required to work with the data they need.

Deleting Permissions

Earlier in this chapter, we showed you how to delete model object permissions. The procedure is the same for hierarchy member permissions. In the grid, click the down arrow next to the row with permissions you want to delete, and click Delete.

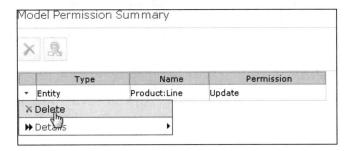

If you want to remove a user so that he or she no longer has MDS access, you need to complete two procedures. First, confirm the user's group memberships. Then, remove the user from the list.

To confirm the user's group memberships, complete the following steps:

1. On the Manage Users page, to the left of the user, click the down arrow.
2. On the submenu, click Edit | Membership. Note any groups the user is a member of.

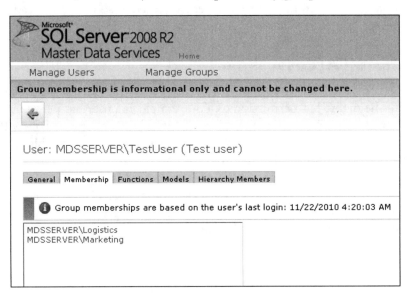

3. If the user is a member of multiple groups, go to the local or Active Directory group and remove the user from the group.

Now remove the user from the list:

1. On the Manage Users page, click the row of the user you want to delete.
2. Click the "Delete selected user" button.

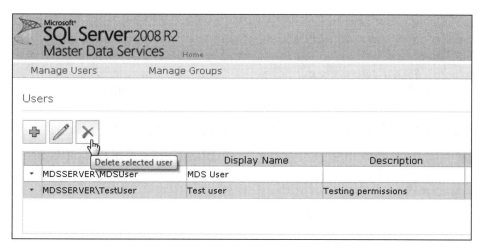

Both of these procedures are required to keep your list of users accurate. Otherwise you might end up with users in the list who don't truly have access.

Hierarchy Member Permissions

In an effort to provide the functional equivalent of row-level member security without providing all of the maintenance nightmares associated with it, MDS provides hierarchy member security. This type of security allows you to assign security to all the members in a node of a hierarchy. The same cascading feature that is found in model object security applies to hierarchy member security.

With MDS, you have the ability to set security on levels of either explicit or derived hierarchies. This powerful feature allows you to limit access to data within MDS on a number of axes simultaneously (one axis from model object permissions, and a second axis from hierarchy member permissions, as was shown in Figure 11-1 at the beginning of this chapter).

Because you may have thousands or millions of members, hierarchy member permissions are applied only periodically. In the MDS database, in tblSystemSetting, the SecurityMemberProcessInterval determines how often these permissions are applied. The default setting is 3600 seconds, or 60 minutes, but you can update this to be more frequent. Note that even if you set it to every 10 seconds, you must wait

60 minutes for the 10-second intervals to start. Be aware that 10 seconds may not be enough time to fully apply permissions to all of your members.

You can also run a stored procedure to apply hierarchy member permissions immediately. Details are provided in the "Procedure: How to Apply Hierarchy Member Security Immediately" section a bit later in this chapter.

Hierarchy member permissions are based on a version of a model and are copied forward on subsequent models. So if you set permissions on a hierarchy in Version 3, those permissions don't exist in Version 2, but they will exist in copies of Version 3. Be sure to consider that your users might have unintended access to data in earlier versions of your model if you set hierarchy member permissions in later models.

Quick Facts About Hierarchy Member Permissions

Things to remember about hierarchy member permissions include the following:

- ▶ They are optional.

- ▶ They determine which members a user can view or update (as opposed to which attributes).

- ▶ They apply to all lower-level members unless another permission is explicitly assigned.

- ▶ They are not applied immediately, unlike model object permissions. You must wait until a specific interval of time has passed. This interval is based on SecurityMemberProcessInterval in tblSystemSetting.

- ▶ You can run a stored procedure to force them to be applied immediately.

- ▶ They are version specific. You set them for a specific version and they apply to that version and all future copies of that version. (They do not apply to any previous versions.)

- ▶ You should not set permissions on explicit cap or recursive hierarchies. Security for these hierarchies is not supported.

Procedure: How to Assign Hierarchy Member Permissions

To assign hierarchy member permissions to a group, complete the following steps:

1. On the Master Data Manager home page, click User and Group Permissions.
2. On the menu bar, click Manage Groups.

3. To the left of the group you want to edit, click the down arrow.

4. On the submenu, click Edit | Hierarchy Members.

5. From the lists, choose the model, version, and hierarchy you need. Keep in mind that permissions will apply to the version you select and later copies of that version.

6. At the top of the page, click the Edit button.

7. Expand and collapse nodes of the hierarchy as needed, or search for a specific node. Notice that individual members are not displayed. You are setting permissions for all members that are in one or more specific nodes.

8. Right-click the hierarchy node you want to give permission to, and from the menu that's displayed, click Update, Read-only, or Deny.

9. Click Save.

Because the Main Street Clothing Company's models are fairly limited, the following example may not necessarily have real-world use, but it should help you understand how these permissions work.

In this example, the user has Update permission to two attributes for the Product entity: Color and Design.

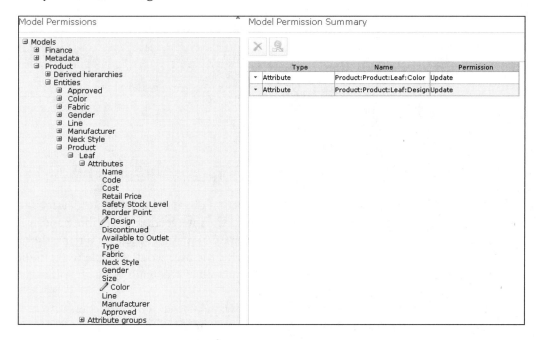

On the Hierarchy Members tab, the user is assigned Update permission to the Female node. Permission to access all other nodes at the same level or higher is implicitly denied.

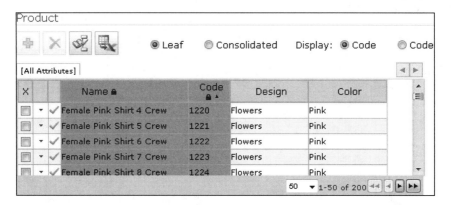

After the hierarchy member permissions interval has passed and permissions are applied, the user can update only the Color and Design attributes for the Female members. The Male members (those with Male as the Gender) are not displayed.

In this example, you can start to see the intersection of model object and hierarchy member permissions. (You can also think of this as the intersection of attribute and member permissions.) If you were to keep this hierarchy member security but, on the Models tab, give Update access to the Product entity, the user would be able to see these same 200 members in hierarchies and collections as well as the main grid. The other 200+ Male members would always remain hidden.

Because hierarchy member permissions must always be used with model object permissions, there are rules for how these permissions are combined. For more information, see "Determining Which Permissions Apply" a bit later in this chapter.

Overlapping Hierarchies

If you've assigned hierarchy member permissions to more than one hierarchy, there is a good chance that you've assigned overlapping permissions to some members. If you do assign permissions to multiple hierarchies and those hierarchies contain the same members, the following rules apply:

▶ If one hierarchy node is assigned Update permission and another is assigned Read-only permission, then the members in the node are Read-only.

▶ If one hierarchy node is assigned Update or Read-only permission and another node is assigned Deny permission, then the members in the node are not displayed.

Procedure: How to Apply Hierarchy Member Security Immediately

While it is generally discouraged to manipulate MDS at the database level, a number of functions in MDS are only available through the use of stored procedures. These stored procedures require specific database access to run successfully.

One of these stored procedures is the one that you run to apply hierarchy member security immediately. If you are testing or don't have too many members, you can use this procedure to quickly see the results of the permissions you've assigned.

To apply hierarchy member security immediately, open SQL Server Management Studio and connect to the instance that is running MDS. Create the following query:

```
USE [MDS_database];
GO


DECLARE @Model_ID INT;
SELECT @Model_ID = ID FROM mdm.tblModel WHERE [Name] = N'Model_Name';
EXEC [mdm].[udpSecurityMemberProcessRebuildModel] @Model_ID=@Model_ID,
@ProcessNow=1;
GO
```

Replace *MDS_database* with the name of your server, and replace *Model_Name* with the name of your model. When you run the query, hierarchy member security is applied.

Determining Which Permissions Apply

Permissions are applied in the following order of operations:

▶ **Permissions for each attribute are determined (model object permissions)** Permissions assigned on the Models tab cascade down the tree structure and are applied to all objects. In this way, permissions for every attribute in the model are determined.

▶ **Permissions for each member are determined (hierarchy member permissions)** Permissions assigned on the Hierarchy Members tab also cascade down the tree. In this way, permissions for all members in the model are determined.

▶ **Attribute and member permissions are combined** Permissions are combined and access to each individual attribute value is determined.

This workflow is shown in Figure 11-2.

Combining Permissions

When attribute permissions (assigned on the Models tab) are combined with member permissions (assigned on the Hierarchy Members tab), the following rules are applied:

▶ Read-only overrides Update.

▶ Deny overrides all other permissions.

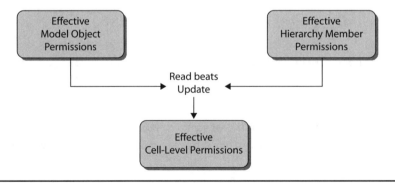

Figure 11-2 *Permissions workflow, showing the combination of model object and hierarchy member permissions*

The following example shows how this works. First, on the Models tab, assign Update to the Product entity's Color attribute. This gives the user the ability to update the Color attribute for all members.

Then, on the Hierarchy Members tab, open the Product by Gender hierarchy and assign Update to the Female node and Read-only to the Male node.

If you apply the rules, all attributes for all members in the Male node should be Read-only. Because Read-only overrides Update, the user cannot update the Color for the Male members.

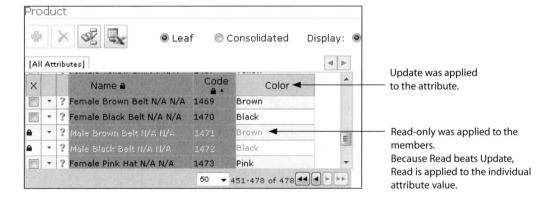

Combining Users and Groups

We've mentioned many times that life gets confusing when you assign permissions both to a user and to the groups the user is a member of. But if you decide you really need to do this, the web UI helps you determine which permissions are applied.

Whenever you open a user account, on both the Models and the Hierarchy Members tabs, you can select Effective from the Permissions list to refresh the web UI and display the results of any overlapping user and group permissions.

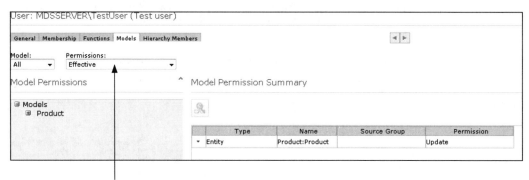

Select Effective to compare user and group
permissions and determine which take effect.

This same list is not available when you're viewing groups; it's available only when you're viewing users.

If you want to understand how the combination of user and group permissions works in more detail, read on and we will attempt to clarify it for you.

The rules that apply when combining user and group permissions are

- ► Deny overrides all other permissions.
- ► Update overrides Read-only.

This means that if the user is assigned Read-only permission but the group is assigned Update permission, the applied permission is Update. MDS makes the assumption that if there is an overlap, the least restrictive permission should win. For example, if Bob is covering for a coworker while that person is out, and you add Bob to the other group temporarily, Bob keeps his existing permissions but also gains those of his coworker.

Figure 11-3 shows the additional complexity that occurs when you have overlapping users and groups as part of the security workflow.

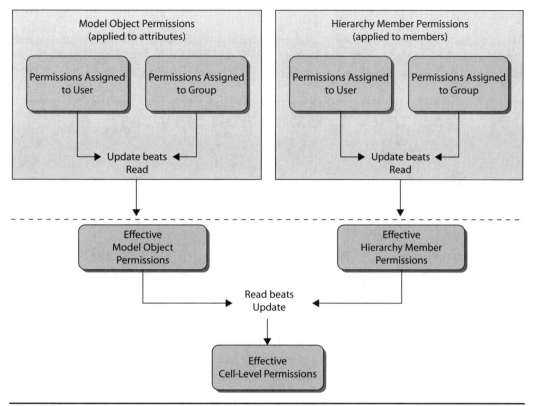

Figure 11-3   *The addition of overlapping users and groups to the security workflow*

A Matter of Distance

Unfortunately, overlapping users and groups is slightly more complex than these simple rules and Figure 11-3 can show. The cascading inheritance in the tree also plays a part. If two or more objects have permissions assigned to them, the "Update beats Read" rule applies. However, if an object has a different permission assigned and it's closer than the permission from the other user or group, then the closer permission applies instead.

For example, if a user has Read and a group has Update to the same model object, then Update is applied. However, if a user is assigned Update to an entity and a group is assigned Read-only to an attribute (a lower level than entity), then Update applies for the entity but the attribute is Read-only.

These same rules apply to the Hierarchy Members tab.

Thankfully, the UI does this calculation for you. On both the Models and Hierarchy Members tabs, click Effective in the Permissions list to display a user's effective permissions.

Overlapping Functional Areas

Users and groups can also have overlapping permissions to functional areas. Functional area permissions are additive: if a user has permission to Explorer and a group has permission to Version Management, then the user has permission for both areas.

Setting Security by Using Web Services

All security in Master Data Services is managed using two web service objects:

▶ **SecurityPrincipal** Security principals correspond to Active Directory users or groups. While users may be in a group that exists in MDS, users will be managed in MDS only after they have logged on to the system through the web UI or web service (or some custom component built on the web service).

▶ **SecurityPrivilege** All distinct permissions within MDS are stored and managed as privileges. In most cases, only explicitly set permissions will be returned from the web service.

Retrieving Users and Groups

The GetSecurityPrincipals operation, shown next, returns all current users and groups that match the criteria passed into the request. Only users that have used MDS through either the web service or web UI will be returned, even if they are members of an Active Directory group with access to MDS.

NOTE

You must be a model administrator to perform this operation.

```
public OperationResult GetSecurityPrincipals()
{

    //Create Request, Response, and Criteria Objects
    SecurityPrincipalsGetRequest Request =
    new SecurityPrincipalsGetRequest();
    SecurityPrincipalsGetResponse Response =
    new SecurityPrincipalsGetResponse();
    Request.Criteria = new SecurityPrincipalsCriteria();

    //Sets the type of principals to return either Group or User
    Request.Criteria.Type = PrincipalType.UserAccount;
```

```
    Request.Criteria.ResultType = ResultType.Details;
    Request.Criteria.All = true;

    //This sets the result type for each type of security
    //Three Options (Details, Identifiers, and None)
    Request.Criteria.FunctionPrivilege = ResultType.Details;
    Request.Criteria.ModelPrivilege = ResultType.Details;
    Request.Criteria.HierarchyMemberPrivilege = ResultType.Details;
    Response = mds_Proxy.SecurityPrincipalsGet(Request);
    return Response.OperationResult;
}
```

Retrieving User or Group Permissions

The GetSecurityPrivilege operation returns privileges matching the criteria provided.
These privileges will be related to the user or group that the permission is provided to.

```
public OperationResult GetSecurityPrivilege(
Identifier PrincipalID, PrincipalType PType)
{

    //Create Request, Response, and Criteria Objects
    SecurityPrivilegesGetRequest Request =
    new SecurityPrivilegesGetRequest();
    SecurityPrivilegesGetResponse Response =
    new SecurityPrivilegesGetResponse();
    Request.Criteria = new SecurityPrivilegesGetCriteria();

    //Set PrincipalID and Type passed into the procedure
    Request.Criteria.FunctionPrivilegesCriteria =
    new FunctionPrivilegesCriteria();
    Request.Criteria.FunctionPrivilegesCriteria.PrincipalId =
    PrincipalID;
    Request.Criteria.FunctionPrivilegesCriteria.PrincipalType =
    PType;
    Response = mds_Proxy.SecurityPrivilegesGet(Request);
    return Response.OperationResult;
}
```

Adding Users and Groups

While the CreateSecurityPrincipals operation includes "Create" in its name, it is really used to load preexisting Active Directory users or groups into MDS. This operation will also be used to update some user-specific properties that are stored directly in MDS.

```
public OperationResult CreateSecurityPrincipals()
{
    SecurityPrincipalsRequest Request =
    new SecurityPrincipalsRequest();
    Request.Principals = new SecurityPrincipals();

    // Create some user objects
    Collection<User> users = new Collection<User>();

    // Add each new AD user to the user or group collection
    users.Add(new User());

    //Create new Identifier for each user
    users[0].Identifier = new Identifier();
    users[0].Identifier.Name = "JDoe";
    users[0].DisplayName = "John Doe";
    users[0].EmailAddress = "Jdoe@someurl.com";
    users[0].EmailFormat = EmailFormat.HTML;
    users[0].SID = Guid.NewGuid().ToString();
    //Replace this Guid with the security ID from AD

    // Add each new AD user to the user or group collection
    users.Add(new User());

    //Create new Identifier for each user
    users[1].Identifier = new Identifier();
    users[1].Identifier.Name = "PPiper";
    users[1].DisplayName = "Peter Piper";
    users[1].EmailAddress = "PPiper@someurl.com";
    users[1].EmailFormat = EmailFormat.Text;
    users[1].SID = Guid.NewGuid().ToString();
    //Replace this Guid with the security ID from AD

    //Add user collections to request object
    Request.Principals.Users = users;
    SecurityCreateResponse Response =
    mds_Proxy.SecurityPrincipalsCreate(Request);
    return Response.OperationResult;
}
```

Assigning Permissions

All types of security privileges for users and groups can be created simultaneously with the CreateSecurityPrivileges operation. Multiple users or groups can be secured within the same operation as well.

```
public OperationResult CreateSecurityPrivileges
(User user, MemberIdentifier hierParentMemberID)
{
    SecurityPrivilegesRequest request =
    new SecurityPrivilegesRequest();
    request.Privileges = new SecurityPrivileges();

    // Create a functional privilege
    FunctionPrivilege fp = new FunctionPrivilege();
    fp.Function = FunctionalArea.Explorer;
    fp.Identifier = new Identifier();

    //Functional privileges only support boolean authorization
    fp.IsAuthorized = true;

    //Set the PrincipalType and ID for the principal assigned the
    //privilege
    fp.PrincipalType = PrincipalType.UserAccount;
    fp.PrincipalId = user.Identifier;

    //Add the function privilege to the privilege collection
    Collection<FunctionPrivilege> FunctionPrivileges = new
    Collection<FunctionPrivilege>();
    FunctionPrivileges.Add(fp);

    //Add collection to privilege request
    request.Privileges.FunctionPrivileges = FunctionPrivileges;

    //Create a model privilege
    ModelPrivilege mp = new ModelPrivilege();

    //Set the model permission object type,
    //support any type of object in MDS
    mp.ObjectType = ModelObjectType.Model;
    mp.ModelId = new Identifier { Name = "Product" };
    mp.ObjectId = mp.ModelId;
```

```
//Model permissions support Update, ReadOnly, Deny, and None
mp.Permission = Permission.Update;

//Set the PrincipalType and ID for the principal assigned the
//privilege
mp.PrincipalType = PrincipalType.UserAccount;
mp.PrincipalId = user.Identifier;

//Add the model privilege to the privilege collection
Collection<ModelPrivilege> ModelPrivileges = new
Collection<ModelPrivilege>();
ModelPrivileges.Add(mp);

//Add collection to privilege request
request.Privileges.ModelPrivileges = ModelPrivileges;

//Create a hierarchy member privilege
HierarchyMemberPrivilege hmp = new HierarchyMemberPrivilege();

//Set the HierarchyType and ID
hmp.HierarchyType = HierarchyType.Derived;
hmp.HierarchyId = new Identifier { Name = "Product"};

//Model permissions support Update, ReadOnly, Deny, and None
hmp.Permission = Permission.Update;
hmp.PrincipalId = user.Identifier;
hmp.PrincipalType = PrincipalType.UserAccount;
hmp.ModelId = new Identifier { Name = "Product" };
hmp.VersionId = new Identifier { Name = "Version_1" };
hmp.EntityId = new Identifier { Name = "Product" };
hmp.MemberId = hierParentMemberID;

//Set an identifier for the new permission
hmp.Identifier = new Identifier();

//Add hierarchy member privilege to the privilege collection
Collection<HierarchyMemberPrivilege> HierarchyMemberPrivileges =
new Collection<HierarchyMemberPrivilege>();
HierarchyMemberPrivileges.Add(hmp);
```

```
    //Add collection to privilege request
    request.Privileges.HierarchyMemberPrivileges =
    HierarchyMemberPrivileges;
    SecurityCreateResponse response =
    mds_Proxy.SecurityPrivilegesCreate(request);
    return response.OperationResult;
}
```

Summary

In this chapter, we explained the details of configuring security in MDS. We showed
the process for assigning model object and hierarchy member security, and how
the combination of the two determines cell-level security. We discussed model
administrators and how to create and update them. We gave best practices for assigning
security and talked about what happens when users belong to groups and security is
assigned to both. Finally, we showed how to use the web service to view and assign
permissions.

Chapter 12

Publishing Data to External Systems

In This Chapter

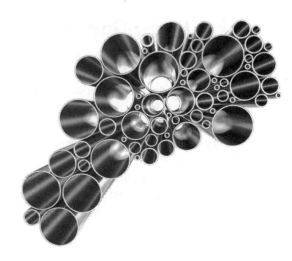

lthough the ability to manage data is an important feature of Master Data Services, the ability to export data to other systems in the enterprise is equally if not more important. MDS the export process by providing subscription views that you can create on any entity or derived hierarchy object within the MDS system.

In this chapter, we describe the different types of the export views that can be created and the format of each of these views. We discuss some tips and tricks for creating a proper view depending on the type of downstream system that will be loaded. We also provide an example of loading a downstream system from an export view we create. While Master Data Services provides no direct ETL features of any kind, the Integration Management functional area of the Master Data Manager web application (or "web UI") can facilitate your integration processes by providing a wide variety of views to assist in the loading of downstream systems.

Exporting Data to Subscribing Systems

Master Data Services can provide value for a project that keeps the data locked in its entities by providing process around the data management; however, to meet the operational or analytical needs of a master data management project, organizations need to transport stored data downstream to subscribing systems. To insulate organizations from the complex object model necessary to manage performance and the customization necessary within MDS, a subscription view layer was created.

You can create subscription views within the Integration Management functional area of the web UI, or by using the web service. The web service refers to these views as export views, but we'll use "subscription views" and "export views" interchangeably.

Subscription View Formats

The following table shows the available subscription view formats. When you create a subscription view, you have to choose which format you want. There are really two major types of subscription views within MDS: attribute views and hierarchy views. Attribute views display the data stored for leaf, consolidated, or collection members in an easily consumable tabular view. Hierarchy views provide relationship data for all types of relationships in MDS, whether explicit or derived hierarchies or collection members. Collection member relationships can only be displayed in a parent-child format. An additional view is available for derived and explicit hierarchies. It contains a row for each member and the parentage all the way to the top consolidation in the hierarchy.

View Format	Description of View
Leaf attributes	Shows leaf members and their associated attribute values
Consolidated attributes	Shows consolidated members and their associated attribute values
Collection attributes	Shows collection members and their associated attribute values
Collections	Shows collections and their members in a parent-child format
Explicit parent child	Shows explicit hierarchy structures for an entity in a parent-child format
Explicit levels	For the entity, shows all members in all explicit hierarchies in a level-based format
Derived parent child	Shows all derived hierarchy members in a parent-child format
Derived levels	Shows all derived hierarchy members in a level-based format

Common View Architecture

Many of the columns in Master Data Services' subscription views are identical across view types. The columns provide either context for the data displayed in the view or additional system information for the records contained in the view. Subscribing systems can use this information to update a subset of records based on validation status or last updated statistics.

Column	Description
VersionName	The version name for the current version being displayed. If this is a view based on the version name, this value will never change.
VersionNumber	The version number for the current version being displayed. If this is a view built on the version name, this value will never change.
VersionFlag	The current version flag for the displayed version. If a view is based on a version flag, then this column will remain constant and the VersionName and VersionNumber column values will change as the version flag is moved between versions.
EnterDateTime	The date and time the member was first entered into MDS.
EnterUserName	The user who initially entered the member into MDS.
EnterVersionNumber	The initial version this member was created in.
LastChgUserName	The user who last updated this member in MDS.
LastChgVersionNumber	The number of the version this member was last changed in.
ValidationStatus	The current validation status for the member. Validation status is discussed further in Chapter 9. Validation status only exists for leaf, consolidated, and collection attribute views, because there is no validation stored for relationship members.

Procedure: How to Create a Subscription View

To create a subscription view in Master Data Manager, complete the following steps:

1. On the Master Data Management home page, click Integration Management.
2. On the menu bar, click Export.
3. On the Subscription Views page, click the "Add subscription view" button.

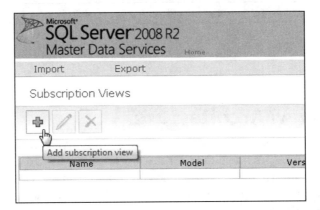

4. In the Create Subscription View Definition pane that is displayed at the bottom of the page, enter a name for the view and select a model from the Model list. In this example, select Product and call the view **ProductsForPOS**.

   This UI can be a bit confusing. There are three columns here and the radio buttons apply to the two options shown in each column.

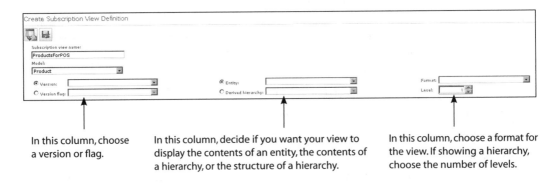

In this column, choose a version or flag.

In this column, decide if you want your view to display the contents of an entity, the contents of a hierarchy, or the structure of a hierarchy.

In this column, choose a format for the view. If showing a hierarchy, choose the number of levels.

5. In the first column of choices, select either Version or Version flag and then select from the corresponding list. As a best practice, you should create a subscription view based on a version flag. Then, as you create new versions, you can move the flag to the latest version and you don't have to update your subscription view. If you created a version flag in Chapter 9, you can select it here. Otherwise select the version that contains the data you want to export.

6. In the next column of choices, select either Entity or Derived hierarchy and then select from the corresponding list. Your subscription view can show the contents of an entity or the structure of a hierarchy. For this example, select Entity and choose the Product entity from this list.

7. In the third column of choices, from the Format list, select Leaf attributes. This determines the format of your view. If you were creating a view of a hierarchy, you would be prompted to select a format for the view and to choose the number of levels you want to show.

8. Click Save.

The subscription view is now displayed in the top pane of the Subscription Views page. If you decide you want to change it, click the row and then the Edit button. You can also delete it if it's no longer necessary.

Scroll to the far right to view the Changed column. This column is important to note. If objects in the model structure change, this column changes to True. At that point, you need to edit the subscription view and save it again (you don't need to make changes to it; just edit and then save). This ensures that the view will still return accurate results based on the latest changes to the model.

Viewing a Subscription View in SQL Server

Now you can open SQL Server Management Studio and take a look at the view. As shown in Figure 12-1, all of the members and their attributes are shown in a format that is easy for subscribing systems to consume.

For each domain-based attribute that is displayed in a subscription view, three columns are displayed. The "_Code" and "_Name" columns display the name and code. The "_ID" column displays the system key for the member. This is an internal key and should not be used in subscribing systems.

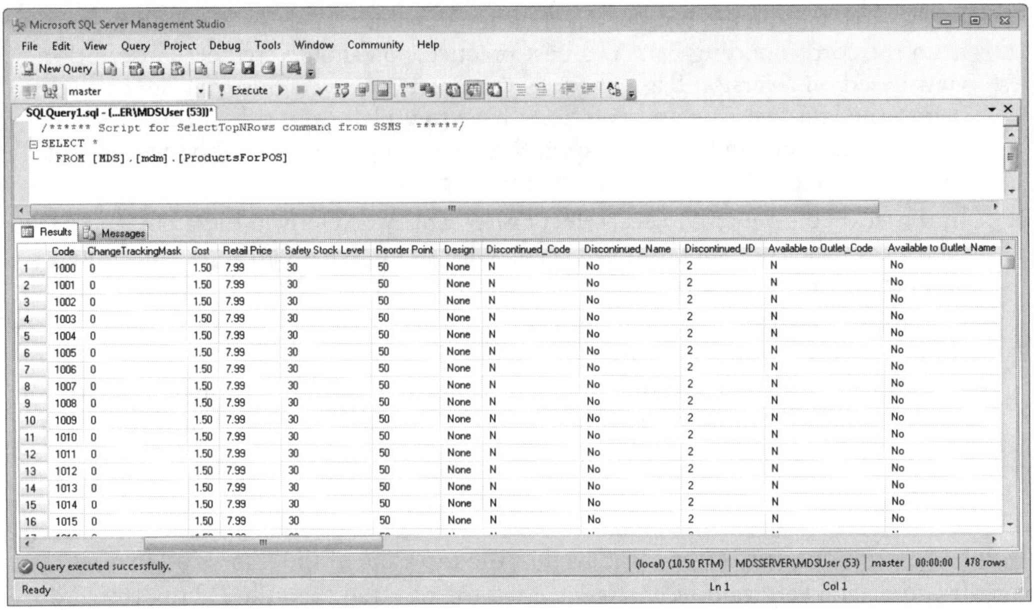

Figure 12-1 *Opening a subscription view in SQL Server Management Studio*

Subscription Views and Model Deployment

In the SQL Server 2008 R2 release of MDS, a shortcoming of model deployment is its lack of support for subscription views. If you create subscription views for an entity or derived hierarchy, these views will not be re-created when moving model deployment packages between development, test, and production servers. This leads to manual intervention that may lead to unforeseen issues or manual errors when moving to production.

Creating a Subscription View with Web Services

All subscription views in MDS are created using the ExportViewCreate operation. Depending on the type of view being created and whether you create the view based on version or version flag, different parameters are required.

Creating Entity Views

This operation creates an entity-centric subscription view for a specified model and entity. This procedure can support explicit hierarchy leveling and either method of version management.

```
//Create any type of subscription view
public OperationResult EntityExportViewCreation(string ModelName,
```

```
      string EntityName, string ViewName,ExportViewFormat ViewFormat,
      VersionFlag Flag, string VersionName, int NumofLevels)
{

    //Initialize the new request object
    ExportViewCreateRequest request = new ExportViewCreateRequest();
    request.ExportView = new ExportView();

    //Set Model, Entity and view name
    request.ExportView.ModelId = new Identifier { Name = ModelName };
    request.ExportView.EntityId = new Identifier { Name = EntityName };
    request.ExportView.Identifier = new Identifier { Name = ViewName };

    //If VersionID is 0, then use the flag identifier
    if (VersionName == null)
        request.ExportView.VersionFlagId = Flag.Identifier;
    else
        request.ExportView.VersionId = new Identifier {
        Name = VersionName };

    //if ExportViewFormat supports levels you can restrict
    //the number of displayed levels
    if (ViewFormat == ExportViewFormat.ExplicitLevels &&
    NumofLevels > 0)
        request.ExportView.Levels = NumofLevels;
    ExportViewCreateResponse response =
    mds_Proxy.ExportViewCreate(request);
    return response.OperationResult;
}
```

Creating Derived Hierarchy Views

This operation encapsulates the creation of derived hierarchy subscription views. Because the level setting is only valid when the chosen format is "derived levels," this parameter is ignored for other view types.

```
//Create any type of derived hierarchy subscription view
    public OperationResult DerivedHierarchyViewCreation(
    string ModelName, string DerivedHierarchyName, string ViewName,
    ExportViewFormat ViewFormat, VersionFlag Flag, string VersionName,
    int NumofLevels)
    {
        ExportViewCreateRequest request = new ExportViewCreateRequest();
        request.ExportView = new ExportView();
```

```
                     //Set model, derived hierarchy, and view name

                     request.ExportView.ModelId = new Identifier { Name = ModelName };
                     request.ExportView.DerivedHierarchyId = new Identifier {
                     Name = DerivedHierarchyName };
                     request.ExportView.Identifier = new Identifier { Name = ViewName };

                     //if  VersionName is null then use the flag identifier
                     if (VersionName == null)
                         request.ExportView.VersionFlagId = Flag.Identifier;
                     else
                         request.ExportView.VersionId = new Identifier {
                         Name = VersionName };
                     if (ViewFormat == ExportViewFormat.DerivedLevels && NumofLevels > 0)
                         request.ExportView.Levels = NumofLevels;
                     ExportViewCreateResponse response =
                     mds_Proxy.ExportViewCreate(request);
                     return response.OperationResult;
             }
```

Deleting Views

The following code deletes a subscription view from Master Data Services no matter
what the format of the subscription view. No data within the entity related to the
export view will be changed in any way by this process. This call returns an operation
result that will contain any errors that occurred in the deletion process, although these
will be rare in this simple process.

```
            //Delete a subscription view by name
            public OperationResult ExportViewDelete(string ViewName)
            {
                ExportViewDeleteRequest request = new
                ExportViewDeleteRequest();
                request.Identifier = new Identifier { Name = ViewName };
                ExportViewDeleteResponse response =
                mds_Proxy.ExportViewDelete(request);
                return response.OperationResult;
            }
```

How Main Street Clothing Company Uses Subscription Views

With all of the processes around maintaining location, product, employee, and
account data now in place, Anthony must build the integration plan for passing and
synchronizing data from MDS into all downstream systems.

The first step in building this plan is to determine the accuracy and accountability required for each subscribing system. Some systems require data that has been validated and version information that has been rigorously tracked. Other systems need data that is more recent and may still contain minor errors. MDS can provide this data for either purpose based on the type of version that is consumed. Version flags, as discussed in Chapter 9, also support this important distinction.

For each downstream system, Anthony must decide what type of subscription view provides the best format for consumption. Does this system require consolidation information? Does this system need attributes related to consolidated members? Anthony determines the best subscription view for each downstream system. As you can see from the following table, systems vary widely on the quality level required.

System	Data Needed	Quality Level
Online Retail System	Product (pricing and stock levels), Customer (contact information, orders)	Highly accurate (valid and committed)
Point of Sales Systems	Product (pricing)	Highly accurate (valid and committed)
Warehouse Management System	Product (stock levels), Suppliers (contact information)	Valid
Data Warehouse (Test)	All domains	Latest data
Data Warehouse (Production)	All domains	Highly accurate (valid and committed)
Finance	Products and Accounts	Approved, committed not required

The point of sale (POS) systems in each of the stores must be updated nightly with the latest product lists and prices. Anthony decides the best way to do this is to use the data presented in his subscription views to export the data he needs. He uses SQL Server Integration Services to create a package that runs on a nightly schedule. Each morning when the managers come to work, their POS systems are already updated with the latest product information.

Procedure: How to Export Subscription View Data

To export data from a Master Data Services subscription view to another data source, complete the following steps:

NOTE

This procedure is just one example of how to get data out of MDS and into a subscribing system. Your process may differ.

1. Open SQL Server Management Studio.
2. Right-click the MDS database.
3. From the submenu, select Tasks | Export Data.
4. On the Welcome page, click Next.
5. On the Choose a Data Source page, leave the defaults (it should be pointing to your MDS database) and click Next.
6. On the Choose a Destination page, in the Destination field, select Flat File Destination.
7. Browse to a text file name, select the "Column names in the first data row" check box, and click Next.

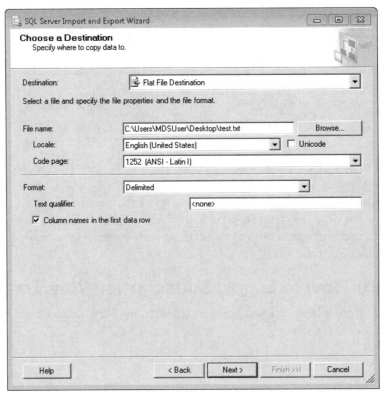

8. On the Specify Table Copy or Query page, select the "Copy data from one or more tables or views" radio button and click Next.

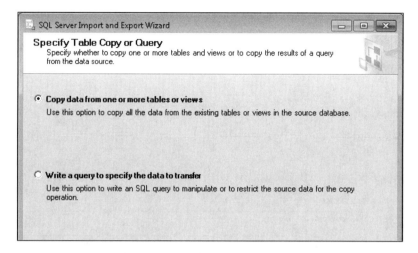

9. On the Configure Flat File Destination page, in the "Source table or view" list, select the view. In our case, it's the view: [mdm].[ProductsForPOS].

10. Click the Edit Mappings button. In the Column Mappings dialog box, ignore all of the Destination columns except: Name, Code, Retail Price, Discontinued_ Code, Type_Code, Gender_Code, and Manufacturer.

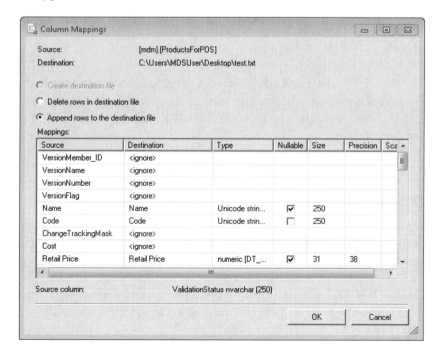

11. Click OK to close the dialog box. Then click Next.

12. On the Save and Run Package page, leave the Run immediately check box selected and select the "Save SSIS Package" check box.

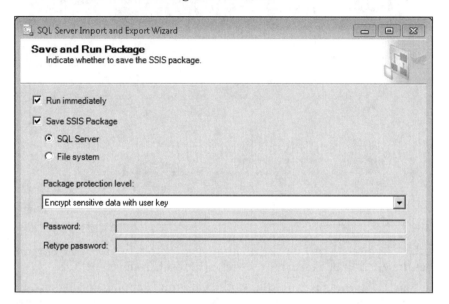

13. Click Next.

14. On the Save SSIS Package page, type a name and description for your package, leave all other defaults, and click Next.

15. On the Complete the Wizard page, click Finish.

The SSIS package is saved and Main Street Clothing Company can schedule the package to run nightly. When the package runs, the contents of the view are saved as a flat file to a file share. A separate batch system transfers the file to each of the 14 stores. The POS systems retrieve the data from the file, and each morning when the stores open, the POS systems have the latest prices and information.

Summary

Consuming data from the Master Data Services system requires analysis of the subscribing system's needs. These needs should be evaluated against the supported export formats. Subscription views provide a number of columns that can help filter and manage ETL processes into subscribing systems at an individual record level. Model deployment does not deploy subscription views from packages. If an organization has a lot of subscription views, it can programmatically manage these views through the MDS web service.

Chapter 13

Extending MDS with Web Services

In This Chapter

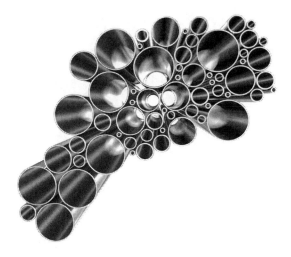

I n this chapter, we explore in more depth the web services layer provided by Master Data Services. Every operation in MDS is exposed within the web service. Despite the large number of operations, any developer can be productive working against the web service by focusing on a few high-value operations. These operations can be used to create a customized UI tailored to your solution or to integrate existing applications with MDS.

Exposing the Web Service

For security purposes, MDS does not publicly implement the web service when you first install MDS. If you are using MDS with prebuilt applications, then exposing the web service publicly from MDS Configuration Manager is the only step required. If you are going to build your own solutions or use the samples listed in this book, then you must also expose the Web Services Description Language (WSDL) in order to compile against the service interface.

Procedure: How to Enable the Web Service

To enable the web service, complete the following steps:

1. Click Start | Programs | Microsoft SQL Server 2008 R2 | Master Data Services | Configuration Manager.
2. In the left pane, click Web Configuration.
3. Select the web site and web application.
4. In the Web Services section, select the "Enable Web services for this Web application" check box.

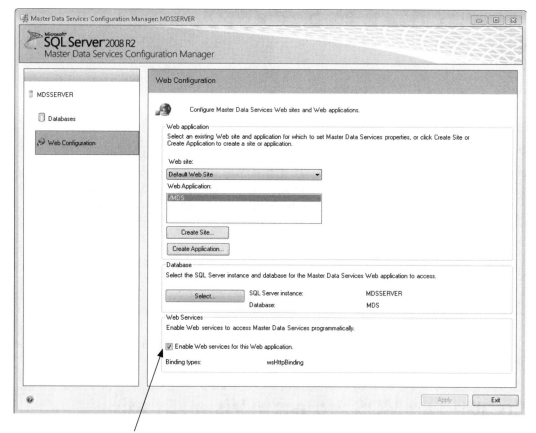

Click to enable the web service.

5.   Click Apply.

Exposing the WSDL

To expose the WSDL, you must modify the web.config file directly. This file is in the WebApplication directory where MDS is installed. If you installed MDS in the default location, the full path is C:\Program Files\Microsoft SQL Server\Master Data Services\WebApplication\web.config.

Procedure: How to Enable the WSDL

Open the web.config file with either Notepad or Visual Studio 2008. Find the following section:

```
<serviceMetadata httpGetEnabled="false" httpsGetEnabled="false"/>
<!-- Enable to allow clients to see service exception details -->
<serviceDebug includeExceptionDetailInFaults="false"/>
```

Change the setting for httpGetEnabled and includeExceptionDetailInFaults to true. Then save the file. This enables the web service to expose the WSDL. If you have configured SSL, as described in Chapter 2, you should change httpsGetEnabled to true.

If you receive an "Access is denied" error when you save, check the security on the file. When you install MDS, permissions are set on this file so that only the users in the local Administrators group have full control.

You may also have User Account Control (UAC) running. You can disable UAC temporarily; unfortunately, you will have to restart your computer when you do this. To disable UAC, open Control Panel and click "System and Security." Under Action Center, click "Change User Account Control settings." In the User Account Control Settings dialog box, slide the bar to the bottom so that you are never notified. Click OK to save. In the confirmation dialog box, click Yes. Restart your computer, and you should be able to edit the web.config file.

Creating an MDS Project in Visual Studio

Now that the web service is exposed, you can create your first project in Visual Studio. All of the code examples in this book use Visual Studio 2008.

Procedure: How to Create an MDS Web Service Application

To create an application that uses the MDS web service, you must first create a project and then add the web service as a reference in the project. Depending on your needs, you can create any type of application you choose. In this book, we've created wrapper classes that can be used in any type of application.

Create a Project

To create a project in Visual Studio, complete the following steps:

1. Open Microsoft Visual Studio.
2. Click File | New | Project.
3. In the New Project dialog box, in the Project types section, under Visual C#, click Windows.
4. In the Templates section, choose the application type. In this example, we chose Class Library.
5. In the Name box, type a name for your application.

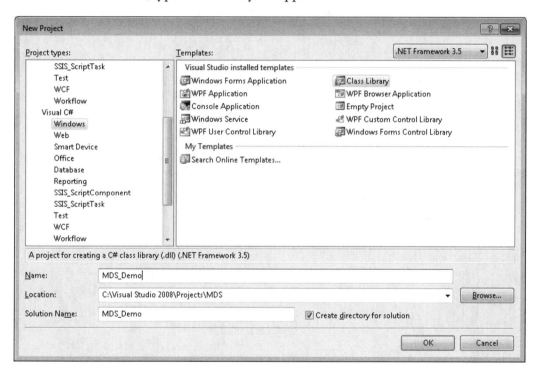

6. Click OK.

Add a Service Reference

To add a service reference to the project, complete the following steps:

1. In Visual Studio, with your project open, click View | Solution Explorer.
2. In the Solution Explorer pane, right-click References and click "Add Service Reference."

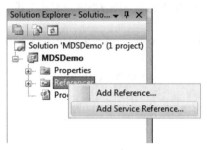

3. The Add Service Reference dialog box is displayed. In the Address box, type the URL for the MDS service. This is usually your URL followed by "/service/service .svc." For example:

    http://MDSSERVER/MDS/service/service.svc

4. Click Go. The service is displayed in the Services section.

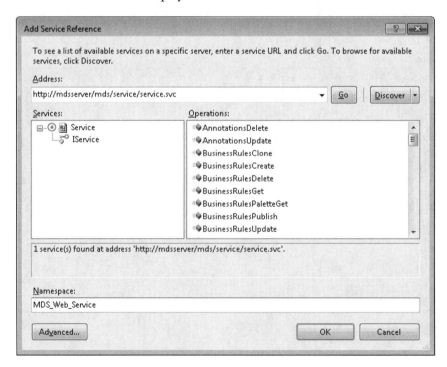

5. In the Namespace box, type a name for the service namespace. This can be anything you want.

6. Click OK.

Creating an Abstraction Layer

The MDS web service is built on Windows Communication Foundation (WCF). Many of the initial calls can seem daunting or overly complicated if you are a first-time user. The web service operations seem complicated because they must be generic in order to port all the model types and data schemas created in disparate implementations. The operations have been built to support all possible configurations and uses of the application.

Most people, however, are only interested in a small subset of configurations and a small subset of the application features exposed to the web service. When you are getting used to the MDS web service, there a few tips and practices that can help you more quickly integrate your organization with MDS. One of these is to create an abstraction layer.

An abstraction layer can do a number of things:

▶ It provides other developers with only those calls that you wish them to program against.

▶ It ensures that everyone uses a similar standard when writing code against the web service.

▶ It enables you to provide complex calls in a far more consumable fashion.

MDS Web Service Operations

While there are more than 50 operations supported by the MDS web service, most people only need to focus on a few of these operations to handle the majority of their routines. MDS operations can be grouped by the MDS objects they control. These groupings are listed in order of importance in the following sections.

Members

Retrieving and updating master data is by far the most frequent procedure you will want to automate. All of the operations for working with members are listed in the following table. For examples of these operations, see Chapter 7 and Chapter 11.

Operation	Description
EntityMemberAttributesGet	Retrieves a specified set of attribute values from a specified list of members. This call must be used to return the File attribute type; files cannot be returned in an EntityMembersGet response.
EntityMembersCopy	Copies selected members and their attribute values to new target members.
EntityMembersCreate	Used to create new members only. Existing members are not updated.
EntityMembersDelete	Soft deletes selected members in a specified version.
EntityMembersGet	Retrieves a set of members and their attribute values from an entity. These results can be filtered by search terms.
EntityMembersMerge	Creates new members and updates existing members. We recommend using this operation when managing most members programmatically.
EntityMembersUpdate	Updates existing members. New members are not created.
HierarchyMembersGet	Retrieves parent-child members from a hierarchy relative to a parent node. To filter results, this operation allows the use of a more advanced hierarchy location as well as search terms.

Bulk Operations

Although many of these operations are called ModelMembers, that is a misnomer. The major distinction for these operations is that they leverage staging to bulk load records into MDS. When loading more than a few thousand values (members times attributes), these calls should be used. For examples of staging operations, see Chapter 5.

Operation	Description
ModelMembersBulkDelete	Uses staging to bulk delete members from MDS.
ModelMembersBulkMerge	Uses staging to asynchronously create and/or update member data across one or more entities.
ModelMembersBulkUpdate	Uses staging to asynchronously update member data across one or more entities.
ModelMembersGet	Retrieves entire models, entities, and/or hierarchies. This can be used for bulk data output.
StagingClear	Clears batches from the three staging tables.
StagingGet	Retrieves the contents of the three staging tables.
StagingProcess	Sweeps existing unbatched records in the staging tables into a batch and triggers the batch to process.

Validation

In this first release of MDS, a large portion of the data quality proposition is working with validation results from business rules created in the application. While there are a number of operations necessary to create business rules, only two operations manage the results of these rules. Examples of these operations are provided in the section "The Most Frequently Used Operations," later in this chapter.

Operation	Description
ValidationGet	Retrieves filtered validation results and summary information from a model in MDS.
ValidationProcess	Can trigger validation processes (applying business rules) for selected members within a model.

Transactions

All data changes made through the web service or the web application UI are saved in the transaction table. These transactions can be retrieved or reversed by using the following operations. Examples of these operations are also provided in the section "The Most Frequently Used Operations."

Operation	Description
TransactionsGet	Retrieves a filtered list of transactions from a model.
TransactionsReverse	Reverses one or more existing transactions by transaction ID.

Annotations

Either members or transactions on those members can be given further explanation through annotations. Annotations are useful in providing further detail in workflow processes.

Operation	Description
AnnotationsDelete	Deletes an existing annotation by ID.
AnnotationsUpdate	Updates an existing annotation by ID.
EntityMemberAnnotationsCreate	Creates new annotations attached to a member record.
EntityMemberAnnotationsGet	Retrieves annotations that are attached to a member.
TransactionAnnotationsCreate	Creates new annotations that are attached to an existing transaction made within MDS.
TransactionAnnotationsGet	Retrieves a filtered list of transactions from a model based on transaction ID.

Subscription Views

External access to MDS managed data is enabled through views that are based on versions and view type. The following export operations manage these views. For examples of some of these operations, see Chapter 12.

Operation	Description
ExportViewCreate	Generates or regenerates provided export views.
ExportViewDelete	Removes an existing export view by ID.
ExportViewListGet	Retrieves a list of existing export views and their IDs.
ExportViewUpdate	Updates existing export view settings and regenerates the view.

Metadata Structures

Because MDS contains descriptive metadata, the naming convention for the following operations is confusing. These operations will create any of the model objects supported by MDS. For examples of some of these operations, see Chapter 4.

Operation	Description
MetadataClone	Creates an exact copy of metadata components from another MDS source, retaining the GUIDs of the original objects.
MetadataCreate	Creates new objects in MDS (attributes, attribute groups, entities, collections, hierarchies, and models).
MetadataDelete	Deletes metadata objects passed in the request object.

Security

While MDS security relies on Active Directory, MDS authorization requires that users be added as principals either by their username or an Active Directory group they are a member of. Users and groups must be assigned both functional and member privileges to have access to MDS. For examples of some of these operations, see Chapter 11.

Operation	Description
SecurityPrincipalsClone	Replicates users, groups, permissions, and their GUIDS within the security model from another external source.
SecurityPrincipalsCreate	Adds AD users and groups to the MDS security model.
SecurityPrincipalsDelete	Deletes user and group associations from MDS.
SecurityPrincipalsGet	Retrieves the security principals associated with MDS.

Operation	Description
SecurityPrivilegesClone	Replicates permissions and their GUIDS within the security model from another external source.
SecurityPrivilegesDelete	Deletes permissions from MDS.
SecurityPrivilegesGet	Retrieves functional, model, and hierarchy member security permissions for selected principals and/or models.

Business Rules

The management of business rules in MDS is best left to the Master Data Manager web UI. The following operations are complex in their object model and not well documented. For examples of some of these operations, see Chapter 8.

Operation	Description
BusinessRulesClone	Re-creates new business rules that are exact copies of business rules from another MDS source, while retaining the GUIDs of the original objects.
BusinessRulesCreate	Creates new business rules with both conditions (optional) and actions.
BusinessRulesDelete	Deletes a business rule or the components of rules.
BusinessRulesGet	Retrieves business rules for specific context provided in the request.
BusinessRulesPaletteGet	Retrieves available business rule components with which to build business rules (the component palette).
BusinessRulesPublish	Publishes business rules for a model type, entity type, or member type.
BusinessRulesUpdate	Updates preexisting business rules by identifier.

System Settings

There are a number of system-wide settings that allow system administrators to customize their MDS implementation. These settings are stored in tblSystemSetting and managed in MDS Configuration Manager.

Operation	Description
SystemDomainListGet	Returns a localized fixed list of choices based on a list code.
SystemPropertiesGet	Retrieves immutable properties about the system.
SystemSettingsGet	Retrieves a list of MDS system settings.
SystemSettingsUpdate	Updates system setting values.

User Preferences

These user preference calls support the MDS web application and have limited value for external systems. Leveraging these calls in your own custom UI work is not suggested.

Operation	Description
UserPreferencesDelete	Deletes the current user's preferences for the MDS web UI.
UserPreferencesGet	Retrieves the current user's preferences for the MDS web UI.
UserPreferencesUpdate	Updates the current user's preferences for the MDS web UI.

Miscellaneous Operations

The remaining operations are not easily grouped into categories.

Operation	Description
EntityMemberKeyLookup	Retrieves either a member code or an internal ID based on the other member code or internal ID and the provided context.
ServiceCheck	Checks the availability of the web service.
VersionCopy	Creates a copy of the model version.

The Most Frequently Used Operations

The examples in this section show you how to build an abstraction layer for the most frequently used operations that are needed to integrate with MDS. We highly recommend that when you build applications against MDS, you focus on the operations provided in this section.

The operations that we do not address tend to be more complex and less useful to everyday consumers. For instance, triggering validation programmatically may be very useful for end users. Business rules, on the other hand, are complex to build in a user interface and difficult to manipulate programmatically. Because of this, creating business rules outside of the MDS application holds less value. Security is another area where most of you will not need to build additional UIs. Ignoring these two areas can greatly reduce the time to implement a customized solution.

Searching for Members

To return data from an MDS entity, you must provide a valid identifier for the model, version, and entity. To further limit and refine the results that are returned from an EntityMembersGet operation, you can provide search terms.

All filters types that are available in Explorer when you're viewing members in the Master Data Manager web UI are supported by the search term parameter in the EntityMembersGet operation. The following table lists all of the filter operators, the corresponding search term syntax, and an example of each. In the Search Term Syntax column of the following table:

- ▶ A stands for attribute.
- ▶ V stands for generic value.
- ▶ S stands for similarity.
- ▶ T stands for match type.
- ▶ C stands for containment bias.

Most of the examples in this table come from the Product entity in the Main Street Clothing Company example.

UI Operator	Search Term Syntax	Example
Is equal to	A = V	[Code] = '1005'
Is not equal to	A <> V	[Color] <> 'RED'
Is like	A LIKE V	[Name] LIKE 'M Red Shirt*'
Is not like	A NOT LIKE V	[Name] NOT LIKE 'M Red*'
Is greater than	A > V	[Size] > 5
Is less than	A < V	[Size] < 3
Is greater than or equal to	A >= V	[Cost] >= 2
Is less than or equal to	A <= V	[Price] <= 10
Matches	A MATCH V S T C	Examples are provided in the section "Using Matching in Search Terms" later in this chapter.
Does not match	A NOT MATCH V S T C	See "Using Matching in Search Terms."
Contains pattern	A REGEX V	[Email] REGEX '@MSTClothing.com'
Does not contain pattern	A NOT REGEX V	Email NOT REGEX '@MSTClothing.com'
Is NULL	A IS NULL	[Color] IS NULL
Is not NULL	A IS NOT NULL	[Name] IS NOT NULL

Getting Members by Using the SearchTerm Property

The following code provides an EntityMembersGet example that uses the SearchTerm property. In subsequent examples, we show only the highlighted SearchTerm portion.

```
public EntityMembers GetEntityMembers(string modelName,
string entityName, string versionName)
{
    EntityMembersGetRequest Request = new EntityMembersGetRequest();
    EntityMembersGetResponse Response = new EntityMembersGetResponse();
    Request.MembersGetCriteria = new EntityMembersGetCriteria();

    //Set the MembersGetCriteria identifiers
    Request.MembersGetCriteria.ModelId = new Identifier { Name =
modelName };
    Request.MembersGetCriteria.EntityId = new Identifier
        { Name = entityName };
    Request.MembersGetCriteria.VersionId = new Identifier
        { Name = versionName };

    //This is the single search term string for the request
    //Combine terms here
    Request.MembersGetCriteria.SearchTerm =
        "[Name] = 'M Red Shirt 5 V Neck'";

    //Select the member return option. This determines whether
    //EntityMemberInformation, EntityMembers, or both are populated
    Request.MembersGetCriteria.MemberReturnOption =
    MemberReturnOption.Data;
    Response = mds_Proxy.EntityMembersGet(Request);
    EntityMembersInformation tEMI = Response.EntityMembersInformation;
    return Response.EntityMembers;
}
```

Combining Multiple Search Terms

Multiple search terms can be combined with the use of the AND operator between each criteria, as shown next. Like the UI, search terms in MDS do not support complex conditions like OR or grouping.

```
    Request.MembersGetCriteria.SearchTerm =
        "[Color] = 'Red' AND [Size] = 5";
```

Using Matching in Search Terms

In the Explorer functional area of the Master Data Manager web UI, you can use the Similarity operator to find matches similar to your search terms. However, you can use the MDS web service to create a much more robust process.

The following table shows the four types of similarity matches you can do programmatically. In each of these cases, 1 indicates an exact match and 0 indicates no match.

ID	Match Type	Description
0	Levenshtein	The Levenshtein distance is based on the number of edits (for example, adds or deletions) that it takes for one string to match another. This is the default match for MDS.
1	Jaccard	The Jaccard index works best when trying to match multiple strings.
2	Jaro-Winkler	The Jaro-Winkler distance is best used for finding duplicate person names.
3	Longest common subsequence	A *subsequence* is when the letters in a pattern appear in order, although they can be separated. For example, MDS is a subsequence of MaDneSs.

Levenshtein Search Term Example   The Levenshtein distance is the default type of match and does not require any additional parameters. Only Minimum Similarity and Type are supported.

```
Request.MembersGetCriteria.SearchTerm =
    [Name] MATCH 'M Red Shirt 5 V Neck' 0.8 0";
```

Jaccard Search Term Example   The Jaccard search supports an additional parameter of containment bias.

```
Request.MembersGetCriteria.SearchTerm =
    " M Red Shirt 5 V Neck' 0.8 1 0.32";
```

Jaro-Winkler Search Term Example   The Jaro-Winkler match results are the least restrictive with our sample data. This method returns more results than any other method. The Jaro-Winkler type does not support containment bias.

```
Request.MembersGetCriteria.SearchTerm =
    " [Name] MATCH 'M Red Shirt 5 V Neck' 0.8 2";
```

Longest Common Subsequence Search Term Example   Longest common subsequence does support an extra parameter of length threshold. This is provided in a decimal percentage between 0 and 1. The default is .62, and a lower threshold will increase the number of possible matches returned.

```
Request.MembersGetCriteria.SearchTerm =
    " [Name] MATCH 'M Red Shirt 5 V Neck' 0.8 3 .35";
```

Understanding the EntityMembers Object

The EntityMember class centers on a collection of members. If retrieving EntityMembers using the EntityMembersGet operation, a number of additional objects will be populated depending on the type of criteria supplied. This same EntityMembers class needs to be created and populated by the call when creating new members in MDS.

Figure 13-1 shows the EntityMembers class object and all possible members. In these class diagrams, the type of relationship between classes is denoted by 0, 1, and *. If a 1 is stated, the object is required or always provided. 0 means the class is optional, and * means multiple items can be added to the class collection.

Summarizing Member Data

When you use the web service to select data by using the EntityMembers object, you do not get summary data that is useful for pagination or for otherwise showing record counts. To get this type of information, you can use the EntityMemberInformation object. This object contains the following attributes:

▶   **MemberCount**   The member count of the records returned in the current request. This will be based on the paging information provided.

▶   **PageNumber**   The current page number returned in this request.

▶   **TotalMemberCount**   The total member count for the current request. The MembersGetCriteria must remain constant for this total member count to stay consistent.

▶   **TotalPages**   The total number of pages for the current request. The MembersGetCriteria must remain constant for this page count to stay consistent.

Working with Metadata

All of the objects within MDS are created using the same operation: MetadataCreate. This operation creates models, entities, attributes, attribute groups, collections,

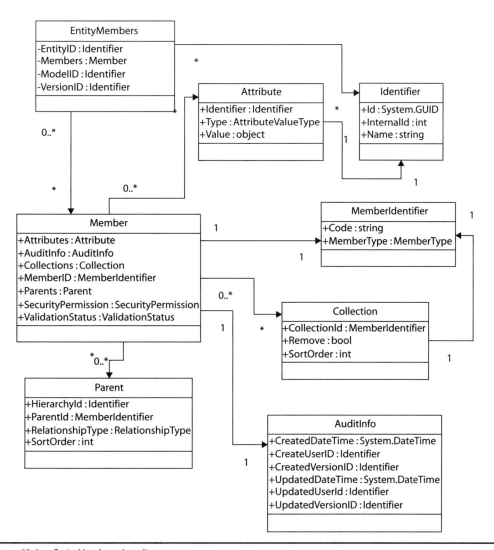

Figure 13-1 *EntityMembers class diagram*

and hierarchies. Throughout the book, there are examples of how to create these metadata objects.

As discussed in earlier chapters, MetadataCreate and MetadataClone are overloaded operations that allow you to create models, entities, and attributes within the MDS system. To create or return these objects, you must navigate the Metadata class and its child classes. Figure 13-2 shows a map of the Metadata class.

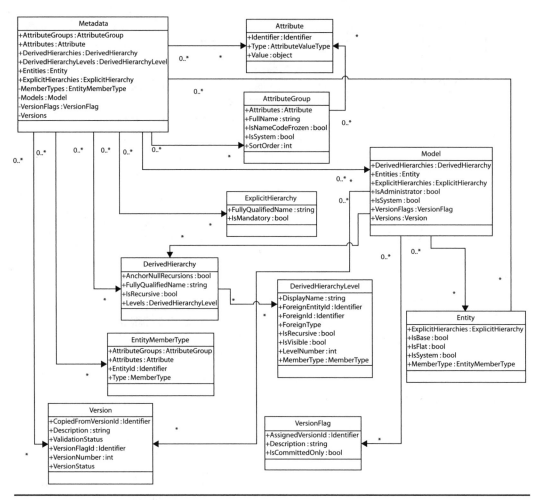

Figure 13-2 *Metadata class diagram*

Validating Records in MDS

As an organization begins to interact programmatically with MDS, it may become necessary to trigger validation on specific members or an entire entity. Once validation has completed, users may need to retrieve validation issues that have been discovered. We have not had a chance to discuss these web service operations earlier in the book, so we'll provide some examples here.

ValidationGet operations can be tricky because they seem to support a wide variety of parameters, but only a few combinations will return results. These combinations seem to align with the UI controls for validation issues. Three valid examples are explained next.

ValidationGetByVersion Example

This operation gets all validation issues for a model and version combination. This would be used as part of the commitment process for a version.

```
public Collection<ValidationIssue> ValidationGetByVersion(string
ModelName, string VersionName)
{
    ValidationGetRequest Request = new ValidationGetRequest();
    ValidationGetResponse Response = new ValidationGetResponse();

    //Instantiate the ValidationSearchCriteria and add the
    //identifiers for Model and Version
    Request.ValidationSearchCriteria = new ValidationSearchCriteria();
    Request.ValidationSearchCriteria.ModelId =
      new Identifier { Name = ModelName };
    Request.ValidationSearchCriteria.VersionId =
      new Identifier { Name = VersionName };
    Response = mds_Proxy.ValidationGet(Request);

    //Return the collection of current validation issues
    return Response.ValidationIssueList;
}
```

ValidationGetByUser Example

This operation returns the results that correspond to notifications that were sent to a user.

```
public Collection<ValidationIssue> ValidationGetByUser(string ModelName,
string VersionName,string EntityName, int UserId)
{
    ValidationGetRequest Request = new ValidationGetRequest();
    ValidationGetResponse Response = new ValidationGetResponse();

    //Instantiate the ValidationSearchCriteria and add the internal
    // UserId who is a member of the notification group for the issues
    Request.ValidationSearchCriteria = new ValidationSearchCriteria();
    Request.ValidationSearchCriteria.ModelId =
      new Identifier { Name = ModelName };
    Request.ValidationSearchCriteria.VersionId =
      new Identifier { Name = VersionName };
    Request.ValidationSearchCriteria.UserId =
```

```
    new Identifier { InternalId = UserId };
  Response = mds_Proxy.ValidationGet(Request);

  //Return the list of current validation issues for the specified user.
  return Response.ValidationIssueList;
}
```

ValidationGetByMember Example

This operation returns results related to a member or set of members. In this example we pass in a single member.

```
public Collection<ValidationIssue> ValidationGetByMember(
string ModelName, string VersionName, string EntityName, string MemCode)
{
  ValidationGetRequest Request = new ValidationGetRequest();
  ValidationGetResponse Response = new ValidationGetResponse();

  //Instantiate the ValidationSearchCriteria and add
  //all relevant identifiers
  Request.ValidationSearchCriteria = new ValidationSearchCriteria();
  Request.ValidationSearchCriteria.ModelId =
    new Identifier { Name = ModelName };
  Request.ValidationSearchCriteria.EntityId =
    new Identifier { Name = EntityName };
  Request.ValidationSearchCriteria.VersionId =
    new Identifier { Name = VersionName };
  Request.ValidationSearchCriteria.MemberTypeId = MemberType.Leaf;

  //Create a member identifier for each member
  MemberIdentifier newMem = new MemberIdentifier { Code = MemCode };

  //Add Members to the members collection for which you
  // want to see validation issues
  Request.ValidationSearchCriteria.Members =
    new Collection<MemberIdentifier>();
  Request.ValidationSearchCriteria.Members.Add(newMem);

  //Return the collection of current validation issues
  Response = mds_Proxy.ValidationGet(Request);

  return Response.ValidationIssueList;
}
```

ValidationProcess Example

ValidationProcess will validate a model and version combination or it will validate a set of members passed into the operation. You can use an EntityMembersGet operation to retrieve a set of members related to a group of search terms and then loop through those members. In this simple example, we will validate only a single member and pass back all validation issues found.

```
public Collection<ValidationIssue> ValidationProcess(string ModelName,
string verName, string EntityName, string memCode)
{
    //Instantiate all request and response objects
    ValidationProcessRequest Request = new ValidationProcessRequest();
    ValidationProcessResponse Response =
      new ValidationProcessResponse();

    //Instantiate the Criteria and Options objects
    Request.ValidationProcessCriteria =
     new ValidationProcessCriteria();
    Request.ValidationProcessOptions = new ValidationProcessOptions();

    //Set Model and Version Identifiers - these will be
    //required in all instances
    Request.ValidationProcessCriteria.ModelId =
      new Identifier { Name = ModelName };
    Request.ValidationProcessCriteria.VersionId =
      new Identifier { Name = verName };
    Request.ValidationProcessCriteria.EntityId =
      new Identifier { Name = EntityName };

    Request.ValidationProcessCriteria.Members =
      new Collection<MemberIdentifier>();
    Request.ValidationProcessCriteria.Members.Add
    (new MemberIdentifier { Code = memCode });

    //Options can return validation results or trigger the commit
    //of a version (when validation is already successful)
    Request.ValidationProcessOptions.ReturnValidationResults = true;

    Response = mds_Proxy.ValidationProcess(Request);
    return Response.ValidationIssueList;


}
```

Managing Transactions

Transactions can provide users and managers with a complete record of all changes that have been made in the system. Model administrators will be able to see all transactions made within a model, while each user will have access to their own changes. These transactions also support reversal.

TransactionsGet Example

TransactionsGet operations return a list of transactions that meet the provided search criteria. Transaction search criteria only support values that are equal, so these criteria are exposed as identifiers attached to the criteria.

```
public Collection<Transaction> TransactionGet(string ModelName, string
EntityName, string verName)
{
    TransactionsGetRequest Request = new TransactionsGetRequest();
    TransactionsGetResponse Response = new TransactionsGetResponse();

    //Instantiate the TransactionSearchCriteria class and add the
    //criteria to filter your results
    Request.TransactionSearchCriteria = new TransactionSearchCriteria();

    //TransactionSearchCriteria can consist of any of the
    //attributes of transaction management
    Request.TransactionSearchCriteria.ModelId =
      new Identifier { Name = ModelName };
    Request.TransactionSearchCriteria.EntityId =
      new Identifier { Name = EntityName };
    Request.TransactionSearchCriteria.VersionId =
      new Identifier { Name = verName };
    Response = mds_Proxy.TransactionsGet(Request);

    return Response.TransactionList;
}
```

TransactionsReverse Example

While there may be many programmatic uses for TransactionsGet, TransactionsReverse should be used with caution. TransactionsReverse does not actually reverse the transaction, but rather reverts the current value from MDS to the prior value stored in the transaction log. This procedure can be very valuable when you need to reverse a change after triggering an external action. Make sure that you reverse the most recent transaction.

The following procedure is a simple example of how to reverse a single transaction based on the ID of the transaction. This procedure will throw an error if an invalid transaction ID is provided. You could add a conditional statement around the TransactionsReversed return statement to handle this case.

```
public int TransactionReversal(int TranId)
{
    TransactionsReverseRequest Request = new
    TransactionsReverseRequest();
    TransactionsReverseResponse Response = new
    TransactionsReverseResponse();

    //Instantiate the transactions object and
    //add the integer ID for the transaction to reverse
    Request.Transactions = new Collection<int>();
    Request.Transactions.Add(TranId);
    Response = mds_Proxy.TransactionsReverse(Request);
    return Response.TransactionsReversed[0].NewId;
}
```

Handling Errors in the Web Service

All MDS web service calls return an OperationResult object within their response messages. This OperationResult object contains a Request_ID to manage long-running requests and any errors that occurred as a result of the request. These errors can provide immediate feedback to client-side developers who need to find problems with their requests. These errors can range from useful to baffling, and sometimes it will take some trial and error to determine what is wrong. Each error will populate a portion of the following properties:

► **Code**   Error number specific to the type of error encountered. A general classification for web service errors is provided in the following table.

► **Description**   Localized text describing the error.

► **Context.FullyQualifiedName**   The fully qualified name of the object involved in the error. Some names are only unique within their context. An entity would be qualified with a model name prefix such as *ModelName : EntityName*.

► **Context.Type**   The type of object related to the error.

► **Context.Identifier**   The identifier of the object involved in the error.

▶ **Context.Identifier.Id**   The unique GUID of the object, if specified or available.

▶ **Context.Identifier.Name**   The name of the object, if specified or available.

▶ **Context.Identifier.InternalId**   The internal key from the MDS system tables.

Area	Error Number Range
Common	100000–199999
Metadata Operations	200000–299999
Master Data Operations	300000–399999
Business Rule Operations	400000–499999
Security Operations	500000–599999

Summary

The MDS web service provides complete access to all of the functions that are found in the product. While many of the operations are detailed in other chapters of this book, this chapter acts as a reference to help you find the operations you need, and provides more detailed examples. After reading this chapter, you should be familiar with the main groupings available so you can programmatically access all that MDS has to offer.

Index

347